BLACK AND PRO-LIFE IN AMERICA

Robert W. Artigo

Black and Pro-Life in America

The Incarceration and Exoneration
of Walter B. Hoye II

IGNATIUS PRESS   SAN FRANCISCO

Cover photograph of Walter B. Hoye
by José Luis Aguirre/*Catholic Voice*, Diocese of Oakland

Cover design by Enrique J. Aguilar Pinto

Published in 2018 by Ignatius Press, San Francisco
© 2018 by Robert W. Artigo
All rights reserved
ISBN 978-1-62164-048-6
Library of Congress Control Number 2017947381
Printed in the United States of America ∞

For my mother, Barbara Ann, and Walter's mother, Vida Mae, with deepest love, gratitude, and appreciation for all you did and suffered for us. You didn't live to see this book published, but these pages would be empty if not for the lessons and the faith you taught us.

For a black man, when you set out to do this, you lose your family, you lose your community, you lose your church.

—Walter B. Hoye II

CONTENTS

FOREWORD

Nearly two decades ago I met Reverend Walter Hoye and his wife, Lori. I remember thinking what a humble man Walter was. He and Lori were already civil rights icons, though they didn't wave their testimonies, trials, and victories in our faces. They were living epistles back then. They still are.

Walter is a man of quiet courage and deep convictions. I remember watching him at his home church at the turn of the century. He was deep into proclaiming the gospel of life. Standing before the elders gathered in the church sanctuary that morning, Walter reminded me of my uncle, Reverend Dr. Martin Luther King Jr., and my father, Reverend A.D. King. In the twentieth century Daddy and Uncle M.L. often stood before panels of elders who wanted them to "turn down the heat" and "stop stirring up trouble". Such was the path that Walter Hoye was on in the early twenty-first century. His peers and elders were uncomfortable with his radical gospel message—that life is sacred to God from the womb to the grave and into eternity.

It was no surprise that Walter's pastoral board soon gave him an ultimatum: give up pro-life activism or give up ministry at the church. There was no longer room for both in Walter's life. Undaunted, he walked further into his destiny, which would include being uprooted from his familiar pastoral duties. Over the years, in rapid succession, he was thrown into the depths of the horrors of abortion and catapulted into the heights of his calling from God to proclaim, "No more!"

Walter's "pro-life calling" isn't new. As early as the premature birth of his son years ago, Walter knew that a preborn baby is a person. Seeing the tiny body of his little son charted Walter's pro-life course, changing his heart forever. "Abortion is a form of discrimination," Walter continues to proclaim.

Robert W. Artigo has embarked upon a "labor of love" in bringing the life and legacy of Walter Hoye to the printed pages of history.

9

As we turn each page and follow Walter's journey, let us thank God. Let us also take special note of Walter's helpmeet, dear Lori, as we glean the truths of love, joy, and victory to be found even in the darkest days when Walter was incarcerated and Lori's continual message to well-wishers was "It is well."

I often find myself reflecting on the marches, prayer vigils, strategy meetings, and so much more that Walter remains involved in. Through it all, we must remember that Walter is an ordained Baptist minister with the call to preach the fullness of the gospel of life. This book is a journal of Walter's journey. It is a testimony to read and to be inspired by; then as the last page is turned, it will be time to rise and join Walter as the mission continues.

Evangelist Alveda King
May 4, 2018

INTRODUCTION

There are five distinct parts to this book. The first part is an account of Walter B. Hoye II's early life and the formative events that shaped his Christian faith and view of the world. Walter's origins, including his ancestry, are placed within their historical context. As the pages that follow illustrate, the man was as much shaped by history as by his personal struggles and triumphs. His story begins in the American South, and its development parallels a changing nation, particularly as it changes with respect to black Americans.

The second part looks at Walter's pro-life conversion, and it contains an overview of abortion in Oakland, California, where Walter first became active in sidewalk counseling. It relates the events and the people who inspired him to post himself outside an abortion clinic one day each week. Coinciding with his pro-life outreach is the action of the City of Oakland and its officials who collaborated with interested private persons and for-profit businesses to craft a law that eventually ensnared Walter.

Several chapters are dedicated to the prosecution and the trial of Walter Hoye, and they are based on court documents and recollections of witnesses both inside and outside the courtroom. This third part of the story is largely the legal drama that unfolded around Walter, and the facts of the case speak for themselves. Conclusions can easily be drawn, but those will be up to the reader.

The fourth part of the story, in chapters interspersed throughout, records Walter's experiences in jail. These chapters are a combination of Walter's recollections and my later observations while touring the facility in Alameda County, California. They include descriptions of some of the sights and the sounds in a level of detail that most people simply cannot recall years after the experience. The observations are not used to embellish, however, but rather to enliven the reading experience. Without the benefit of video recordings or transcripts used in other parts of the book, dialogues inside the prison cannot be confirmed. In such cases, the utmost care was taken to avoid direct quotes unless Walter could recall exact words. These interactions should be clear to the reader.

The closing chapters focus on what happened after the trial and Walter's time in jail. They include the results of his appeals and other court challenges. Then there's a look at Walter Hoye's most recent activities and hopes for the future.

A word about sources. A good-faith effort was made to reach the people identified in this text. They were contacted by letter and by phone and offered an opportunity to contribute their interpretations of the events recorded in this book. Not many people from the pro-abortion side agreed to be interviewed, but those who did provided helpful information, for which the author is grateful. In some cases, the names of sources were kept confidential due to their positions of authority and the political sensitivity of the issues involved. Most often these individuals only elaborated on information available through public records. Documentation for all this can be found in the source notes.

Full disclosure: I am Catholic and pro-life. But Walter's story did not have to be told from my perspective. I told Walter as much when we first met. All we needed to do was tell the truth to the best of our ability. I am an investigative journalist, and I applied the highest standards of my profession to the telling of this story. I could not have written it any other way. Some readers may be disappointed that this book is not an indictment of abortion. At the same time, abortion supporters will no doubt also be disappointed.

The story of Walter Hoye is not just about abortion, and it would be a mistake to construe these events as just an anti-abortion story. It is a story of the American political and legal system, which has often failed to fulfill its promise of fair, equal, unbiased treatment toward all, particularly toward black Americans. It is also a free-speech story, and by the end of the book, the courts will have spoken on that First Amendment right. Even before the courts spoke on the issue, some people who self-identified as pro-choice called out the Oakland City Council for what they considered a chilling attack on political speech.

The question this story asks is not "Is abortion wrong?" but rather "Do American citizens have the right to say that abortion is wrong?"

I

Hunger for Justice

On Friday, March 20, 2009, fifteen months after the City of Oakland passed a law making it illegal to approach a woman entering an abortion clinic without her consent, Walter B. Hoye II stood in Alameda County Superior Court to hear the penalty he would suffer for allegedly violating the law. Jail was very likely, but at least he had some idea of what it would be like. He had been in a prison before, but not as an inmate—a fact that could have been otherwise, given his early life in Detroit, where going to jail was a common occurrence among young black men. There were times when the allure of belonging to a neighborhood gang tempted Walter, but his parents made it very clear to him that a hopeful future would not be found on that path, and he managed to avoid the kind of trouble that led to jail.

As Superior Court Judge Stuart Hing deliberated, Walter pondered what awaited him in jail. Images of San Quentin easily came to mind because he had accompanied Chaplain Earl Smith on visits to the state penitentiary. Intimidating and foreboding, San Quentin sits on a promontory in San Francisco Bay and houses California's most dangerous lifers and death row inmates: men such as Morris Solomon Jr., a serial killer who was also convicted of a variety of sex crimes in the Sacramento area. His favorite victims were prostitutes. Scott Peterson, also on death row, was convicted for the murder of his wife, Laci Peterson, and their unborn son in Modesto, California. Then there was San Quentin's most famous inmate, Charles Manson, the subject of books, movies, and ultimately the NBC TV series *Aquarius*, which elevated the murderer to cult-figure status. Manson died at San Quentin in November 2017.

Of course, the majority of inmates at San Quentin were not famous, just extremely dangerous. Some of the men doing life for murder outside the prison had also killed fellow inmates. Violence regularly broke out over prison politics and gang rivalries. Conflicts were endless, no matter how hard the state worked at addressing the issues that caused them, because in prison there are more calls for revenge than offers of forgiveness and more acts of violence than deeds of kindness.

During his visits to San Quentin, Walter had offered an alternative to the constant posturing and bullying. With a soft voice and kind eyes, the Baptist elder had sought to see Christ in the inmates so that they could see Christ in him, and in each other. His counsel and prayers, offered without regard for the crimes they had committed, had been well received. And like Chaplain Smith, Walter had been a link to the outside that lies beyond not only the walls of the prison but also the walls inmates build for themselves. Walter would not be going to San Quentin, *thank God*. Still, he was minutes away from becoming a guest of the correctional system with its many physical dangers. Although nothing could have completely prepared him for this fate, his knowledge of how prison hierarchies work, how inmates relate to each other, would come in handy.

Choosing Prison

Walter knew how the judgment would play out because he and his lawyers had previously agreed on a plan. His lawyers would decline the lesser sentence, which offered a choice between jail time and community service, and take the predictably harsher punishment at the discretion of the court. In the long hours since agreeing to this plan, however, Walter found himself stripped of confidence and struggling to console himself. He wondered whether he would make it through his first night in custody without needing to fight physically to defend himself.

Some members of the courtroom audience groaned as Walter's legal counsel explained his decision to refuse the lesser sentence of three years' probation, thirty days in jail or a sheriff's work program, and a $1,300 fine. They were the same people who had erupted with exuberant cheers when the jury announced his guilt. But there were others in the audience who were silently praying on his behalf, and

Walter leaned on the quiet strength of their presence in the rows behind him.

Deputy District Attorney Robert Graff responded to Walter's defense by requesting a harsher punishment. "If Mr. Hoye is rejecting probation," Graff said, "then the sentence of two years in county jail, each count carries one year, so the people are asking for two years."

Walter Hoye's position had been unwavering since the first sentencing, when he told the judge, "I believe an unjust law is no law at all. . . . It is my intention to continue my efforts to save the life of the unborn child, by reaching out to men and women going into the abortion clinic, with the love of Jesus Christ, my Lord and Savior." The part of the sentence that Walter considered particularly unjust and intended to defy was the stay-away order. This order would prevent him from being within one hundred yards of Oakland's Webster Street abortion clinic.

"Once the stay-away order was added to the package," Walter's attorney Michael Millen clarified, "at that point it became so onerous that it was something Mr. Hoye could no longer consider."

Several times, Deputy District Attorney Graff argued that Walter's intention to defy the stay-away order warranted the maximum possible sentence of two years in jail—a remarkable punishment for a misdemeanor that hadn't existed until Walter regularly visited the Webster Street clinic with a sign that read, "God loves you and your baby. Let us help you."

Rejecting Graff's request for two years in jail, Judge Hing sentenced Hoye to thirty days in Santa Rita Jail, three years of court-supervised probation, and the fine. He also imposed the hundred-yard stay-away order, even though Walter had promised to ignore it.

Walter's wife, Lori, was seated in the first row of seats behind the table for the defense. She hung on every word and nervously twisted the finger where her wedding ring used to be. The night before, Walter took off his wedding band and gave it to her, saying, "It is the knowledge that I will see you again that will give me the strength I need to endure the time away from you. So hold on to this and know that I'm coming back to wear this ring again." In the morning, just hours before the sentencing, Lori removed her own wedding ring and placed it with Walter's in a box. The rings signified not only the spouses' love for each other but their confidence in God's love for them, and as two deputies led Walter from the courtroom, both husband and wife knew that during the next thirty days they would need to rely on their faith in God and in one another more than ever before.

Walter stopped before the courthouse door and waved good-bye to his wife and his supporters. A familiar voice with a distinctive New Zealand accent called out, "We love you, Walter!" The bailiffs assigned to maintain decorum eyed the crowd for another outburst, ready to eject the offender. Nevertheless, Walter's supporters, some with tears in their eyes, smiled at Mary Arnold, the source of the outburst. For a moment, she had buoyed their spirits, as well as Walter's.

The deputies escorted Walter out of the courtroom without handcuffing him first. Defendants remanded to custody are nearly always handcuffed first. Was the break from the usual practice an oversight, an act of sympathy and respect, or an expedient acknowledgment that Walter was harmless? Behind the courtroom door, the bailiffs handcuffed Walter. They led him through an old, dark oak door and a heavy reinforced door to a cement room. Walter was left alone, and in the stillness, his wrists absorbed the weight of the metal cuffs as the impression left by his wedding ring faded.

The Questions

The literal emptiness of Walter's stomach was joined by a nervous sick feeling as he sat waiting alone in the first holding cell, just steps from the courtroom. His cheekbones were more pronounced than usual, as he had been losing weight, and he was resigned to shedding more pounds in the coming days. It was not a matter of a loss of appetite due to stress, but rather of a juice-and-water fast in observance of 40 Days for Life, a globally coordinated pro-life effort to fast and pray during Lent for an end to the "injustice of abortion". It left him a little weak and lightheaded at a time when he needed his wits about him, and he stared at the floor in the eerie silence.

The close atmosphere created an echo chamber that amplified even the ringing in his ears. Every sound he made—rustling his clothes, shuffling his feet, rattling his handcuffs—reverberated in agonizing decibels. The distinct sour odor of nervous sweat seemed to exude from the walls as if bonded with the paint. It was the smell of an endless string of men and women who, like Walter, had sat there and wondered, *What next?*

Walter prayed and raised the inevitable question, quoting Christ on the cross, "Why have you forsaken me?" Just as the loneliness was overtaking him, the door opened and a deputy entered. He led Walter down a hallway to the second waiting room, which was occupied by other detainees. *Perhaps being around other people would help?* It would not. In fact, the presence of the other prisoners just made things worse.

For those newly admitted to the system, fresh from court, like Walter, the standard dress is come-as-you-are civilian attire. Walter wore his standard black suit and white cotton T-shirt, which easily placed him in the best-dressed category. Inmates who were there to make various court appearances were in prison uniforms. The ones in blue were low-level offenders, nonviolent. Red was worn by violent felons or protected inmates, and green by those destined to return to the mental ward. Looking more like a lawyer than an inmate, Walter knew he would attract attention, the one thing no one wants in an overcrowded room of incarcerated people. It was an incendiary environment, filled with angry, scared, and trapped men, for whom prying into other people's business is a common distraction. It would be only a matter of minutes before Walter would hear, "Hey, man. Why are you here?"

Walter swallowed hard as he considered his options. He knew he couldn't keep his head down. He couldn't allow these men to see weakness. This lesson he had learned even before his conversations at San Quentin. He had gleaned it in the years he spent surviving the streets of Detroit. Walter answered deliberately in a low, even voice, "I was convicted of the crime of holding a sign that said, 'God loves you and your baby. Let us help you', in front of an abortion clinic."

"Come on, yo, you're a drug dealer or something, right?"

"No. I was arrested at the clinic on Webster in Oakland. They charged me with violating a so-called bubble law."

"He's lyin', dude," said another inmate.

In Walter's weakened state, the talk made his head spin. He tried to stay focused. "No," he insisted, "I'm serious. You see, I believe the abortion clinics are destroying black people and it's no accident. It's a genocide." Aside from being a prime motivator of his sidewalk counseling efforts, Walter's concern for "black people" was a good thing to mention in that room, given the race of half his audience.

"Come on, yo, that's not even law. Abortion? Man, forget it."

"Told you he's lyin'."

The eyes upon Walter were skeptical at least, accusatory at worst. He could see that the men didn't want to believe him. Some of them were becoming angry and getting rough with him. He was drawing more attention to himself, exactly what he didn't want. It was so crowded that there were seven or eight guys standing right next to him, prodding him to come clean with the truth. The thought occurred to Walter that there was no security in the room. If something went down, there would be no way to stop it. He did his best to hold himself together.

Walter enjoyed a brief reprieve from the harassment when all of them were taken to the jail transport bus. "They separated us by class of crime, locking the most dangerous and violent criminals down for the ride," Walter said. "I'm sitting there, and some of the guys just admitted to the crimes they were in for, saying they just got caught. I just felt like a criminal. I thought, 'How did I get to this point?'"

Throughout the American justice system, everything about prison life is divided by a class structure of sorts, some of it official and some of it unofficial. It starts with segregation by clothing, then by level of crime for transport, but it doesn't end there, not in the least. The divisions are born out of necessity, and in many respects inmates govern themselves.

The ride from the county courthouse in downtown Oakland to the Alameda County Santa Rita Jail in Dublin is about an hour, but for Walter "it seemed like a very, very long ride." From his seat, he saw mostly black and brown faces among the passengers. The guards were mostly white. The men talked more quietly, but they still singled out Walter. His street smarts helped him to keep his cool as he responded to their questions, suspicion, and derision. He spoke deliberately in the same even tone. As a result, the inmates became convinced that he was some kind of high-level, lying dope dealer.

The Lockup

The bus arrived at Santa Rita a few hours after the gavel fell at Walter's sentencing. The guards on the bus had made it clear that they were in charge and that following orders was the only way to avoid trouble. There was the easy way, and there was the hard way. As they filed off the bus, the inmates seemed as though they had every intention of doing things the easy way. The prisoners were again segregated. The violent reds were kept apart until they could be taken, one at a time, back to their cages in the jail. The psychiatric greens were divided into small, manageable groups and then returned to their cells. Along with the inmates in blue and the others in civilian clothes, Walter was taken to another holding room. The new inmates waited as the crowd wearing blue dwindled. Then they were called for booking photos and strip searches.

As Walter waited for his turn to be booked and searched, a sense of dread came over him. He found himself back in the echo chamber, where every noise had a tinny after-presence, like a drip of water in a large sewer pipe. As before, some men asked Walter questions, but as the inmates became restless and hungry their focus shifted away from him. Some of them banged on the walls, demanding to be fed. They looked as though they were ready to riot just to get a sandwich. Walter couldn't help but think about how he hadn't eaten for three weeks.

The guards used the opportunity to make a show of force. They arrived in intimidating numbers, properly equipped to put down any problems. The leader of the guards issued a stern statement that included a warning. Only then was lunch served. The customary, rather dull, bologna sandwich was greeted with a bit of a cheer. Walter took his sandwich and held it in his hands. It was wrapped in plastic, with the bread and the two slices of bologna separated, and the condiments in little packages. There was also a piece of fruit, an orange. At Santa Rita, the days of oranges in such lunches were numbered. Eventually they would be declared contraband after the discovery that they were being used to make pruno (an alcoholic beverage). Walter was one of the few men in that holding cell who had entered the jail without any personal effects other than the clothes on his back. He had no watch, no ring, no wallet; he left everything at home or with his wife. That sandwich was hardly a replacement for the missing wedding ring, but there it was, in a peculiar way, his only possession in the world—and he couldn't eat it.

Some of the inmates began harassing a young inmate, trying to get him to shut up. He was whining about still being hungry. The kid lacked the instincts to recognize how dangerous it was to draw attention to himself in a room full of men desperate to relieve stress. Walter called out to him, and his weak voice stopped all the reprimands. He gave his sandwich to the young inmate, and just as quickly as the tension had escalated, it calmed down again.

The guard called Walter's name. It was his turn for the strip search. "I hated the strip search," Walter said of the experience. He described standing behind a bathroom-stall-like partition and exposing his private parts to a perfect stranger with a clipboard. "You had to bend over and spread your legs and turn around and do it again. I really hated that." It was only the first strip-search the system had in store for him.

The indignity was quite a descent from his experience only forty-eight hours earlier, when, wearing the very same suit, Walter Hoye walked the halls of American power in Washington, D.C. He met with Representative Jessie Jackson Jr., other members of the Congressional Black Caucus, and Representative Trent Franks to discuss Colorado's abortion clinic bubble law. In two days he had gone from Capitol Hill to Santa Rita Jail. And he faced a new round of questions.

It may have been a guard asking the questions this time, but his answers were met with the same disbelief. In a way, the guard's reaction was worse than the inmates', because whether he thought Walter was an uncooperative liar was a matter of utmost seriousness. At first the guard hit Walter with questions riddled with popular street lingo and jail speak. But he changed his language when he noticed Walter's obvious confusion. He began with questions about health, and those were easy enough. Walter didn't have anything to report. He had no venereal diseases, chronic health problems, or addictions. The guard moved on to the reason Walter was in jail.

"I was convicted of holding up a sign at an Oakland abortion clinic," Walter explained. But the guard's face turned to stone. He warned Walter that evasive answers would not be tolerated. It was a test. Was Walter going to follow the rules and respect the authority of the guards and other staff, or was he going to be a problem, someone who would need an attitude adjustment in isolation? There was a pause, and the man's eyes demanded a response, a truthful response.

"It's a new law, an abortion clinic bubble law," Walter added. But just like his fellow inmates, the guard judged him to be a liar, a defiant troublemaker. The guard searched the county database on his computer, but he found no such crime. He looked at Walter and warned him again about lying. Walter did his best to elaborate. "I know, it's pretty unbelievable, but it's true."

Walter Hoye looked around the processing unit and felt an intense sense of humiliation and isolation for which he hadn't been prepared. He couldn't have been prepared, and he finally began to break down inside. *God, where are you? This is real now.*

2

Old Memories

Walter Hoye sat in a Union City, California, coffee shop next to Lori, his wife, and reflected on the events that led up to his prosecution, incarceration, and exoneration. It all seemed so long ago, but Walter isn't the type to forget. The life lessons that forged his Christian faith and his commitment to the pro-life cause guided him through his darkest hours. Some of those memories were old indeed, drenched in chapters of American history, both glorious and ignominious.

From the outset of Walter's life there were forces aligned against him. Some of these were the odds against a black boy flourishing in white America. But some of the opposition came from unexpected sources, from Walter's black peers. In his view, these men were on the wrong side of some issues, such as abortion, that have had a negative impact on blacks in the United States. Walter believed that many black leaders failed to speak out against abortion because they had forgotten key lessons of the past, or had chosen to ignore them, in order to make compromises for the sake of their personal ambitions.

Walter, a descendant of slaves, called these lessons the "old memories" that must be kept alive in order not to shortchange the pursuit of full equality and participation for blacks in American society. For Walter, these old memories run as a connective tissue through time and space and anchor him to his identity and his place in history. Forgetting and compromising are the enemies of black progress, he said, an affront to those who are laboring to complete the unfinished business of race in America.

The Legacy of Slavery

Black American history is shot through with missed opportunities, beginning with the tragic compromises made by the nation's founders. Despite being a slave owner, Thomas Jefferson opposed the continued practice of slavery in America. When he penned the Declaration of Independence, Jefferson, then a member of the Continental Congress from Virginia, included a scathing rebuke of taking people from a foreign land and enslaving them in the American colonies. He declared it, in the name of the colonies, an outrageous act, for which he laid responsibility squarely at the feet of Parliament and King George III. This revolutionary stance did not make it into the final version sent to the king and recorded in the annals of history. The Southern colonies threatened to pull out of the independence movement if the statement were left intact, and the Continental Congress chose the path of least resistance in order to preserve the unity of the thirteen colonies in 1776. It was a political decision, a compromise for the momentary greater good. Jefferson said at the time, however, that the issue of slavery must be settled soon, or worse would follow. "Nothing is more certainly written in the book of fate", Jefferson wrote in his memoir, "than that these people are to be free." *But when?*

As Congress drafted the Constitution in 1789, it again appeased the Southern plantation owners by tabling the debate over slavery and agreeing not to outlaw the importation of slaves until 1808. Under the leadership of Jefferson, as the third president of the United States, Congress criminalized the international slave trade in 1807. Although Jefferson proposed various plans for giving American slaves their freedom, he failed to free more than a few of his own, and upon his death his remaining 130 slaves were sold to pay his debts.

The failure to eradicate slavery at the foundation of the United States not only led to the Civil War in 1861, fulfilling Jefferson's prophetic warning, but also engrained the subjugation of an entire race of people into the culture of the Southern states. From there, a condescending attitude toward blacks spread and infected the growing nation at every turn and twist, almost irreversibly. Its impact was at its most personal in the lives of individual black men and women. On plantations, blacks were given just one name and cut off from their own bloodlines, in an effort to dehumanize them. Families were broken up when slave owners sold family members separately. Slaves were property, and nothing more, to be bought and sold or traded. It is no wonder that, when looking back and researching family histories, the trail for many black Americans ends in the 1860s. This appears to be where the trail ends for Walter, and where his story really begins.

Walter's great-grandfather on his mother's side, John Odum, was born into slavery in the state of Georgia, the birthplace of the cotton gin, around 1858. Early records describe him as black, but at least one government document classifies him as mulatto. At the time of the 1860 U.S. census, there were more than a million residents of the state of Georgia, nearly 600,000 categorized as free and 462,000 registered as slaves. Although there were some free black property owners who owned black slaves, John Odum was most likely owned by a white man with the same last name because children born into slavery were often given the surnames of their masters. There are records of an Odum plantation in Putnam County, about twenty-five miles from the central-Georgia region where John Odum eventually raised his family.

When Odum was about five years old, slavery was abolished by President Lincoln's Emancipation Proclamation. Many freed slaves had nowhere to go, however, and continued to live and work on the plantations that had owned them. Wherever Odum finished his growing up and learned his skills as a carpenter, by 1910 he was officially known as a farmer. Thus Odum came of age during the post–Civil War period known as Reconstruction. It was a rocky period for both whites and blacks, but it was made worse by those who resisted change and held on to postwar animosity. Many people in the South harbored resentment toward blacks and toward the Yankees who had stolen their way of life. The outcome of the war was hardest on the poorest whites who had sacrificed much for the losing side.

The Ku Klux Klan and the White League were an outgrowth of poor white bitterness and hatred. The Klan formed in 1866, almost immediately after the Civil War, and by 1870, the secret—actually not-so-secret—organization had spread throughout the South. Dwindling numbers of federal soldiers couldn't stop Klan lynchings of blacks and their white sympathizers, which were frequent and horrifying. The Klan's conduct was so violent that today the Klan would be declared a terrorist organization.

The forces of white racism wielded other means to resubjugate blacks. When the close results of the 1876 presidential election were disputed, the Democratic Party conceded to Republican Ruther-ford Hayes in exchange for an end to Reconstruction. All remain-ing federal troops were withdrawn from the former Confederate states, which were allowed to pass laws against blacks with impunity. Betrayed by the Compromise of 1877, many blacks left the Repub-lican Party. After anti-black laws were passed, blacks were hindered from voting. As a result, by the late 1800s, the Democrats had won back control of most of the former Confederate states.

Having won the war against Reconstruction, the Klan faded into the background as its usefulness, influence, and membership dimin-ished. But the organization rebounded in the early twentieth century, thanks to the silent 1915 film *The Birth of a Nation*, which romanticized early Klansmen and demonized blacks. Grossing astronomical sums at the box office, the film left an indelible mark on the American psyche and inspired a number of similar films. Klan membership came roaring back, and black Americans found themselves on an even steeper climb toward realizing true freedom.

A Hate Crime

In a few years, the resurgence of racism would scorch a path right through Walter Hoye's family tree. John Odum married Mary LeSeuer, who was about ten years his junior and had some French Canadian ancestry. Family oral history had always suggested that the LeSeuers had some Ojibwe blood. Since the tribe was known for a migration route that ran along the Great Lakes, and since the French Canadians were known for intermarriage with the natives, it was quite possible that LeSeuer was part Ojibwe.

John and Mary had their first child, a daughter, in 1893 and named her Viola. Thirteen more children followed. Meanwhile, John gained a reputation as fine builder. He eventually bought some land and built his own home in Hawkinsville, Pulaski County, Georgia. As often happened in the black communities of the South, friends and rela-tives gathered to help build the Odum house. Large as it was, it could barely accommodate the family of sixteen.

For some whites, the Odum house was a source of irritation—or, more accurately, envy. As Hollywood churned out lesser-quality imitations of *The Birth of a Nation*, there was a dramatic increase in animosity toward black Americans in the South, and in a tiny part of Pulaski County, that ill will began to focus on the Odum family. White buyers made offers on the house, but it wasn't for sale. It was well crafted, beautiful, and comfortable—more than a black family deserved, in the opinion of some people.

According to firsthand accounts supported by historical circumstantial evidence, sometime in 1921 or shortly thereafter, while the Odum family slept, at least six men came calling. They came to get the patriarch out of bed, and they did not knock. They may have been wearing hoods or other face coverings, but it didn't matter much to John and Mary as they were dragged outside. The men's intentions were as clear as the glow of their flickering torches when they set the Odum home ablaze. The house was made of wood, and the fire spread quickly. The men restrained John and Mary as the fire licked the outer walls. Their terrified children decided to wait inside for as long as possible, hoping the fire would burn so hot that the men would assume they were dead and leave. To protect their younger brothers and sisters for as long as possible, some of the older children sacrificed their lives.

Meanwhile, the men tortured and dismembered John Odum. They cut off his genitals, stuffed them in Mary's mouth, and gagged her with a rag. While John lay dying they raped Mary and finally left her for dead. By then the Odum children had to flee the burning house. Viola, in her thirties, grabbed two of her siblings and dragged them outside. Then she turned and ran back inside, vanishing into the black smoke that billowed from every window and doorway. Somehow, she cut through the flames and the choking smoke and emerged with another child. Her burned skin draped from her scorched arms like thin layers of wax. Leaving the three siblings, she went back inside for another child. She went back and forth until her body gave out and the house was completely engulfed in flames. The six survivors Viola saved were William, Alijah, Mary, John, Robert, and fifteen-year-old Bessie Kate, the future grandmother of Walter Hoye.

With half the family and all their possessions lost, Viola and the rest of the children turned to the very same community that had helped them to build the house. They were as reliable as ever, but before a new house could be built, Viola had to be brought back from the edge of death. There were no doctors available, but caregivers and healers applied remedies developed over hundreds of years of slavery, one of which was the lard treatment. They covered Viola in lard, herbs, and spices and buried her in the ground up to her neck. She remained in the ground for three months as her neighbors fed her and cared for her. Viola recovered, but she bore the thick, debilitating scars of that night for the rest of her life. In spite of chronic, crippling health problems, she lived to a ripe old age.

To the children of her brothers and sisters, and their children, Viola was known as Annie (derived from "Auntie"). The story of her heroics was passed down to Bessie Kate's daughter Vida, Walter's mother. Vida Pickens Hoye said the story was always told with respect for the faith that carried the family through that trial and many others. Their faith was a reason to be thankful and to persevere. The story is more about the family and the community pulling together and helping each other than about the evil that had been done, Vida said. Walter Hoye echoed his mother, "We held together as a family."

The Great Migration

After the murder of her father, mother, and siblings, Bessie Kate Odum accepted the invitation to live with her older sister Mary Odum Bell in Atlantic City, New Jersey. Bessie Kate was about seventeen years old and had no idea just how important the trip north would be—and not just for herself, but for millions of black Americans. She was part of the Great Migration, which was caused, in no small part, by the rise in Klan violence and which would reshape America. Between 1916 and 1970, six million blacks from the rural South took all they had and moved to the Northeast, the Midwest, and the West. They took wagons, trains, and cars, and some of them even walked, in search of opportunities.

Atlantic City at the dawn of the Roaring Twenties must have seemed like another planet to Bessie Kate. It was during Prohibition, and there were bootlegging mobsters and speakeasies. There were new and daring styles of clothes and hats. But Bessie Kate was more interested in jazz than in any of the other fashions of the time. She was even more interested in a particular young man: Eltee Pickens. In his early twenties, Eltee was from Anderson, South Carolina, where he had been part of the Royal Oak Baptist Church from an early age. He was the son of Hettie and Kata (or Cater) Pickens, who had brought him up right. Once Bessie Kate met Eltee, she had little to fear. The raging world around her seemed to be quieted by the man who became her "one true love and companion", as Eltee would be described decades later in her obituary. Bessie and Eltee were married on June 6, 1923, and soon afterward the tide of hope that lifted so many others carried them along as well. The couple headed to Detroit, Michigan, where the auto plants were expanding and hiring workers.

The Pickenses found their way to Hartford Avenue, where they rented one of the many bungalows within the original city limits of Detroit. Not forgetting where they came from, they promptly joined a small but respectable congregation, the Hartford Avenue Baptist Church. The pastor there since 1920 was the Reverend Charles Andrew Hill Sr. The congregation didn't number much more than thirty-five at the time and had room to grow. The Pickenses figured it was a good fit, and they were right. Eventually they played important roles in the church: Eltee became a deacon, and for Bessie Kate there wasn't a job within the community that she couldn't handle.

Eltee discovered that factory jobs were not as plentiful as he had hoped. The 1930 U.S. census recorded him as a chauffeur, but he was doing right by his own and paying the bills. There was Bessie Kate, keeping things straight at home, and, of course, the little girls who had come to make sure that life would not be predictable. In 1930, Bernice was four. And Vida Mae? Well, the census man, practicing his fractions, reported that the baby was a mere four-twelfths of a year.

To help make ends meet, the family shared the house with Eugene and Martha Thomas, who were just a bit older, thirty-five and twenty-nine, respectively. Four years later, Mary Louise Pickens joined the family. She had turned six when the census man came around again in 1940. By that time, Eltee had finally landed a job at Chevrolet and moved the family, sans Mr. and Mrs. Thomas, up the street. Life was good for Bessie Kate and Eltee Pickens. God willing, it would stay that way.

3

Detroit

On August 20, 1956, Detroit, Michigan, welcomed another native son, Walter Brisco Hoye II. The little bungalow on Hartford, where he spent his first night in the comfort of his mother's arms, was just like the one his grandparents occupied when they arrived in Detroit. The city was in its heyday; the great industrial powerhouse was the center of the booming American auto industry. But its preeminence and prosperity would erode during Walter's boyhood, as would the viability and the stability of his community. Neighborhoods built on the strong foundation of Christian families and churches would crumble before his eyes.

Walter's grandparents had been part of that foundation. By 1940 Bessie Kate and Eltee Pickens had carved out a hopeful slice of the American dream in the Motor City. Eltee Pickens had a good job at Chrysler, and his family had grown to five with the addition of Mary Louise, by then six years old, Vida Mae, age ten, and fourteen-year-old Bernice. A framed portrait of the daughters, taken a few years earlier, adorned a shelf in their humble home. It was one of those priceless images that would survive the years, passed along in family collections. The young ladies wore dresses, and their dark locks were twisted into abundant silky curls in the style popularized by Shirley Temple. The girls each wore a large ribbon tied neatly around the head with a big bow on the side. Only Bernice managed to offer the slightest smile.

Eltee Pickens served on the deacon board at Hartford Avenue Baptist Church. The Pickens family worshipped at the makeshift chapel on Hartford when the congregation, established in 1924, was still small. Eventually a larger church was built near the corner of Hartford and Milford, only two blocks from their home. The Pickens family walked to church on Sundays, and social time and fellowship always followed services. The congregation grew to a thousand by 1945.

Bessie Kate was a mother and a housewife. She was also about as active as anyone could be at Hartford Avenue Baptist. She sang with the choir, served on the committee for church bylaws, and helped those in need with the Jolly Matrons, sometimes called the Jolly 24. Every Friday they would pool money for the cause. At Thanksgiving and Christmas, they would buy clothes and food to distribute. But service didn't stop there. Across the street a widow was struggling to raise her three sons. Eltee took it upon himself to mentor the boys. He helped them to understand the proper way to show respect for their mother and for every woman. It was a role he played in various ways for many young boys at his church. "It wasn't enough to just go to church," Vida Mae Hoye later recalled. "My father taught us that we had to become a church and commit to helping others as part of our everyday lives."

A Future Full of Hope

For Eltee and Bessie Kate, their northern urban neighborhood was more than just miles away from the rural South. They were raising children in one of the fastest-growing cities in the nation, one of the prized destinations for black Americans taking part in the Great Migration. They had brought with them their commitment to faith and family, but Detroit offered them something the South could not provide: a good education for their children.

According to Vida Hoye, her parents cherished Jesus Christ, family, education, and respectability, in that order. She developed an appetite for learning and found in her own family history plenty of inspiration to learn all she could about folk medicine. She studied old remedies, including the one that saved the life of her aunt Viola, and she might have made a good doctor if the times had been right, but eventually she gravitated toward education and teaching. Vida was a standout athlete. She played basketball for Northwestern High School and also excelled at softball, tennis, and field hockey. While her athletic prowess developed, she grew into a real beauty. Her jump shot improved, and so did her chances of going to the prom with the best-looking young man at nearby Cass Technical High School, someone she had known since she was a little girl.

Walter B. Hoye was from Mississippi and came to Detroit at a young age with his parents, William Horace Hoye and Loubertha (Bertha) Hoye (née Stewart). They were regular members of Hartford Baptist Church, which is where Vida and Walter met. On the day Walter Hoye married Vida Pickens, the bride-to-be was assisted into her magically flowing Italian lace gown by her sisters, who labored lovingly over every detail. As Bernice stood up for her sister as the maid of honor, the Reverend Charles Hill presided over the nuptials at Hartford Baptist, where the couple was serenaded by a singer and a string ensemble performing "Calm Is the Night".

The first child to arrive was Walter II. Vida's labor lasted only an hour, just long enough for her son to be born in a hospital bed. A year later, Walter's sister, Jo-Ann, came even more quickly, making her entrance into the world in the hospital elevator. Vida Mae enrolled Walter and Jo-Ann at Detroit's Winterhalter Elementary School, at the corner of Cortland and Broadstreet, not far from their home on Pasadena Street. Established in 1922, the school was named for Admiral Albert G. Winterhalter, a Detroit native who commanded the United States Navy Asiatic Fleet in 1917. It was unique for having a half-grade system. Walter and Jo-Ann were required to show proficiency in grade 1-A, for example, before moving on to grade 1-B.

Walter and Jo-Ann were latchkey kids from the start, but they were expected to obey a strict set of rules that every family on Pasadena knew and enforced. Children were supposed to be home before dark, for example, or risk the wrath of their parents. Then there was Miss Brookes, a neighbor who kept a close grandmotherly eye on the Hoye children. While their parents were at work, Walter and Jo-Ann reported to her about where they were going and what they were doing. Heaven help them if she found out they were misbehaving. To preempt the inevitable call to their parents, they would rush home to plead their case to Mom and Dad. At least they could give their side of the story, which might soften the blow.

Pasadena Street was just a couple of miles from Vida's childhood home on Hartford, where her parents still lived. When Walter and Jo-Ann were on Hartford, they were known as the Pickens kids, and they were there a lot. Spending a weekend with the grandparents was a reward for good behavior, Jo-Ann said. "I would break my neck to get through the week to go to Grandmom's," she said. "In the mornings, there were biscuits and fresh pancakes. You just knew when Granddaddy was awake. And he played with us." The weekends usually included Sunday service at Hartford Baptist, followed by dinner with the grandparents. For Jo-Ann, the weekend was a complete loss without that last part. She was inconsolable if Mom and Dad tried to take her home before the meal. The major holidays were also spent on Hartford. Not a Thanksgiving or a Christmas would pass without festivities at the home of Granddaddy and Grandmom.

Over on Pasadena, life was more ordinary. In addition to their school assignments, which their parents made sure they completed, the children had chores to do. One of Walter's boyhood chores was quite unpleasant—burning trash in the alley behind the house. The job was also dangerous. Despite being feet from his home, the alley was dark and foreboding, a place where people sometimes did things they shouldn't. Walter's life wasn't all drudgery, however; he also enjoyed some childhood fun. Jo-Ann recalled Walter's active imagination and how he and his friends would don sheets for capes and pretend to be Superman. She would roll her eyes as they took turns leaping off the garage roof and impersonating their hero. To this day Walter bears a scar over his left eye, a memento of a time when he was rudely reminded that he was a mere mortal.

Last Survivor

Walter was hardly more than three years old when Tamla Records bought a house at 2648 West Grand Boulevard in Detroit. The humble two-story bungalow sent shockwaves through the entertainment world as from it grew the Motown music empire, driven in large part by the pen of Berry Gordy Jr., the company's owner. Walter would grow up loving Motown favorites—Smokey Robinson and the Miracles, Diana Ross, and the "wicked" Wilson Pickett. Add the Temptations and Marvin Gaye, and one understands how the house on West Grand came to be nicknamed Hitsville, U.S.A.

Detroit's music scene in 1959 was emblematic of the growing influence of black American culture. What began as a trickle with jazz had become a transformational wave with the Motown Sound, which was a combination of jazz, rhythm and blues, and gospel. It not only changed the way Americans sang and danced; it caused them to think across racial boundaries.

Six hundred miles away, on New York's legendary Broadway, another cultural breakthrough occurred when a modest-sounding stage play opened. *A Raisin in the Sun* was written by black playwright Lorraine Hansberry, who took the title from the poem "Harlem" by Langston Hughes. The play tells the story of a black family's experiences on the South Side of Chicago. Sidney Poitier played Walter Younger, whose ambition for wealth clashes with his black identity and his obligations to his family's cultural legacy. Walter Hoye had little idea, if any, about the success of *A Raisin in the Sun*, but a version of Walter Younger's struggles was set to play out in Detroit with Walter Hoye as its central figure.

By the mid-sixties, the newfound influence of black Americans, and the subsequent national awakening, manifested itself in authentic change. In Washington, D.C., President Lyndon Johnson signed the Voting Rights Act. And in Detroit, Motown was basking in its heyday. The Temptations hit number one on the pop charts with "My Girl", and Tamla-Motown launched in London. Black musicians were touring the capitals of Europe and becoming international celebrities.

On every corner of Detroit, it seemed, were groups of young men and women showing off their talents in hopes of being discovered and signing a recording contract. The starry-eyed wannabes, enraptured by the allure of the rising stars, emulated their look and sound. But there was a downside to this movement. For every success story, there were thousands more young people who would never make it big. If they didn't invest in their education, they might not make it all. A criminal element was growing in Detroit, and a lot of young black men were "doing things they shouldn't have been doing," Walter said. For impressionable ten-year-old Walter, it wasn't easy to tell right from wrong when everyone seemed to be having such a good time, and he jumped right into the action. "I wanted my hair conked," he said, referring to slick hairstyle of Chuck Berry and James Brown. "I wanted the black jacket, to chase women, and to do the things that gang members were doing."

Walter was a standout student, and he advanced faster than his classmates. The school district even wanted him to skip a grade. His academic success boded well for his future, and it was a source of tremendous pride for his parents. The trouble was that bookworms were a lonely lot at Winterhalter. Walter got the grades, but what he wanted was what everyone else wanted, to have friends. To Walter, it seemed as though the tough kids running the streets had all the friends they wanted. Those boys didn't go to school, however. They were robbing, stealing, and lying. The worse they behaved, at least as Walter saw it, the more the girls liked them. So Walter grew tired of being smart. First, he ignored this or that assignment, then he brushed off his studies, and then he stopped reading altogether. He had been such a good student until then, getting not just good grades but great grades, that the change was striking. The school district decided that Walter was not as smart as had been thought and elected not to move him ahead. Walter's parents knew that he most certainly was that smart and sadly realized that he was intentionally rebelling and sabotaging his future. Detroit's ugly side had drawn in their son.

During Walter's bad-boy act, he asked his mother for a switchblade. It was the sexy weapon of the street and a symbol of cool, and it was also useful for personal protection. Looked at from the viewpoint of an aspiring tough, it was a mistake to ask his mother for the knife. "She wasn't having any of it," Walter recalled. "The way we grew up in my household, when you're told no, that was all you needed to hear." A couple of years later Walter was in a situation in which a switchblade might have come in handy, but it also might have led to such a disaster that, in retrospect, asking his mother for a knife might not have been a mistake after all.

The situation unfolded at the Winterhalter baseball field, where Walter was practicing his pitch with his friends from Little League. He knew he wasn't much of a pitcher, but he wanted to be better. He had only one pitch, a fastball, and generally it would travel right down the middle of the plate, handing a fine opportunity to the batter. When practice with his friends ended, he stayed at the field a little longer to work on his game, but eventually he had to head home, alone. He didn't make it to the fence. "A couple of guys jumped me," he explained. "We fought a little bit, and they threw me down." Soon they had him pinned, he said. One of the boys struck a match. "They were going to burn my eyes out." If only he had a knife, he thought at first, but then he realized there are other weapons besides violence. "Lord," Walter prayed, "you've got to help me. I can't physically get out of this."

Some might say that what happened next was just dumb luck. It sure didn't feel that way to Walter. With the older boys leaning over him, and the flame blurring everything, Walter glimpsed a bicycle tire and part of a person's leg. Then he heard a voice: "There's a white guy in the alley." Immediately the boys let go of Walter and ran off toward the alley. The possible misfortune of someone else saved Walter, and his reaction was understandable. He just thanked God and ran as fast as he could to the schoolyard exit.

There was one thing about running home that hadn't yet occurred to him. He would have to run right by the alley where some white guy was surely being beaten up by those boys. As he got closer to the alley, he thought of that person and felt a sudden tinge of fear for him. But when he arrived, no one was there. The alley was empty. Walter was convinced that there never had been a white guy in the alley. He had the feeling that the person on the bicycle was an angel, an answer to his prayer. Maybe his faith saved him, but what if it hadn't? Would a switchblade have been the answer? Walter doesn't think so. Without the sober guidance of his parents, who wanted more for him than being a hoodlum, he might have had a knife and might now be dead. "I'm probably the only one that's left alive," Walter said, "that grew up on my block on Pasadena, in Detroit."

The Spiritual Fire

In late 1967 a remarkable thing was happening to Walter B. Hoye. He was falling in love. For the eleven-year-old, the street scene and the glamour of the world were losing their appeal. His previous ambitions seemed to shrink away from his consciousness little by little. What took their place was a smoldering fire in his belly just waiting to burst into a raging blaze. That fire was his growing love for God and for his people.

After Congress had passed various civil rights laws in the early sixties, there was more reason for optimism than ever before in the black

American community. Yet there was still plenty of racism, enough to thwart the progress that blacks were trying so hard to make. Walter's experiences with racism reminded him of "how difficult it was going to be to grow up in this society, to be a man in this society." He developed an aversion to white people, and so did many others in the predominantly black communities of Detroit. It was commonplace and, under the circumstances, not the least bit shocking. Encountering racism "makes you want to stay with your own," Walter said. "You become very close to your people." Walter was hardpressed to find any place that made him feel closer to his people than church. "It was a place where you could go and be with your own, and Christ was celebrated." It was a place of refuge.

Racism wasn't the only factor that deepened Walter's appreciation for his church. At the peak of his rebellion, when school and discipline appeared to be the enemy, when he fantasized about the rewards of being Bad Walter, there was one problem: he wasn't any happier. He wasn't any more popular than before and still had very few friends. The sense of identity and belonging that he had sought on the streets had eluded him. He felt anxious, confused, and sad. He was beginning to see that apart from his family, the only other place that offered him real support was Hartford Avenue Baptist Church.

On an October Sunday in 1967, Walter experienced an epiphany that would change the course of his life. He was sitting in the second row in church with his sister, Jo-Ann. In the row just behind him sat his mother and father, and his grandmother Bessie Kate Pickens. Up front, in the section where the church leadership sat, was his grandfather. As the preacher began his sermon, Walter's mind was on his frustrations. *How come I have no friends?* By all accounts he was getting straight As in the How to Be Bad class in the school of hard knocks. *So how come I haven't reaped a single reward?*

"All things are possible with God," said the preacher, interrupting the monologue in Walter's head. "All things," he added, "if you accept Jesus Christ as your Lord and Savior."

If I would only trust him, Walter responded in his mind. *If I'd put all my hope and faith in him ...*

"Can I believe this?" Walter asked. Only this time his words came out of his mouth. "God," he spoke out loud, so loudly that the people around him could hear, "can I believe what the preacher just said about you?" All eyes from all directions turned toward the young man.

"I heard God's voice audibly," Walter recalled. "God just said, 'Yes you can.'"

It was all Walter needed to hear. He stood up and headed for the preacher, who had invited forward those who were ready to give themselves to Jesus. In Walter's faith tradition, one gives his hand to the preacher and his heart to God. Jo-Ann got up and followed him. "That was the day we both got saved," Walter said.

Jo-Ann remembers the day too. Grandaddy Pickens had advanced lung cancer and had been in and out of the hospital for months. No one knew for sure, but he had only a few months left to live. As Walter rose from his seat, Jo-Ann felt a strong desire to see Grandaddy Pickens smile at them both, she said. That was why she followed Walter and gave her hand to the preacher.

Walter's new commitment to Christ put a new kind of pressure on him, but with it came a new kind of strength. He no longer tried to be bad, but whenever he was bad, he felt remorse; when he was tempted, it was easier to resist. Moreover, his inner turmoil gave way to a peace that allowed him to be more himself. He could smile again.

4

Lockdown

Midnight on Saturday, March 21, 2009, was the start of a new day. But Friday hadn't ended yet, *had it*? For Walter B. Hoye, time had lost its reference points. He was like a gambler inside a casino where flashy lights and ubiquitous pings and bells work on people's minds to keep them playing all night without realizing how much time has passed. At least Walter had also lost the sense of hurry-up-and-wait urgency that dominated the last so many hours. He was outfitted in his new blue, wrinkle-free jail clothes and standing in a hallway of pale lime-green brick walls. The migrating smells of bodily fluids and nervous sweat hadn't entirely faded but were fainter. Was he getting used to them?

Things had quieted down, but the longest Friday of Walter's life wasn't over, and neither were the questions. Walter had one last, but not less taxing, session with a jail official, which included a good introduction to the facility and the rules. At least listening was easier than answering questions.

Walter had become BGR852, a registered prisoner in the care of the county Department of Corrections. The inmates had been sizing him up all along, and the guards were finally having their chance. Walter had never been known as a liar or even an inventor of tall tales, but during his first day in custody virtually everyone around him assumed he had to be lying. He couldn't possibly be in jail for carrying a "God loves you" sign. That would be absurd.

After hours and hours of questioning, the guards, at least, seemed to soften a little in their skepticism, though not entirely, because the so-called bubble law was so new that it hadn't yet found its way into the county data system. But something was happening just a few miles away that would erase all doubt about why Walter was in jail.

Around the time Walter was putting on his jail clothes, in nearby Walnut Creek, Bay Area News Group was churning out the Saturday morning edition of the *Oakland Tribune*. The papers fresh off the press were piled up in orderly bundles and wrapped with a plastic band, awaiting delivery. Several bundles were destined for Santa Rita Jail. The vindication that would result from their arrival was the furthest thing from Walter's mind as he walked bleary-eyed to Housing Unit 34, carrying the bed linens for his bunk.

Inside Unit 34

As Walter stepped inside the common area, it must have seemed like a soundstage for a movie set. There was a large three- to four-foot-square metallic box with a red digital display. With its hinges, the box resembled a small refrigerator, but as Walter would later discover, it kept things hot, not cold, and was used to deliver food at mealtimes. Beyond the box were circular stainless-steel tables, each with six permanently affixed stools. Hovering just above them, and adding a sci-fi effect, was an octagonal guard station with mirror-tinted windows.

Opposite the tables were six cages, or pods—three on the second story, the upper pods, and three on the first floor, the lower pods. Each pod housed two rows of bunks. The main doors opened, and Walter and the other inmates entered their assigned pods. Sleeping inmates groaned over the intrusion, but some inmates were awake and milling about in various stages of undress.

When Walter walked into his first-floor F-pod cage, one of the inmates asked, "Did you bring the drugs?" A bit startled, Walter nevertheless looked the man in the eye and answered no. He set his linens down on a lower bunk but was quickly admonished by an inmate, who snapped at him to take an upper one. Walter took note: lower bunks were a sign of status; a new guy doesn't deserve one. He was still on the upward slope of the first-timer learning curve. The experienced inmates and the guards knew the system. A newcomer like Walter must learn the unwritten rules and the unspoken hierarchy through hazing.

Walter took the top bunk chosen for him, and when he spread the sheet across the mattress and tugged at a corner to secure it, he

discovered that it was too small to tuck underneath. Suddenly an inmate flashed a contraband razor blade, and Walter's pulse kicked into
high gear. But the man wasn't threatening him; he was introducing himself as an ally by offering to fix his bedsheet. "He must have
just had pity on me," Walter said. The man was in his thirties, also
black, and a little taller than Walter. He sliced through each corner
of the sheet to create an attached ribbon of fabric about an inch
wide and several inches long. He then tied the corners to the bunk
springs. The razor blade vanished as quickly as it had appeared. The
experienced inmate's workaround was a gift, Walter said, a sponta-
neous act of kindness from a stranger. It was even more beautiful in
that place, after all Walter had been through in the last dozen hours
or so.

Looking around the cage, Walter realized that all the other alpha
males were also black—a lucky break, because in most California
jails and prisons, the Mexican La Familia gang rules the roost. When
Walter asked for the time, he was surprised to hear that it was three
o'clock in the morning. He mustered the energy to say thank you
and climbed onto his bed. As his head hit the pillow, the lights went
out. Despite his racing thoughts and rising fears, exhaustion overtook
him and pulled him into a deep sleep.

Overcrowding

Walter's nap was brief because Santa Rita keeps military hours.
Breakfast is served before dawn, sometimes as early as three o'clock
in the morning. Also before dawn, would-be visitors line up outside
the jail to get on the visitor list. Appointments to see inmates are set
for later in the day or in the evening and are granted on a first-come,
first-served basis. Visiting hours for each housing unit occur only
three days a week. Unit 34, Walter Hoye's temporary address, had
visiting hours starting at noon on Saturdays. As Walter awoke early
that first Saturday morning, Lori Hoye was already outside, waiting
for a chance to see him.

"You had to get out there in the dark to get your name on the list
so you could come back and get a piece of paper to go in and visit
the person," Lori said. She had been up all night Friday, and when

she called Santa Rita in the wee hours of the morning to find out when she could visit Walter, she was first told that Walter wasn't there. After the jail employee finally figured out that he was a newly processed inmate, she told Lori to come as soon as she could if she wanted to see Walter that day. She quickly showered and drove about twenty-five minutes to the jail, and although it was still dark when she arrived, there were already two long lines of people waiting to make visitor appointments. "Some people had folding chairs as if they were going to a soccer game," she said. Some of them were wrapped in blankets, and some were even sleeping.

Lori didn't know where to go, or which line to choose. She instinctively chose the longer line, which turned out to be a good move. Later she found out that the other line was shorter because it was for visits to prisoners in maximum security. When Lori returned for her first visit with Walter, the security check was thorough and the rules were outlined clearly. She put a quarter in the coin-operated locker and left all her belongings inside. The key from that locker was about all she was allowed to take with her inside the walls of Santa Rita. She also had Walter's reading glasses, which she turned over to the guards with the request that they be delivered to her husband. Even that simple request involved red tape. It would take two days for the glasses to reach Walter in his cage.

The visit that day was as refreshing as it was surreal for Walter and Lori. After the odyssey of the past twenty-four hours, they were happy to see each other, even if separated by a several-inches-thick slab of bulletproof glass. They spoke to each other through telephones, but the cords were so short that they had to sit on the edges of their stools and crane their necks so that their ears would reach the receivers. After seeing and talking with Lori, Walter returned to his cage with a renewed sense that things were going to be okay.

While Walter's so-called crime put a harmless man in a crowded jail, prison overcrowding put a dangerous man on the streets. Five months before Walter was locked up in Santa Rita, Lovelle Mixon was released from the state penitentiary at Susanville after serving nine months for a parole violation involving possession of stolen property. Before he was sent to Susanville, Mixon was on parole for good behavior after five years in a state prison for an assault with a deadly weapon and a carjacking in San Francisco. In spite of a history of violent crime, he was released early from Susanville because of overcrowding, and he returned home to East Oakland, to one of the city's most troubled neighborhoods.

An Oakland Shooting

At 1:08 P.M., on Saturday, March 21, 2009 (about the time Walter and Lori Hoye were talking with each other at Santa Rita), two Oakland motorcycle police officers stopped a burgundy 1995 Buick driven by Lovelle Mixon. For reasons known only to Mixon, he exited the car with a pistol and opened fire. Some accounts say he stood over the dying officers before running away from the scene. Oakland police launched a full-scale manhunt with the aid of multiple agencies. They located Mixon after he had barricaded himself inside an apartment in his neighborhood. A SWAT team closed in and made entry with full tactical force. Again, Mixon opened fire, shooting and killing two more police officers and wounding another. In the short, violent engagement, Mixon was shot and killed. People wondered why he lashed out in one violent final act, but the most compelling explanation was also the most likely—he simply did not want to return to prison. If there was another reason, it was buried with him.

Santa Rita Jail established a lockdown following the first reported shooting in Oakland. There was, in effect, a state of emergency among law enforcement agencies across Alameda County. Calls for assistance were answered by officers throughout the area and from agencies outside the area as well. The sheriff's department shifted to minimum staffing at the jail to maximize support for Oakland's search for a cop killer.

The garbled lockdown announcement echoed off the walls not long after Walter returned to his cage in Block 34. The inmates, wherever they were—the visiting room, the work details, or the common area—shuffled with urgency back to their cages. Their pained groans followed the automatic bolting of the cage doors. Guards swept swiftly through the unit, counting heads and making sure everyone was where he was supposed to be. The inmates dreaded being cooped up for long hours, and because they had no idea why they were on lockdown, they had no way of knowing how long it would last. After only thirty minutes in lockdown, some men started to go stir-crazy. Walter's ignorance of lockdown made it easier for him to cope. For all he knew, it happened all the time and lasted just an hour. He sank back into his bunk and stared at the ceiling. He didn't know what to think about the lockdown, but he was beginning to have some very clear thoughts about something else—pornography.

Like the razor blade that was used to modify his bedsheet, pornography was contraband. Walter's sheet fell into the contraband category the moment it was cut. Some things are bigger problems than others, and guards had to choose their battles to keep peace in their cell blocks. Pornography was banned but conveniently overlooked. Walter, however, found it impossible to overlook, particularly in the shower, where it papered the tiles. He tried to keep his back to the images and to keep his eyes closed whenever he had to face them. Other than that, there was nothing he could do about it—*or was there?* The situation awoke the pastor in him. But there was the lockdown to contend with first.

"Some of the men were nervous, kind of fidgety," Walter said. Some were pacing back and forth. There was a single long aisle between the bunks. On one end were the bathroom and the shower, and on the other end was Walter's bed. The aisle was wide enough to fit only one man, so there was a certain decorum and pecking order in terms of who had to yield to whom when men passed each other. Some inmates were releasing their pent-up energy by pounding on the cement walls. Other inmates killed time by talking themselves up and telling stories about their exploits on the outside. Walter, the ordained minister, prayed for the right way to insert himself into the lives of these men.

Meanwhile back at home, Walter's wife, a huge sports fan, tried to calm her uneasy mind with basketball. Watching March Madness college games proved to be a good distraction, especially when Demetri Goodson made a game-winning running bank shot with less than a second on the clock, lifting Gonzaga over Western Kentucky, 83 to 81. Lori, a sports statistician, saw the inspiring win as a comforting sign. It was fleeting, however, for the news bulletin on the Oakland shooting snapped her back to reality. Lori turned off the television and turned on her computer to write Walter a letter.

Babe,

You don't know how good it was to see your face this afternoon. Even though I couldn't reach out and touch you, I was
grateful to God to see you and see that you are safe and sound.
I pray that the Lord will keep a hedge of protection around
you and give you favor. God is using you already.... I console
myself by sleeping in sweatshirts (it will have to keep me warm
until you get home).... You are my HERO!

5

Made by History

On April 4, 1968, a soft-point, metal-jacketed bullet fired from a Remington .30-06-caliber rifle ended the life of Martin Luther King Jr. as he stood on the balcony outside his room at the Lorraine Motel in Memphis, Tennessee. It was a violent end to a life defined by nonviolence. The rifle belonged to a forty-year-old Tennessean by the name of James Earl Ray, who confessed to the crime. Ray was a small-time criminal who had, a year earlier, escaped from the Missouri State Penitentiary in Jefferson City. He was convicted of murder and died in prison while serving a life sentence. Whether Ray acted alone on the basis of his well-established racism or was set up and framed by others, as he later claimed, the result of King's assassination was the same: waves of shock, grief, and righteous indignation spread through the country, particularly through the black community, including the family and friends of Walter Hoye in Detroit.

In a sermon published in 1963, Martin Luther King Jr. said, "We are not makers of history. We are made by history." Like Walter Hoye, King had roots in Georgia, where race, racism, slavery, and Reconstruction shaped the lives of his forebears. After the Civil War, black Americans in Georgia experienced rapid progress, made possible in large part by political gains. Under the skilled leadership of Georgia's first black state senator, Tunis Campbell, the Republicans built a solid black political base that gave the GOP control of the state government in Savannah. Many laws were passed that protected the newly won rights and freedoms of blacks.

Jim Crow

A violent pushback, inspired and led by the Ku Klux Klan, reversed the advancement of blacks in the South. Murder, intimidation, and coercion targeted anyone who worked toward equality, whether white or black. In 1871 the Republican governor of Georgia, Rufus Bullock, was forced to resign and to flee the state. Although in 1872 President Ulysses S. Grant, a pro-Reconstruction Republican, won reelection, Georgia, including Campbell's senate seat, was lost to the Democrats. So effective and pervasive was the violence, and sometimes paid voter suppression, that in three Georgia counties critical to the survival of Reconstruction, not a single vote was cast for President Grant, although the counties had large black voting populations. When leadership in Savannah reverted to the Democrats, Campbell was imprisoned on trumped-up charges, and all his work on behalf of black Americans was dismantled as Jim Crow segregation laws were passed to keep blacks on the margins of white society.

When Martin Luther King Jr. was born in 1929, blacks throughout the South were treated as second-class citizens. In his home state of Georgia, public facilities segregated black people and offered them inferior service. Private enterprises, too, such as diners and movie theaters, kept blacks apart from whites and treated them with contempt. Segregation meant that King attended all-black schools until he graduated from Morehouse College with a sociology degree in 1948. He experienced culture shock when he did his graduate theological studies at Crozer Theological Seminary in Pennsylvania, followed by Boston University, which were predominantly white. By the time King became a pastor of Dexter Avenue Baptist Church in Montgomery, Alabama, he was committed to changing the unjust system that described its treatment of blacks as "separate but equal".

With nonviolence as a guiding principal, King spearheaded the civil rights movement by leading its first major protest, the Montgomery Bus Boycott, which was inspired by Rosa Parks' refusal to vacate her seat for a white passenger and move to the rear of a city bus. During the 1957 boycott, which lasted 382 days, King was arrested and his house was bombed. In the end, the Supreme Court declared the bus segregation unconstitutional.

Soon afterward King began campaigning for the removal of laws that prevented or hindered blacks from exercising their right to vote, which the Fifteenth Amendment to the Constitution had granted. He was put on the cover of *Time* magazine and met with President Dwight D. Eisenhower and later President John F. Kennedy. In the meanwhile, King, the voice and the face of the movement, continued to lead nonviolent demonstrations against segregation in the South. As a result, he also continued to be the target of attacks and arrests. In his famous "Letter from Birmingham Jail", King wrote, "I am in Birmingham because injustice is here. . . . Injustice anywhere is a threat to justice everywhere."

Walter Hoye would one day come to a very personal understanding of those words. Until then, growing up in Detroit, he was inspired from afar by what King was saying and doing. Yes, for blacks, injustice in Birmingham was a threat to justice in Detroit, Chicago, Montgomery, and everywhere else. Likewise, no matter where King brought the fight for justice, his victories were victories for everyone.

The Dream in Detroit

Segregation was not the law in the North, as it was in the South, but it was legal. In Detroit, for example, before the Fair Housing Act of 1968 there was legal discrimination against blacks by landlords and sellers of residential property. People could simply refuse to sell houses to blacks. In some places, new houses could not be built unless cement walls were erected to keep houses for blacks and whites separate. They came to be known as segregation walls. The Detroit Eight Mile Wall was built in 1941 as a barrier between whites and blacks and still stands today.

In 1963, two months prior to the famous March on Washington and his "I Have a Dream" speech, King spoke before a crowd of about twenty-five thousand at Detroit's Cobo Hall. Throngs in the Walk to Freedom packed Jefferson and Washington Avenues, buoyed by King's powerful oratory and their sense of unity and purpose. The moment stood in striking contrast to the previous summer, when the Twelfth Street riots set the city aflame. They were some of the most violent race riots in American history, described by some as urban revolt. Anger had been simmering for years over segregated schools and housing and growing unemployment among blacks. After a police raid, it exploded into five days of fiery violence,

ending with the deployment of federal troops. All told, thirty-three
blacks and ten whites were killed. Between five hundred and a thousand people were injured. More than seven thousand arrests were
made, and twenty-five hundred businesses were destroyed. Walter
recalled those long nights. "What kept going through my mind was
the question why," he explained. "I could not understand why we
were burning our own community."

Walter's sister, Jo-Ann, has a more detailed memory of the tu-
mult. She remembers the tanks rolling through the streets and the
mounted police employed for crowd control. There was a bomb
threat at their elementary school. The children were first sheltered
in the basement and then let out and told to run home, which
was thirteen blocks away for Walter and Jo-Ann. The curfew added
to their fear, as did the orders for people to stay indoors, to keep
their doors locked and their lights off, and to sleep on the floor.
A few days later, when Walter had football practice, Vida Hoye
decided to drive him to school. She was sick of living in fear, and
with both Jo-Ann and Walter in the car, she drove through the
police checkpoint on Pasadena. At an intersection, Jo-Ann saw a
man throw a brick through a drugstore window and begin looting
the place. "I remember my mom saying to us, 'That's no way to act.
That's not how we act,'" said Jo-Ann.

A year later, the Hoye family was marching with King. By joining
the civil rights movement, they felt that they had become part of the
solution. The atmosphere of fear and despair was gone, and hope had
returned to Motor City. Jo-Ann sat on her father's shoulders as her
family listened to King's thrilling speech. His words made them feel
as though they had risen from the ashes, Walter said. King himself
called attention to the contrast between the peaceful march and the
violent riots. "I think there is something else that must be said because it is a magnificent demonstration of discipline," King told the
crowd. "With all of the thousands and hundreds of thousands of
people engaged in this demonstration today, there has not been one
reported incident of violence." The crowd responded with exuber-
ant applause.

The Detroit speech was famous for being an early rendition of
"I Have a Dream", and it carried no less impact for the people who
were there to hear it. Walter Hoye Sr. and his wife, Vida wouldn't

have missed it for the world. Walter was hardly six years old, yet he too was carried along by the optimism of the crowd. His early years coincided with the beginning of this new and great movement, which made many blacks feel that their time, their moment of real freedom, was at hand. "It would be an understatement," Walter said, "to call it just optimism. We could overcome, accomplish, break through, finally."

The Move to California

Five years later, in 1968, Walter was full of the spirit of the Lord. He had survived his trying time and had been baptized, and life was as good as could be expected. His father, who had been a sports writer and editor for the *Detroit Tribune* and the *Michigan Chronicle*, landed a job with the San Diego Chargers as assistant director of public relations. He was the first black American to hold the position in the National Football League (NFL), breaking the color barrier for that job. Such a great opportunity for a black man was another reason for optimism. For the Hoyes, it was *California, here we come.*

To expedite the move, Walter Hoye Sr. and Vida flew to San Diego while Walter and his sister temporarily moved in with Aunt Mary and Uncle Robert Harris in order to finish the school year. It was a convenient arrangement, but the distance between parents and children soon felt like a million dangerous miles.

As soon as Walter and Vida stepped off the plane in San Diego, they heard about Martin Luther King's assassination. A frantic phone call to Uncle Bob's delivered the news to Walter, but even before he was told, the boy about to turn twelve had already sensed something was amiss in his Detroit neighborhood. Cities around the country, one by one, were already boiling with rage. People were becoming violent in the streets of Detroit, Baltimore, Washington, Chicago, Kansas City, and 120 other cities. Detroit did not suffer the worst of it, but it still suffered.

Certainly the greatest casualty was the optimism that King had inspired. With the flip of a switch, it seemed to Walter, hope had been replaced by uncertainty and dread. "It happened in an instant," he said. "When they killed Martin Luther King, I went from a young man thinking about a positive future, from hope, to no hope, to a gigantic uncertainty."

His mother wanted to fly back home immediately, Walter added, to make sure he and his sister were safe. She knew Detroit had changed and would never be the same for blacks again. But young Walter couldn't quite believe it. "I was thinking it wasn't even that long ago, the Arkansas Nine," he said, recalling the nine black students who were the first admitted to Little Rock High School after it was desegregated. "[Governor George] Wallace was proven wrong," he continued. "We had overcome. We were acting Christlike."

As Detroit and other cities recovered from the initial shock and the public outrage over King's murder, Walter could see with his own eyes that his hometown had changed. An ominous dark cloud of despair had settled over the city. "Mortality was a reality," Hoye reflected. Even harder to accept was the sense of futility. The streets where Walter grew up were never perfectly safe by any stretch of the imagination, but at least he could go outside and play. That freedom ended as his neighborhood became meaner than it had been before.

Tempted to act out with violence like the other young men around him, Walter could have turned from what he had been taught. He also could have been attracted by the appeal of Malcolm X, whose philosophy was spreading in Detroit. His approach to civil rights was far different from King's. Originally a Baptist, Malcolm X became a Muslim and joined the Nation of Islam, a movement to create a separate state for black Muslims in America by violent means, if necessary. When Malcolm X split with the Nation of Islam and began to promote integration with whites, he was murdered in 1965 while giving a speech in New York City. Three Nation of Islam members would eventually be convicted in the killing, including one man who admitted his involvement years later. Walter managed to steer clear of such extremes and looked forward to his upcoming move to San Diego, where perhaps he would be able to rekindle a promising vision for his future. The legacy of Martin Luther King lived on in the young man and would one day consume his every thought.

6

Life Is Not a Game

Walter Hoye finished the sixth grade in Detroit in the spring of 1968 and moved to San Diego. During his first months on the California coast he felt like Dorothy in Oz, but there were no Munchkins, just a lot of Caucasians. For Walter, a kid who knew only his black neighborhood in Detroit, landing in white society was just as odd and fantastic as Dorothy's house crashing in Munchkinland. Even the clothes worn in San Diego seemed like costumes. What the kids there thought were cool clothes, and how much skin they exposed, was mind-boggling. Walter's first steps into this strange world were tentative, given the cultural armor that he had built up almost since birth. He was defensive toward white society, which he assumed was the primary cause of the woes of American blacks.

Amid the mostly white student body at Lewis Junior High, Walter felt like an outcast. "I had no friends," he said. "I didn't see anybody that looked like me. And certainly, nobody thought like me or acted like me." His sister also felt out of place. After Walter and Jo-Ann started to succeed in school, however, they were fine. In addition to good grades, Walter had Pop Warner football. Being part of a team gave him a sense of purpose and belonging. So did his family's membership at Calvary Baptist Church, which they joined in 1969.

The Southeast San Diego church was established initially as Second Baptist in 1889. When it moved from its original location at First and B Streets to Crosby and Julian in 1926, it was renamed. Finding a black church with a strong faith community was the top priority for the Hoyes. Walter Hoye Sr. immediately liked the pastor, Dr. S. M. Lockridge, and the feeling was mutual. The younger Walter grew to love and admire Lockridge, whom he calls "my father in the gospel".

Shadrach Meshach Lockridge was born in Texas in 1913. By the age of sixty he had earned a national reputation as a man of God and a brilliant preacher. He even caught the attention of the nation's best-known preacher, Billy Graham. Lockridge was appointed to the faculty of the Billy Graham School of Evangelism and the Greater Los Angeles Sunday School Convention. He was a mentor to Walter, and the young man aspired to follow his example and become an ordained minister someday. Lockridge surprised Walter with a very convincing argument to skip seminary and to get a master's degree in business administration. "He said the church needed men who knew how to get things done. They needed MBAs." Walter took that advice to heart and applied himself to his high school studies with the goal of applying to Michigan State.

Inside the Locker Room

Walter remained devoted to sports, and the combination of academics and athletics, plus church activities, kept the teenager out of trouble. Like a lot of other starry-eyed high school athletes, he dreamed of becoming a professional ball player. With his father at the helm of public relations for the Chargers, Walter had the kind of access to the NFL that any sports-minded kid would envy. He served as a ball boy for the Chargers, and at Jack Murphy Stadium he witnessed the bigger-than-life athletic men honing their craft on the field and in the gym.

As a ball boy, Walter had access to the locker room, and there he was introduced to the dark side of professional sports. The way the men carried on, in varying stages of undress and without any reservations, was disorienting. The surreal sight of huge and muscular men roving in and out of showers, posturing, and spouting vulgarities made the locker room seem like a foreign country populated by rustics speaking a coarse and unpleasant dialect.

And then there were the prostitutes and the drugs. "The black ball players didn't hide anything from me," Walter recalled. They told him that the drugs were medicinal, that every player, regardless of race, needed them in order to recover from the brutal pounding he received every Sunday.

Some of the black players considered their jobs to be a form of modern-day slavery. They were well paid and famous, yes, but they still served a white master, they said. Like the Roman gladiators, they destroyed themselves for their master and their audience. Walter took the complaints of the black players seriously. From childhood he had heard that whites used blacks to enrich themselves, while keeping the black community down. "It's what my father taught me," he said, and it's what the people at his church said too. As far as Walter knew, American history proved them right, as did his own family's painful past. Walter Hoye had no reason to doubt that he grasped the whole picture of race relations in America.

Yet something did not add up. Perhaps the athletic stars he admired and wanted to emulate were victims of racism and so broken in body and spirit that they needed drugs to dull the pain, but that did not explain why they would try to corrupt Walter—a teenage athlete, a good student, and a Christian. Walter was shocked when one of the Chargers offered him drugs. Maybe he would have been less surprised if he had asked for the drugs or had been a kid with a bad reputation, but neither was the case. "Here was this black man trying to get me hooked on drugs," Walter recalled. "I then realized that the white man wasn't the problem; the black man was the problem. An adult black man was preying on a young black man who was doing the right things. . . . It wasn't a white man trying to ruin my life."

Walter resisted the temptation and refused the drugs. Although shaken a bit, he felt that he had passed a test and proved to himself that he could be both a professional athlete and a practicing Christian. After high school, he went to Grossmont Junior College, where he played football and took general education classes for two years. He continued as a ball boy for the Chargers, but he avoided the off-the-field antics.

Michigan State Football

In 1977 Walter was accepted as a transfer student to Michigan State University (MSU), where he hoped to play football as a walk-on. Uncle Bob and Aunt Mary were more than happy to host him again.

Since he had no scholarships, the housing arrangement helped him financially. Even so, he would need to work hard on and off the field in order both to play ball and to obtain a degree.

Walter's desire to become a minister like his pastor, Lockridge, persisted, though he could not help but dream of the glory of playing MSU football and having a shot at the professional draft for the NFL. He had talent and desire, and he had been around professional players. Ultimately, it was his time with the Chargers that gave him the edge he needed to earn a Spartans jersey—and another lesson in race relations.

Walter suited up as a junior with his mind set on being a running back, but life is rarely a matter of dictation. The coaches pegged Walter as too light for a running back. In that position they preferred the big bruiser types—huge guys who could plow through a line of other huge guys and gain some game-winning yardage. Thus, the coaches made Walter a receiver. He, however, was not mature enough to accept their decision and begrudgingly took his roll with the receiving squad. He had zero respect for receivers, and he conveyed his displeasure with the receiver squad by being disagreeable. God works in mysterious ways, but football players sure don't, and it wasn't long before Walter was sent an unmistakable message.

In those days Walter shared the field with some players who would go on to be famous professional athletes, such as Kirk Gibson, who abandoned a promising football career to play baseball. While playing for the Los Angeles Dodgers in 1988, Gibson earned the National League Most Valuable Player award. But that was not his most memorable feat. In the 1988 World Series, Gibson was hobbled by injuries in both legs and not expected to play at all in the championship games. During the first game, however, he was called from the bench to pinch-hit in the bottom of the ninth inning. Amazingly, he hit a home run and won the game for the Dodgers. His limping around the bases, as he pumped his fist triumphantly, made baseball history.

When Gibson played football at Michigan State, he was the star receiver. He was "not an extraordinarily nice guy," Walter said. But some of the other guys on the receiver squad weren't very nice either. In fact, the words "nice" and "football player" rarely went together when men were posturing on the playing field. Walter acted up too, and even nice guys don't tolerate arrogance in a newcomer.

During one practice, Walter stood behind the end zone, striking a pose that said he was too good for it all. He was asked to run a route, and he thought, *How hard can it be just to run down the field, turn around, and catch a ball?* But his half-hearted efforts to learn the plays made this play harder than it seemed. When the center hiked the ball to the quarterback and bodies were moving in all directions, Walter was confused and didn't see the strong safety break free of his coverage. When he finally noticed, it was too late. The safety turned when Walter turned, and they collided. In those days players frequently wrapped their hands, wrists, and arms so tightly with tape that the material was as heavy as a cast. The safety hit Walter and really clobbered him. His fist came crashing down on Walter's helmet, and the impact was so hard that it broke his face mask. Walter's mind was swimming as the world became smaller. All he could see was "a small circle of light". He could hear the other players laughing as he dropped to one knee and came very close to losing consciousness. Somehow he shook the spiderwebs out of his head, pulled himself together, and returned to practice. "The rest of the day was just as brutal. Everybody took turns teeing off on me."

Lesson learned.

The job of the practice squad is to play the part of the opposing team so that the starting players can improve their skills and be ready for the game on Saturday. But during weekday practices, Walter began making too many catches and sometimes showing up the Spartan starting lineup. Annoyed, the coaches moved him to the running-back position. Perhaps they had forgotten that was the position Walter had wanted to play from the beginning. But Walter played running back only at practice. During games, he was back with the receivers, and strictly as an observer.

Although Walter became a dedicated, game-ready player, he remained a benchwarmer. It was no secret that the head coach, Darryl Rogers, was no fan of Walter Hoye. Walter suspects that Rogers thought of him as a black man who didn't know his place. "I was the only brother on the team not living in the hood or the dorms," Walter said. In fact, he lived in the same East Lansing neighborhood as Coach Rogers. Walter's uncle Bob was a music professor at MSU, and he lived in the same style as others who worked for the university. What really bothered Rogers, Walter figured, was that his daughter would sometimes stop by Walter's house. "He didn't like that at all." Whatever the reason for the coach's dislike, the result was that Walter never played in a game—that is, until one early November Saturday.

During a home game, Kirk Gibson was sitting out because of an injury, and the other receivers were not in the best shape either, but MSU was steamrolling the competition anyway. Sixty thousand screaming Spartan fans were cheering on their team to what would be a 44-to-3 rout of Northwestern University. The score was so lop-sided that Coach Rogers turned the game over to his assistants, who decided to give their weakened receivers a break and Walter Hoye a chance.

Walter knew he had earned the respect of the assistant coaches and his peers, even if Rogers wasn't sold, but he was still a bit shocked when he was told to "get in there." He grabbed his helmet and sprinted onto the field. In a momentary lapse in his otherwise steadfast game routine, Walter wasn't warmed up, and he was a bit worried as the quarterback called the play, a long pass to receiver Walter Hoye. The quarterback took the snap of the football, and flashes of Spartan green flew in every direction. Walter sprinted along his route. He was open. The quarterback dug in, dodged a defender, and let it fly. The pass traveled along a beautiful arc. Walter turned and looked up to catch sight of the ball, but it was just over his head and out of reach—an incomplete pass.

Back in the huddle, the quarterback took the blame for a badly thrown pass. He called the same play and said to Walter, "Go deep, the ball's coming to you." The quarterback took the snap of the ball once again, and Walter Hoye sprinted along his prescribed route, running along the white-striped sideline. He knew this was his last chance to prove himself. For a split second, Walter lost track of the ball and felt his chance slipping away. But then he remembered some-thing he had learned as a ball boy with the San Diego Chargers, when he had helped the quarterbacks to warm up. The ball was coming in just over the top of his head, where it was momentarily out of his sight. Walter hoisted his arms into the path of the ball. Then he twisted and tiptoed the sideline just as the professional wide receivers for the Chargers were trained to do in these circumstances. He caught the ball before his momentum forced him out of bounds. Walter

Hoye's name, number, and forty-six-yard catch were announced over the loudspeakers, and the adoring crowd chanted "Hoye, Hoye, Hoye!" Coach Rogers, however, was furious.

At Monday practice Rogers pulled Walter aside. "He told me I would never play again," Walter said. For the 1977 season, Walter Hoye's one catch gave him an average of forty-six yards per play from the scrimmage line. The statistic stands out, because on paper it gave him the highest yardage per play of any player on the team, even the team's star, Kirk Gibson. But none of that mattered to the head coach. "I marched with King. We weren't slaves. No Jim Crow or black codes. Segregation was gone," Walter said. Yet it seemed to him that a white man's animosity could still hold back a black man's progress. While a black professional athlete back in San Diego had unsuccessfully tried to ruin Walter's life with drugs, a white head coach had succeeded in ruining his football career. Walter understood that his future path wasn't going to be easy, and that winning at life was not going to be as easy as winning a game.

The end of football was "a blessing", Walter soon realized. Being told he would never again play in a real game crushed him at first, but just as he regained control of his senses after being nearly knocked out, he quickly reset his equilibrium and left the sport he loved in favor of a full commitment to his pursuit of the ministry. He was not forced to leave the football team. He could have stayed on with the practice squad, but his desire to play football was replaced by the desire to study Martin Luther King. "It was an overwhelming transformation," he said. Walter believed that his one great catch was Christ's gift to him, an affirmation of his faith, athletic skill, and commitment, but that it was a parting gift. God seemed to be beckoning Walter Hoye, and Walter gave himself over to that calling.

Walter and King

Walter hung up his cleats and went to work on his studies with a renewed focus. He moved into a place of his own because Uncle Bob Harris had taken a position at Northwestern University. He also met a young woman. She didn't steal him away from his studies, but she sure had a grip on his heart. It proved to be a fruitful time in Walter's life. With his football dream replaced by a powerful desire to serve God, Walter began drawing inspiration from his hero, Martin Luther King. "I decided that I wanted to figure out how to have some kind of impact in the world, the way Martin Luther King Jr. did," he said, "and it occurred to me that the best way to do that was to learn about MLK."

He turned his focus away from football and set his gaze on furthering his knowledge of the Word of God, studying Martin Luther King Jr., and finishing his bachelor's degree in sociology. And there was another piece in the puzzle—a romantic relationship. Everything went very well, mostly. The MSU library became his new sanctuary, where he often went to immerse himself in the study of King's life and works. He discovered a seemingly endless number of letters, papers, and books written by the slain civil rights leader and another endless number of letters, papers, books, and films about him. In the audiovisual section of the library, the twenty-year-old listened to recordings of King's sermons and speeches on reel-to-reel tapes, and he watched footage of key moments in the civil rights movement. Walter Hoye received his bachelor's in sociology (the same course of study King had undertaken), but he wasn't through with school. He wrote to the King Center in Atlanta, requesting the opportunity to study King's legacy there. He didn't get the reply he wanted, but he received a gracious letter from King's widow, Coretta Scott King, explaining that the school was undergoing renovations and not accepting new students that year. It left him with little choice but to stay on at MSU, where he completed a master's degree in sociology in 1980.

During this period, Walter's admiration for King and his doctrine of nonviolence deepened. King not only preached nonviolence; he also lived it, even to the point of suffering criticism from his own community. Walter found in King an understanding of something he had learned during his childhood in Detroit—that violence only causes division, hatred, and more violence. He also came across a quote from King that became the foundation of his later defense of the unborn: "The Negro cannot win if he is willing to sacrifice the futures of his children for immediate personal comfort and safety. Injustice anywhere is a threat to justice everywhere."

7

Self-Will

In spite of the way his football career ended, and the fact that his girlfriend broke his heart by choosing to see other guys after he asked her to marry him, Walter had learned to live mostly on his own terms at Michigan State University. And he still believed that his worthy aspirations, for the ministry and for a role in the noble cause of civil rights, would surely be achieved. Whatever barriers were before him, he thought, could be overcome by his determination alone. Herman Melville's Ahab said, "What I've dared I've willed and what I've willed I'll do." Walter's will was also strong, but like the doomed captain of the *Piquod*, Walter was about to find out that his will was worthless unless it was conformed to the will of God.

Walter returned to San Diego with set plans for his future, yet internal doubts and conflicts soon surfaced. During his years at Michigan State he had grown a lot, achieved many life goals, and established his independence. Back at home, all that progress seemed to belong to the past. Walter felt the way many recent college graduates feel—a little stuck. The steps he needed to take to fulfill his dreams were not entirely clear to him.

Then he remembered what S. M. Lockridge had said years before—that the ministry needs people with business training. Seeing that a business degree was helping other young black men to succeed, Walter's father also had encouraged him to study business. The time had come, Walter realized, to heed the advice of both men. He took a job at Allstate and enrolled in postgraduate business classes at the United States International University of San Diego (now Alliant University).

The Word of God

On his own, Walter continued to study the Word of God. Whenever he listened to recordings of sermons, the burdens of life seemed lighter and the fire in his belly grew hotter. He listened to preaching while driving to work, while walking down the street, and even while taking a shower. When he wasn't listening to the preaching of others, he was doing some preaching of his own. Whereas others sang in the shower, Walter preached, and loudly. "I loved preaching with a passion and craved it. I felt an insatiable need for it," he said.

Walter did not realize that his love for the Word of God was a sign that God was calling him to the ministry. Then he met a preacher who helped him to discern that God was indeed calling him. "He was talking about 1 Timothy 3:1, where Paul says to a young Timothy that if a man desires the office of bishop, he desires a good work," Walter said. "It became very clear to me that God was calling me to preach."

There was still another step for Walter to take in his discernment process. As a Baptist, he needed to discuss his longing for the ministry with his pastor. He needed his approval and that of the congregation. He met with Pastor Lockridge and described the mysterious inspiration he had been feeling ever since that day at Hartford Avenue Baptist Church in Detroit when he gave his life to the Lord Jesus Christ. What started then as a tugging toward the ministry had grown into a prodding, Walter explained, and sometimes it was so insistent that it felt more like a punching.

S.M. Lockridge already knew Walter and his family well. The Hoyes had been committed members of his congregation from their earliest days in San Diego. Walter had practically grown up in the church, where he had been involved with the Junior Brotherhood and Sunday school. Walter could have a calling, Lockridge thought. To put the calling to the test, he asked Walter to deliver a sermon in the "old church" the following Wednesday night. Based on the sermon, he said, the congregation would decide whether Walter had what it took to be a preacher.

The location of the "old church" was important. It was the original building of Calvary Baptist Church, and many a great preacher had been raised up within its walls. The old building was a monument to the great and sometimes painful sacrifices that had been made to found the congregation, and Walter was both excited and nervous about proving himself worthy in that hallowed place.

He set out to draft the sermon in full, word for word, in longhand. There were many crumpled pages on the floor beneath his desk when Wednesday arrived all too soon. When Walter took his seat in the pulpit next to Pastor Lockridge, the church was packed. The special night had been advertised in the church bulletin as though it were a Hollywood movie premiere, and for most members of the congregation, a young Mr. Hoye preaching his first sermon was a singular, not-to-be-missed event.

From his raised vantage point, Walter looked upon the eager upturned faces of the people who had filled the pews just to hear him. These were the people he had grown up with, who knew him and his family well. Would they see only the boy he had been, or would they see him as a man and accept him as one of their spiritual leaders? His palms were moist, and his heartbeat was keeping pace with his racing thoughts. He took some deep breaths to calm himself, placed his trust in God, and tried not to shift too much in his seat.

Lockridge strode to the podium and warmly introduced Walter B. Hoye II, and Walter felt Calvary's venerable history weighing on him. Would he measure up to the great men who had gone before him, he wondered, as he prayed silently over and over, "Lord, have mercy!"

When the moment arrived for Walter to preach, the friendly faces in the congregation encouraged him. Like a seasoned preacher, he asked everyone to find the Scripture passage that would be the foundation of his sermon. Then he added, "If you've found the text in your Bibles, say amen." The people said amen with a warm chuckle, Walter recalled, because they knew this was his first sermon. Slowly Walter read the verses aloud, emphasizing the words and the phrases that he would comment on later. Then he asked the congregation to bow their heads and pray with him. "O Lord," he began, reciting Psalm 19:14 from memory, "let the words of my mouth, and the meditation of my heart, be acceptable in thy sight, O Lord, my strength and my redeemer. Amen."

The congregation raised their heads and stared expectantly at Walter. Outwardly the young man was smiling, but inwardly he was terrified, and he silently prayed again for the Lord to help him, to speak through him in a mighty way. As he preached, he couldn't stop imagining how the newness of the experience must have been showing all over his face. Each time someone shouted a supportive amen, he struggled to stay on point and to stick to his notes. "Jesus, help me," he kept repeating to himself, "so that I don't leave out anything important."

When Walter was finished, relief washed over him. Lockridge smiled approvingly and returned to the podium, where he announced Walter's intent to become a preacher. In keeping with Robert's Rules of Order, a motion to make him a preacher needed to come from the congregation. "As I sat waiting for the motion to license me to preach the gospel of Jesus Christ in the Baptist Church, I was almost shaking on the inside. Finally, the motion came, and my heart began to feel lighter." After the motion was seconded, the pastor called for a vote. Walter put his head down because he could not bear to watch as the congregation loudly affirmed that the church should license him to preach. As the pastor said amen, Walter felt both gratified and frightened. "What have I done?" he asked himself. "I had the feeling that my life would never be the same."

Back in Lockridge's office, the pastor Walter admired so much signed the document that made him a licensed preacher. The license seemed to Walter further proof that if he willed to do something right and good, with some sweat and elbow grease it was as good as done. At that time in his life he still placed too much stock in his own effort and not enough trust in God, he said.

Perils of Love and Life

Walter's studies were going well, and his preaching was taking off. It would not be long before he would realize his dream of becoming an ordained minister. Yet Walter was still smarting from his breakup with his girlfriend at MSU. He felt a big hole in his heart that he was impatient to fill again. So when he met an attractive woman who was very involved in the life of the church, he decided to court her. With her public speaking abilities and leadership qualities, she seemed to have all the right qualifications to be a minister's wife, and it wasn't long before Walter decided to marry her.

Walter approached the relationship the way he had been approaching everything else lately—by setting his eyes on the prize and overcoming every obstacle. When warning bells began to ring during their engagement, Walter stubbornly chose to ignore them. For one thing, the couple argued a lot, but, determined to make this relationship work, Walter was always eager to reconcile and to carry on. After the couple broke off their engagement a second time, Walter's parents asked him to reconsider the course he was on. His sister was blunter—she told him point-blank not to marry the woman. "But I was going to do it my way," Walter said. "I was not going to let myself be brokenhearted again."

Walter accepted the position of minister of education at St. John Missionary Baptist Church in Oceanside, California. Thinking that a new start in a new city was all he and his bride would need to start their marriage on the right foot, he ignored all the warning signs and tied the knot. He was twenty-five at the time, and she was twenty-two.

It was a short, turbulent marriage with few bright spots. Almost immediately the strains of life were more than the fragile relationship could handle. In the summer of 1984 the marriage was hit with a crisis. Two pounds and one ounce was all baby Walter weighed when he was born at around twenty-four weeks. The preemie's weight soon dropped to 1.6 pounds and headed still lower. He was in grave danger, and the doctors at the midtown San Diego hospital offered next to nothing in the way of good news. Considered a micro preemie, the tiny infant would likely die, they said.

In another twenty years or so, the survival rate for micro preemies would be 15 to 40 percent, but at that time, it was in the single digits. The risk was clear to Walter as the San Diego sky on the morning he noticed that the incubators in the preemie ward had fewer babies in them than the night before. "The day before, the cribs had babies in them and families around them. Then, when I came back the next day, they were gone. The incubators were empty." The babies had not survived the night.

In addition to the health problems the baby already had, the doctors warned Walter about the possibility of tainted blood. People had been infected with the human immunodeficiency virus through blood transfusions, and the blood supply was still compromised. "I can fix that," insisted Walter. "My father and I will donate the blood my son needs." But the doctors came back with the concern that they didn't have a needle small enough for the baby. After one turned up, Walter was left wondering, *What's next?* He was terrified of the answer.

Walter was a man of faith, a preacher, it was plain to see, but the doctors encouraged him to be "realistic", telling him that nothing could alter the baby's fate. Walter then went home and prayed all night, turning the outcomes of his own life and his son's life over to the will of God. "I was desperately waiting to hear from God all night, but the answer never came," Walter said.

The next day the medical staff let Walter hold the baby for the first, and possibly the last, time. The tiny infant fit in the palm of Walter's hand. At the sight of him, love for the innocent, helpless child swept over Walter. "I noticed his fingers and his toes," he said. "I saw his eyes and his nose and recognized that my son looked just like me. And that's when the Lord answered my prayers."

Internally, Walter heard a voice, different from his own, say, "This is what is inside of a pregnant woman. This is a living human being. This is a person." And he realized "what an abortion is and what an abortion does."

The boy in Walter's palm beat the odds and survived. The marriage, however, did not. The problems the couple had encountered in their courtship only intensified during the early years of baby Walter's life. The union resulted in another child, a daughter born in 1986, but the couple could not live amicably together for reasons that Walter prefers to keep private. In 1987, Walter filed for divorce. When he saw that his children were not thriving in the household of his ex-wife and her second husband, Walter fought for full custody of his son and daughter. After several years of battling in court, he was granted legal responsibility for his children.

In talking to Walter about the divorce, one can hear the sadness and regret in his voice and see them in his eyes. But there is also a genuine love for his children and a sincere forgiveness for the woman he rushed to marry.

The painful episode taught Walter to stop relying on his own will. "I learned that no matter what it looks like to me, no matter what my feelings are, I need to trust God with my future, my life. I began to trust God at a much, much deeper level." From then on, Walter would pray for the Lord to show him the way and then follow the path as He laid it out before him.

8

Lori

In the early 1980s Walter sought to capitalize on emerging technology to spread the gospel. Long before the Internet as we know it became a reality, public access to the fledging Web was limited to rudimentary bulletin board systems and basic Internet mail (which we know today as e-mail). Walter was intrigued by the potential of reaching a nearly limitless audience with the message of Christ, but gaining access to it was a difficult task that required programming and code-writing skills. On his own, Walter learned just enough to put a few virtual gears into motion.

Landing a job at the telecommunications giant Pacific Bell, Walter entered the ground floor of the new technology. With the skills he learned there he created an early version of a website that connected people to information and to each other. "It was Christ centered and Bible based," said Walter of what he dubbed the Pro-Christ BBS (or bulletin board system), which allowed him to answer kids' questions about the Bible.

A Balm in Gilead

At the time, Walter was using an Apple IIe—a $1,400 cutting-edge personal computer in early 1983. With its bloated tube monitor affixed to a full-size keyboard, it was the best computer on the market available to the average person. Walter was eager to share the technology and the Internet with the other pastors in local black parishes, but to his deep disappointment, the response was less than enthusiastic. He was told that personal computers were a fad that wouldn't last and that Internet mail would never be practical. This was the first time

Walter and black Christian leadership were on different pages, but it would not be the last.

Undeterred, Walter forged ahead. "We helped a lot of people," he said. The website was offering people the "balm in Gilead", a reference to a passage from the prophet Jeremiah:

> Is there no balm in Gilead?
> Is there no physician there?
> Why then has the health of the daughter of my people
> not been restored? (8:22)

To Walter it was simple: Christ is the Balm in Gilead, and by bringing people to him through the bulletin board system, they were being healed.

While his peers ignored his efforts, the July 1986 issue of San Diego County's Christian newspaper published a story on Walter's work. Then, in June 1994, *New York* magazine mentioned Pro-Christ BBS in an article on Internet "salons". By then, The Balm in Gilead was a recognized 501(c)(3), a California nonprofit corporation. Serving as its president and executive director, Walter continued to connect with people in search of God. He did not expect, however, that the ministry would connect him with a like-minded woman with a penchant for numbers and a willingness to embrace a life dedicated to Christ.

A couple of years after his marriage ended, Walter was splitting his time between working as a technical manager at Pacific Bell and managing the website. During phone conversations with a Pacific Bell co-worker, he discovered a kindred spirit. Walter was in San Diego, and Lori Patrece Woods was in San Ramon, a town 470 miles north, in the San Francisco Bay Area, but they gradually came to realize they were closer than the miles might suggest.

Gifted

Lori was more than a voice on the other end of the line. She was special. By the second grade, she was exceptional with numbers and proficient at just about everything she set her mind to—that is, if she read about it first. Reading was a breeze for the eight-year-old girl who had begun deciphering words before she was two.

Yet, as gifted as she is, Lori almost wasn't born. Her mother was the youngest of five and only a teenager when a man she knew committed what Lori described as "date rape". The resulting pregnancy divided her mother's family. Her mother wanted to keep the baby, as did her maternal grandmother, but her mother's sisters were against the idea. One sister offered a drug to induce an abortion. Though young and frightened, Lori's mother bravely refused the seemingly easy way out of her situation and gave birth to Lori in 1959.

There were no secrets in the family, and from a very young age Lori knew her father's identity. He was the son of a woman described as well-off. She owned a beauty parlor and lived in a neighborhood nicer than Lori's. For the first few years of her life, Lori lived in "the projects" of Chattanooga, Tennessee. Her home was at 203 Thirty-Fourth Street Circle, next to the railroad tracks.

Crossing the tracks on her way to school was dangerous, and not only because of the trains. When Granny, her mother's mother, took her foraging for blackberries in the area, her basket went flying as she ran away from a snake slithering in the grass. The local blackberries made delicious pies, but Lori refused to help pick them. She did help Granny to bake the pies, however. She loved to cook and bake with Granny. "She was my heart," Lori said.

Lori deserved the chance to develop her intelligence, and that chance would soon arrive. When Grandma, her father's mother, moved to San Jose, she learned that there were plenty of phone company jobs in the Golden State and encouraged Lori's mother to apply for one. In the summer of 1965, Lori's mother packed up her daughter and the little they had and moved out West.

Anxiety and homesickness took a toll on Lori. "I missed Granny so much," she said, "that I refused to eat and became ill. The doctor told my mother she had two choices—send me back to Tennessee or watch me die." During Lori's Christmas break from school, an aunt and an uncle drove Lori back to her beloved Granny in Tennessee, where she finished first grade at Calvin Donaldson in Chattanooga.

After some baking bliss with her favorite person in the world, Lori returned to California and enrolled in the second grade at Grant

Elementary. She lived with her mother on Eleventh Street, a few blocks from the school, in a predominantly black and Latino neighborhood east of downtown San Jose. Some of her new neighbors were "white folks", Lori said, the first white people she had ever seen.

San Jose was founded in the late 1700s, when Spanish Franciscan priests arrived from Mexico and established the mission Santa Clara to evangelize the natives. The growth of the city exploded when Hewlett-Packard, Apple, and other companies made the surrounding area the world center of silicon chip technology. And Lori was one of the beneficiaries of the expanding economic opportunities.

One day, when Lori was in the second grade, some "IBM men" came to her school. Lori didn't know where they worked, but they wore the thin ties and the sport coats common among the computer types of the day. The men were there to determine the IQs of the children. They passed out tests and had the students complete them. Lori's score of 172 stood out, and the school recommended her for an immediate jump from second to fifth grade.

Lori's mother was against her skipping so many grades at once. She was concerned about Lori's social and emotional development in a classroom filled with children two or three years older than she. Lori stayed with her peers, but her teachers doubled her assignments, giving her two grades' worth of work at a time. It was the only way they could keep her engaged.

Lori's best friend was a Latina from a large Catholic family. She was the oldest of seven children, and Lori would sometimes go to Mass with her. Lori preferred the Mass to other Christian services because it lasted only an hour and she could be home in time to watch the football games on television. After math, sports was her passion. Aside from being an outstanding student, Lori was an athlete. By high school she was running track, and playing soccer, softball, tennis, and volleyball. She loved basketball.

When her best friend had a crush on one of the boys on the high school basketball team, they conspired to get involved. Statistics was the foot in the door. Although her friend did not stick with it, Lori quickly mastered the complicated number-crunching. Sports statistics became a hobby that would hold her interest through high school and into college at San Jose State University (SJSU), where Lori was awarded a full-ride academic scholarship. As a student at SJSU, she was a Spartan, just like a man she was destined to meet, the one who made one fantastic catch for the MSU Spartans.

In her first year of college, Lori took nineteen credit hours of classes and worked full-time at Pacific Bell. By the end of her sophomore year, her job was more important to her than her classes, and when the company offered her a big promotion, she withdrew from the university.

Baptism and Marriage

Lori was a technical problem solver for the phone company. She had many interactions with co-workers around the state, including a man in the San Diego office on whom she could depend. "He was always so helpful, always available, and he would do things that would help people when they needed it," Lori said of Walter Hoye.

They both worked at night, and they talked regularly about fixing this or that computer problem or glitch. Walter was known to call Lori at two o'clock in the morning. They had a good rapport on the phone and soon became long-distance friends. Sometimes Walter talked about his faith. When Lori told him that she was not active in a church, he encouraged her to do something about that. "Walter led me to Christ," she said. "I found a church and got involved."

When Lori sat down in a church for the first time in years, she read the Sunday bulletin. There was a notice about the need for math tutors. She recalled what Walter had said about getting involved and felt prompted to volunteer. She tutored math and physics, and in the process her faith grew. Like Walter many years before, Lori gave her hand to the minister one Sunday and gave her heart to Jesus.

At her church, baptism was by full immersion. New Christians wore white robes and were immersed underwater by the pastor. The robes were problematic because they became nearly transparent when wet. For the sake of modesty, and at the behest of her grandmother, Lori put a second robe on top of the first one. Then Grandma forced her into a third.

While standing in the baptismal font, Lori leaned back against the pastor's arm and slid into the water, but the pastor wasn't quite able to lift her out. The extra robes soaked with water were heavy.

Feeling as though she were on the verge of drowning, Lori panicked. Clinching her abdominal muscles with all her might, she snapped her upper body forward and gasped as her head sprang out of the water. "Talk about being 'born again,'" Lori said with a laugh.

A little while later Lori heard about a job at her San Ramon office that she thought would be perfect for Walter. She had sensed that he needed a change, and she was right. Walter jumped at the opportunity and moved north. Soon afterward, he and Lori were dating.

In 1988 Walter asked Lori to marry him. "She said no," Walter recalled. "I was trusting God now, so I just took it for what it was. She said no, and no meant no." Walter was convinced that God wanted him to marry Lori, but God hadn't told Lori yet, at least as far as she could see.

Lori knew that Walter was nearing the completion of the long process of ordination, and however much she liked him, she did not want to be the wife of a minster. But she and Walter remained friends, and while her car was in the shop for repairs, she asked him for rides to work. The commute together turned out to be a comfort, because Lori was starting to have some problems at work and found that talking them through with Walter was a big help. Next, they attended an evening Bible study together. And finally, Lori went with Walter to his church.

"I attended church with Walter one Sunday," she said. Two of Walter's friends there tried to convince her that she should change her mind about marrying him. Then the pastor's wife bluntly asked her whether she loved Walter. When Lori said yes, the woman told her to trust God to handle the rest. "Her words stuck with me," Lori said.

Lori began thinking about the sequence of recent events. She traced the car problems and the work problems back to her saying no to Walter's proposal. Then she noticed that these problems had led to a situation in which she and Walter were spending more time together. *Was God trying to tell me something?* Lori wondered. "I prayed and asked God if he was trying to tell me that I should marry Walter. As I considered saying yes, I felt a peace come over me that had been missing from my life since I said no." The next day, she told Walter that she had changed her mind and would marry him. Soon afterward her mechanic called to say that her car was fixed.

Mysteriously, the mechanic couldn't explain what had changed to make the car run again.

Walter and Lori married in a small private ceremony on February 4, 1989. A few months later Walter was ordained a Baptist minister of the gospel of Jesus Christ at Greater Faith Missionary Baptist Church in Stockton, seven years after his first sermon. The pastor of Greater Faith signed his ordination certificate, and so did his father in the gospel, Dr. S. M. Lockridge.

As the first girl in her family, Lori was pressured by her relatives to have a traditional church wedding that they all could attend. Thus, on July 15, 1989, Lori walked down the aisle in a fluffy white wedding gown and a flowing veil to the admiration of all her family members. "She looked good," Walter said, "real good." He did not object at all to repeating the vows that bound him to Lori for life.

Reverend Hoye

Walter's road to ordination had been a winding one. When he took the new job in the Bay Area, he left some painful experiences behind. While his exuberance for spreading the gospel hardly waned, his passion for preaching, once so robust, had been suppressed by pressures at work and memories of past mistakes. The closer he got to ordination, the more discouraged he became. He even found himself looking for ways to avoid the duties that were leading up to "the collar". But "I couldn't get away from them," he said.

During an especially low point, a friend invited Walter to preach at Greater Faith Missionary Baptist Church. He agreed, but his heart was not in the assignment at all. He devised a passive-aggressive, self-defeating plot to miss that sermon—he drove to the church as slowly as possible. As he approached Stockton he discovered that he had neglected to bring the address. Easy remedy there: he would stop somewhere and ask for directions. Surely the delay would make him late, and he would blame his tardiness on getting lost. "That was so I could have a clear conscience," he explained.

He pulled over at a barber shop with surprising signs of life inside. The hours on the door indicated that the shop was closed on Sundays, as barber shops in black neighborhoods usually are, but people were there anyway. Walter walked in and asked if anyone had heard of the church or knew where it was. More surprising, the men knew exactly where it was. That was okay, Walter figured: by the time he arrived, the services would be over since the preacher hadn't shown up.

When Walter at last walked into the church, he was stunned to find the congregation wrapping up only the first part of the service. Next up was the preacher's sermon. He was not only not late; he was precisely on time. By singing longer than usual, the worshippers had exercised a little faith that the preacher would eventually arrive.

Walter was now presented with a new problem—he was not prepared to speak. He hadn't intended to say anything other than "I'm sorry I'm late." Never before had he given a sermon without first writing it out word for word. Then, seemingly out of the blue, the book of Genesis came to mind along with the name Abraham. He recalled a sermon he had given years before and thought he just might be able to deliver it again. "I started, and I found myself flipping to the right text in the Bible. I had a thrilling time, and the congregation loved it." Even better, some people answered the invitation to accept Jesus as their Savior. "The Holy Spirit flowed through me," Walter said, "and I was so happy."

The Lord had indeed given him a gift, Walter believed again, and he was reassured of his divine calling to preach the gospel. The experience restored his desire to preach God's Word and impressed the pastor at Greater Faith Missionary Baptist Church. Walter was immediately offered the duties of assistant to the pastor and youth director. He never preached with notes again.

Eventually, after a few moves and job changes for both Walter and Lori, the couple joined Progressive Missionary Baptist Church in South Berkeley, where Walter became executive elder in 2000. The next leap in Walter's evolving vocation was a few years away, when he would come to grips with the fact that some issues important to the black community were being ignored in the pulpit.

9

Voices in the Wilderness

Two decades after Walter spent a dark night in prayer, searching for God's will in the suffering of his premature son, the new executive elder found himself feeling like something was missing at the Progressive Missionary Baptist Church in South Berkeley. He noticed a disconnect between the words from the pulpit and the words being spoken in the parking lot. "In the parking lot, you could hear this family, that family, this young person, that young person," Walter recalled. "I was tired of the conversations happening in the parking lot never being addressed in the pulpit."

To remedy the situation, Elder Hoye arranged a church-wide conference to be held August 26–28, 2005. He named it Issues That Matter, and memories of baby Walter's scrape with death would be on his mind throughout. The conference "changed everything", Lori Hoye recalled with a chuckle, but, at the time, she and Walter had no idea how profound the change would be.

The main speakers were Star Parker, founder and president of the Center for Urban Renewal and Education, a public policy think tank, and Reverend Clenard H. Childress Jr., the senior pastor of New Calvary Baptist Church in Montclair, New Jersey, and the founder of the website Blackgenocide.org. Both Parker and Childress are black pro-life advocates.

Walter invited Childress to attend his conference after reading his article "Abortion and Race" in *World* magazine, which provides news from a Christian perspective. Childress gladly accepted. He saw an opportunity to cultivate Walter as another ally on the abortion issue. Being pro-life often meant isolation for black pastors, Childress said, because in the black community "abortion is heavily politicized, and pro-lifers are demonized." Many black American leaders present themselves as having *the* platform for upward mobility for blacks, he explained, but they promote policies that devastate the black community. In particular, they support the policy of abortion on demand, primarily because it is a plank in the platform of the Democratic Party and most black leaders are Democrats. "Recognizing that the call from God is stronger than the calls of a political party," Childress said, he challenges black support for abortion, and he found in Walter another black leader willing take on that burden too.

When the Issues That Matter conference ended there was a consensus among the participants: the issue that mattered most was the dignity of human life, and the unborn of the black community needed protection. At Progressive Missionary Baptist Church, abortion became a frequent subject preached from the pulpit and talked about in the parking lot.

Walk for Life

One of the conference participants was Dolores Meehan, an organizer of the Walk for Life West Coast, which first occurred in San Francisco on January 22, 2005. It was not a coincidence that the date was the anniversary of the 1973 *Roe v. Wade* Supreme Court decision, which imposed abortion on demand on all fifty states. The theme of the Walk was "Abortion Hurts Women", and among the event's speakers were women who regretted their abortions.

Meehan was invited to the Issues That Matter conference by Reverend Childress, whom she had requested to speak at the first Walk for Life after discovering his website. Encouraged by his enthusiastic support, she and the other Walk for Life organizer, Eva Muntean, reached out to local black Christians to involve them in the Walk. After Walter received an e-mail about the event, he posted the flyer on his church bulletin board and tried to interest members in going. But apart from Walter and Lori, no one at Progressive Missionary Baptist Church wanted to participate in the Walk for Life, and in the end the Hoyes were unable to attend.

Although Walter and Lori missed the first Walk for Life, when Childress and Parker said that they would both be speaking at the second one on January 21, 2006, "of course, we were going to go," Lori said. Again, Walter put up the poster in his church.

"This time we got one person," said Walter.

"Christiana [Downer]," added Lori. "She was eighty, from Jamaica. The mother of thirteen kids."

"That's all we needed," Walter said. "One member."

Representing their church in the Walk for Life West Coast was an important step for Walter and Lori. They scraped together some money to make a big Progressive Missionary Baptist Church banner that they could carry, and they were joined by Jonathan and Dianne Maddox. All told they had five in their group, just enough to hold up the banner as they walked.

More than fifteen thousand people attended the second Walk for Life, more than double the turnout for the first one. As the speeches got under way, Walter Hoye led his humble assemblage to an area behind the stage. The goal was to listen, but when Star Parker stepped up to the microphone, and it seemed a bit empty on the stage, Muntean and Meehan looked around and spotted the small group from Progressive Missionary Baptist Church. "We were the only black folk standing there," said Walter with a smile, "so they grabbed us and put us right behind Star on stage."

"With the banner and everything," recalled Lori.

"From that point on, I got very involved and was on the stage at all of the walks," Walter added.

The importance of their involvement seemed obvious to the Hoyes, and it was underscored when an elderly white woman asked Lori for permission to take her photograph. The woman said to her companions, "I'm going to send this to my friend in D.C. and let her know that black people do care about life." Her words struck at the heart of the matter for Walter Hoye. Because there were so few black Americans at the Walk, the presence of just a few created a sort of buzz, an excitement. It was a sad reminder that few blacks stood up for the unborn in the public square and that as a result, as Childress had already experienced, being black and pro-life in America was going to be a lonely task.

Family Planning Specialists

That spring Hoye was busy being a hands-on minister, involved whenever and wherever he could share the good news of Jesus Christ.

He was rarely found inside his Berkeley church office, but one day when he happened to be there, he received a phone call from Mary Arnold. She introduced herself as a member of a small group who prayed outside Family Planning Specialists (FPS), an abortion clinic at 200 Webster Street in Oakland. Begun in 2005 by Fredi D'Alessio, the group also offered assistance to women entering the clinic, but it was hard to do that well and to pray at the same time. Would Walter like to help them? she asked.

D'Alessio was an experienced sidewalk counselor, a volunteer who prays and distributes information on abortion and its alternatives to women outside abortion clinics. The practice of sidewalk counseling varies widely from place to place, and D'Alessio had developed his own approach based on the work of Monsignor Philip Reilly, founder of Helpers of God's Precious Infants in Brooklyn, New York. "It helps if there's a group of people praying while someone does the outreach," D'Alessio explained.

D'Alessio had been a regular at Planned Parenthood in San Francisco, where he had met many women entering the clinic who were not seeking abortion. Thinking it might be easier to reach only those who were, he started sidewalk counseling at FPS in Oakland. There he met such a high number of abortion-seeking women that he assumed the clinic provided no other service. He recruited more volunteers and expanded his group's presence from once a week, on Saturdays, to several days per week.

Occasionally the police showed up at FPS while the group was there—each time, it was a different pair of officers who had responded to a call by FPS. The typical interaction was cordial, D'Alessio said. The police would explain the rules of peaceful assembly on a public sidewalk and thank the group for cooperating with them. There were never any arrests, citations, or hostile confrontations.

That is, until three days after the second annual Walk for Life in 2006, when police cited D'Alessio for allegedly interfering with a lawful business, a crime punishable by jail and fines. The citation came at the behest of the abortion clinic manager, who made a citizen's arrest. A police officer is obligated to act when a citizen has made an arrest, whether lawful or not. The misdemeanor charge was dropped later, due to lack of evidence, and switched to a charge of disturbing the peace. Then the city agreed not to prosecute the case in exchange for the group's agreeing to stay three hundred feet away from FPS.

About the time of the citation, it occurred to Mary Arnold that it might help to have a black man with them. Most of the clients at FPS were young women of color, primarily black Americans. All of the sidewalk counselors were white and not so young. Was it possible, Arnold wondered, that they came across as threatening strangers to the women entering FPS? Arnold sent an e-mail to Reverend Childress in New Jersey, whom she had heard speak at the recent Walk for Life in San Francisco. "I didn't have a pastor or priest in mind necessarily, but I asked him if he knew any African American men in the Oakland area who might be interested in doing some sidewalk counseling with us. He recommended Walter Hoye."

Walter described Arnold's call, coming when he just happened to be there, as more than a coincidence. "It was amazing she caught me in my office; I'm hardly ever there," he said. He agreed to meet Arnold, D'Alessio, and another volunteer, Ginny Hitchcock, at his church's library to talk about sidewalk counseling at FPS.

At the meeting, Walter learned that Arnold, D'Alessio, and Hitchcock were Catholics with extensive experience in outreach at abortion clinics. He listened with care as Arnold explained how they legally used the public space in front of abortion clinics to pass out detailed information about abortion and abortion alternatives, something the clinics are not required to provide. Their literature described the development of the child in the womb and listed places that offered free pregnancy testing, counseling, and other services.

Most of the women going into the clinic were black, Arnold said. An African American, especially an ordained minister, would be harder for them to ignore than a group of white people. Perhaps FPS clients would see in Walter Hoye a friendly face, someone they could trust or at least someone they could not easily dismiss. Appreciating their faith and their commitment to help mothers and to save unborn children, Walter agreed to give sidewalk counseling a try. "Walter was very young-looking, handsome, and very receptive," Arnold recalled. The group was thrilled to have him on board.

The subject of law enforcement came up at the meeting, as did D'Alessio's citation. Arnold explained that the clinic staff sometimes called the police. Apart from their citing D'Alessio once, the police only reminded the group of the legal limits to free speech. It would be no different with Walter there, she assured him.

It was different.

The Church of the Eight Steps

The stride of the average woman is about twenty-six inches, little more than two feet. At Family Planning Specialists on Webster Street in Oakland, it took about eight steps for a pregnant woman to travel from the white loading zone at the curb to the nondescript office entrance. Women had been making that short walk to end their pregnancies for decades.

Family Planning Specialists Medical Group was established in 1985 by two physicians and executive director Jacqueline Barbic. Unlike Planned Parenthood, FPS was a for-profit corporation. The clinic's website boasted of the "most experienced surgical team providing first and second trimester abortions". The clinic had a reputation for specializing in the latter, up to the gestational age of twenty-two weeks. It claimed a complication rate of less than 1 percent.

The fee schedule at FPS showed that the further along the pregnancy, the more expensive the abortion. First-trimester abortions were $450 to $520, and second-trimester abortions would cost up to $2,000, which in most cases, according to Barbic, was paid by Medi-Cal, meaning California taxpayers, not the clients. Corporate records show that FPS had a net annual revenue of a little less than $3 million in 2015.

To maximize profit, the operation required competent management that could keep costs down and lots of women moving through the doors. The medical staff at 200 Webster Street performed abortions three days per week. During Walter Hoye's trial, Jackie Barbic testified that FPS terminated about twenty pregnancies on Tuesday, April 29, 2008. It was a guess, she said, explaining that she had no specific recollection. (The date played a significant role in the trial, as will be discussed later.) Another witness, the security guard at FPS, said there were forty appointments on his list that day. While some of the appointments may have been for something other than an abortion, it's possible that the actual total number of abortions was between twenty and forty. If the average of both numbers is a reliable gauge, and the clinic was open all fifty-two weeks of 2008, there were more than four thousand abortions at the Webster Street clinic that year.

Jacqueline Barbic got her start in the abortion industry fresh out of college. Hers is a rather common story. Although private, for-profit facilities like FPS don't have the same presence on college campuses as Planned Parenthood does, they do benefit from Planned Parenthood's outreach and brand. Planned Parenthood does an exceptional job of recruiting college graduates into their workforce. Private clinics benefit from the general acceptance of Planned Parenthood and hire college graduates, but their hires tend to be less-educated than those of Planned Parenthood.

Volunteers

Both Planned Parenthood and private abortion clinics rely on volunteers to escort clients from their parking lots to their front doors. If protestors are present, the escorts try to steer clients away from the pro-lifers who attempt to talk with them or to give them literature. The escorts for FPS and other clinics in Oakland were the responsibility of Barbara Hoke. For years the retired real-estate agent trained and deployed escorts citywide, advising them to wear fluorescent vests and to exercise caution when approaching clients. After all, Hoke would explain, the women are wary of being approached, even if the person is trying to be helpful. At an East Bay nonprofit that gave her an award in 2011, she said that being an escort "requires the tenacity of the devil and the love of a mother."

The San Francisco Bay Area may be a long way from Houston, where Barbara Sue Hoke was born, but the miles have done very little to minimize her Texas drawl. Her voice was among the chorus of supporters who championed the "bubble ordinance" before the Oakland City Council, and she was notable for her behind-the-scenes work to ensure that it would pass. During Walter's trial and during the public debate on the ordinance, abortion advocates such as Hoke argued that escorts are needed at clinics to guarantee that women have a choice.

If clinics really wanted their clients to have a choice, they wouldn't try to prevent them from hearing about alternatives to abortion, said Abby Johnson, a former abortion clinic director for Planned Parenthood. "Escorts are there to take away the choice," she added. Abortion clinics have quotas, she explained, a minimum number of abortions they need to perform to pay their bills and, in the case of private clinics, to make a profit. Women changing their minds about abortion are bad for business, Johnson said. Thus, clinics use escorts to prevent their clients from seeing or hearing anyone who might suggest that they reconsider their decision.

Although abortion is a multimillion-dollar industry, a lot of the women who volunteer or work at abortion clinics do so out of a strong desire to help others, Johnson said. But their motivation is often a little more complicated than that, for about 70 percent of them have had abortions. Johnson describes her previous passion for working at Planned Parenthood as a combination of unconscious remorse for her own abortion and "fierce determination" to help women in difficult circumstances. She didn't know much about Planned Parenthood when she began at the organization in 2001, but she assumed its mission was to help mostly low-income women who lacked access to good health care.

The clinic where Johnson worked relied on volunteer escorts to shield its clients from the pro-life demonstrators outside. Some activists carried large signs with photographs of aborted fetuses. Some screamed obscenities and denounced the women entering the clinic as sinners who were going to hell. Once there was a man dressed as the grim reaper. The offensive spectacle was beneficial to the clinic, Johnson added. "Women wouldn't just walk past these people; they would *run* into the clinic."

These were not violent anti-abortion protests, but violence had occurred at other clinics. Abortion clinics had been the targets of vandalism, arson, shootings, explosions, and bomb threats. Between 1993 and 2015, eleven people were killed in attacks on abortion providers. Among them was Dr. George Tiller, the Wichita, Kansas, specialist in late-term abortions, whom Johnson had known.

In the 1980s, there were many large protests in which pro-lifers would block the doors of abortion clinics. While they saw such trespassing as a form of civil disobedience, justifiable because every abortion kills an innocent human being, it required force, in the form of police action, to stop. During this period, James Kopp broke into FPS and chained himself to a table. In 1998 he shot and killed abortionist Barnett Slepian in Amherst, New York.

Although the use of violence has been rare in the pro-life movement, when Johnson ran an abortion clinic, Planned Parenthood made sure that she and the other staff members never forgot that clinics were sometimes attacked. They sent their clinics a daily "hotspot report" on recent violence or threats of violence. "Fear is perpetuated inside the clinics," Johnson explained. Abortion providers keep the risk of violence alive in everyone's imagination in order to justify their violent killing of unborn children, to keep the teams of people involved in this grisly business intact and in line, and to keep the law on their side.

Johnson's experiences shed light on the actions taken by Oakland abortion providers when Walter Hoye began sidewalk counseling. During the campaign to pass the Oakland bubble ordinance, abortion advocates spoke before the city council about the danger, the fear, and the denial of rights that abortion providers and their clients faced, and they were partly right. The picture they painted, however, was not the whole picture, nor did it apply to the pro-life activities then occurring outside FPS. One woman addressing the council identified herself as an abortion provider and said she was wearing a bulletproof vest because she didn't feel safe. Perhaps she did feel safer wearing the vest, but there was no evidence that she was in danger of being shot by a sidewalk counselor in 2008 Oakland.

The most significant threat to abortion providers, Johnson explained, is not the occasional rude person with a graphic sign or the rare violent extremist, but the pro-lifer who prays and offers support to women outside abortion clinics. The pro-life activities outside her clinic calmed down and became much more effective, she said, when a 40 Days for Life campaign began in September 2004. There were no accusations, no nasty signs—only people praying, fasting, and offering to help. Johnson quit her job with Planned Parenthood after she experienced a change of heart during the campaign.

Mary Arnold, Fredi D'Alessio, and Ginny Hitchcock had always taken a low-key approach to their pro-life work outside FPS. They prayed, they offered support, and they gave out literature to anyone who would take it. They helped some women to choose life for their unborn babies, but their impact was so inconsequential that FPS did not use volunteer escorts. That was before Walter Hoye arrived.

Baby Steps

Walter Hoye had never heard of Family Planning Specialists before he was invited to join the sidewalk counselors at 200 Webster Street. "I was focused on my church, on my congregation and the next conference," he explained. Abortion and its impact on the black community had become issue number one at Progressive Missionary Baptist Church, but Walter had not yet visited an abortion clinic.

Energized by the Walk for Life and intrigued by the possibilities involved in sidewalk counseling, Walter decided to give it a try. With Christiana Downer and Sister Elga Kendall, two women in their eighties from his church, he went to FPS for the first time on Tuesday, March 14, 2006. That very day, FPS called the police. No one was cited or arrested, and Walter and his friends decided to return every Tuesday morning.

During Walter's time slot at FPS, from 8:00 A.M. to 10:00 A.M., he would stand on the public sidewalk near the clinic loading zone and watch for the telltale signs of a woman on her way to an abortion. The pathway to the front door of the clinic, eight steps in length, was on private property and off-limits to Walter. But it was no barrier to the spiritual power of prayer and heartfelt concern that he could exercise from the sidewalk. Walter figured that if by those means he could save just one life each Tuesday, he could save fifty-two lives each year.

Most clients would walk right past Walter, acting as though they didn't see him and his sign, which said, "God loves you and your baby. Let us help you." But once in a while a woman would stop and listen to his soft, comforting voice saying, "Good morning. May I talk to you about alternatives to the clinic?" Sometimes his truthful and hopeful words would change a woman's mind about having an abortion.

Walter's sign was a gift from Mary Arnold. It was a copy of one Arnold used with some success during one of her vigils outside an abortion clinic in Auckland, New Zealand. A Pacific Islander inside the clinic saw the sign through the window and went outside to talk to Arnold. She said that her boyfriend and her boyfriend's father were at home praying for her and that the message on the sign meant a lot to her. She asked Arnold for help, and Arnold assisted her through the pregnancy. They stayed in touch after the birth of the baby, and Arnold has a photograph of the child, which is dear to her heart.

Walter loved the sign and the story behind it, he said. The succinct message summed up everything he would say to a woman in a crisis pregnancy if she would give him the chance. It contained the answers to the three questions women would most often ask him: "Does God love me?", "Does God love me and my baby?", and "Are you willing to help me?" Every time a woman asked Walter one of these questions, he answered yes.

During Walter's visits to FPS he noticed that most of the women seeking abortion were black. Gradually, the number of black clients increased. One Tuesday morning, Walter counted twenty-seven women approaching the clinic, and twenty-five of them were black. Yet the clinic could not perform twenty-seven abortions in a two-hour period, he said. Some of these women, he discovered, came "not because they had an appointment, but because they knew there was a black man out there, a preacher out there, who was helping the women." Word had spread about Walter's two-hour weekly vigil at the Webster Street clinic.

The needs women brought to Walter went beyond those related to pregnancy. "If they were hungry, if they needed a place to stay ... We were literally helping the women," he said. Some women simply needed someone to talk to. "Sometimes we would just go have coffee, lunch, and just talk."

Young men also began coming to Walter, seeking answers and looking for help. Sometimes a pregnant mother dragged along the father of her unborn child, hoping he would listen to Walter. "She wanted him, her boyfriend, to hear me talk about it," he said, referring to the life of the baby and alternatives to abortion.

As members of the local black community, Walter and his companions from Progressive Missionary Baptist Church became the most effective sidewalk counselors outside FPS—so effective that the clinic turned to Barbara Hoke for help.

Antis and Deathscorts

Barbara Hoke calls all of them "antis"—pro-life demonstrators, protestors, and sidewalk counselors. When the "antis" began squeezing FPS financially, the clinic asked her to recruit escorts for their clients.

For their part, the "antis" referred to the escorts as "deathscorts", and when the first ones arrived at FPS two months after black folks began sidewalk counseling there, the reason for them was obvious— to counter the Walter Hoye effect.

Walter and his companions kept their Tuesday-morning appointment at FPS like clockwork. Christiana Downer and Sister Elga Kendall went to their usual curbside spots and handed out literature. Walter, in his early fifties, moved back and forth in his own area, closer to the white loading zone. "I would say to the women, 'Good morning. May I talk to you about an alternative to the clinic?', so they would know I wasn't crazy," Walter said. If a client chose to listen, she would walk closer to him.

The first sign that FPS was worried about Walter Hoye was the increase in visits by the police. They started to come at regular intervals. As had been the case before, the police would leave without making any arrests. There were federal and state laws governing activities outside abortion clinics, some of them strongly worded and court tested, but what Walter was doing remained in compliance with those laws. He was holding a sign and offering an alternative to abortion on a public sidewalk. There was no law against that. Officers would arrive, briefly talk to Walter, and then quickly leave. Those police visits were a blessing in disguise, Walter said. "They were actually helping me be a better sidewalk counselor," he explained. "I obeyed everything they told me to do. Women were still stopping."

When the first escorts arrived at FPS, they were cold and hard toward Walter, as if he were a dangerous enemy. But their treatment didn't bother him. He was as open and friendly with them as he was with anyone else, and it wasn't long before they began talking to him when no clients were around. The conversations were unavoidable

since the escorts shadowed Walter's every move by standing or walking right next to him. The topics ranged from the trivial to the more
serious and personal. Walter was training to run a marathon, which
one escort found interesting. Another escort wanted to talk about her
gravely ill mother, and Walter listened to her concerns with kindness
and sympathy.

Walter looked upon these conversations as opportunities to share
the love of God with the volunteers. One escort, one of the few
black volunteers, stopped coming to the clinic. "She saw what I was
seeing," Walter said. "She knew what was going on, and she got to
the point where she never came back. She just couldn't do it anymore." Her departure became another problem for the clinic.

After a while, the escorts stopped talking to Walter, and he and his
companions concluded that the clinic had ordered the escorts to stay
away from him. "They would come out and say, we can't talk to you
anymore, Walter. We can't talk to you," he said. The escorts then
waited in their cars or in the lobby for clients to arrive.

In April the escorts began more aggressive tactics. As they stood
next to Walter or walked alongside him, they blocked his sign or
his face with blank whiteboards. "In some cases, I was literally sur-
rounded and followed by four white women wherever I went," he
said. The spectacle slowed traffic on Webster Street as drivers rubber-
necked to see what the fuss was about.

Sidewalk counselor Mary Arnold recalled how the circus caused
clients to approach her with questions about what was going on. It
was an open invitation for her to reach out. It worked for a while,
but the constant harassment by the escorts ultimately caused Arnold
to give up, leaving Walter there with his two elderly companions.

By November 2006 there was public talk about crafting a bubble
law for abortion clinics in Oakland. The clamor for action against
Walter Hoye had reached City Hall, where abortion providers had
powerful allies who proved willing to go to extremes to stop him.
"They were afraid that if one black pastor was out there, more would
come. They couldn't let one black pastor get away with counseling
black women about alternatives to abortion," he said.

Forces Rally against Walter

Nancy Nadel received a master's in geophysics from the University of California, Berkeley, but her first job after graduation was with an association of abortion and health clinics. The Oakland Feminist Women's Health Center had its roots in the late sixties, when it was started by some women working to legalize abortion. Following the 1973 *Roe v. Wade* decision, they founded their first abortion clinic. Nadel's job was administrative—collecting payments, paying the bills, and managing computer data. In time, the health center folded, but the abortion clinics continued to operate in Oakland under different management. Working at the center, Nadel learned that abortion clinics were subject to harassment. She said that her job gave her stomachaches, but she admitted that money troubles, not anti-abortionists, were the cause of her digestive problems.

Nadel was elected to the Oakland City Council in 1996, representing District 3, where most of the city's abortion clinics were. Shortly thereafter, former colleagues from her abortion clinic days reached out to her. They included long-time clinic-escort coordinator Barbara Hoke and Jackie Barbic, director of Family Planning Specialists on Webster Street. Hoke and Barbic told Nadel that there was harassment going on at FPS and that the police department was not doing enough to protect them. Nadel's perception was that the police treated clinic workers and pro-life demonstrators equally as citizens with rights to assemble, which to her seemed unjust. From her point of view, the abortion providers were helping patients, while the pro-lifers were harassing them.

Bubble Law Beginnings

Nadel and her staff began to meet regularly with Hoke and others and eventually formed a working group to help the clinics and the police to communicate better. That led to the idea of crafting a bubble law for the city of Oakland, similar to the one enacted in Colorado in 1993. But there was stiff opposition from a powerful constituency that financially backed most of the elected officials in Oakland: labor unions, including the Service Employees International Union (SEIU), that did not want to be barred from picketing health care facilities during strikes.

When the state codified the Freedom of Access to Clinic Entrances Act (FACE) in October 2001, Nadel gave up on pursuing a bubble law. FACE mirrored federal law concerning access to abortion clinics and made it a misdemeanor to interfere with or to intimidate their patients or staff. In a speech the following year to a pro-choice group, Nadel said she was pleased that laws were in place to protect abortion providers.

A few years later, however, it became apparent to Nadel's friends at FPS that FACE was not enough to keep pro-lifers away from their clinic. Fredi D'Alessio began his outreach ministry at 200 Webster Street, and it grew. Efforts to get D'Alessio arrested failed until he was cited in early 2006. Then Walter Hoye showed up at the clinic, which called in escorts to counter his effectiveness. One of the volunteer escorts was Berkeley family law attorney Jane Kaplan. She made it her responsibility to track the case against D'Alessio through the district attorney's office, and she became the district attorney's liaison to FPS escorts.

Deputy District Attorney John Creighton got the D'Alessio case, to the chagrin of Nadel's abortion access group, which shared pessimistic e-mails about its eventual outcome. The group lacked confidence in Creighton, and they met with District Attorney Tom Orloff to push the case against D'Alessio. In a November 16, 2006, meeting set up by Nadel, some of the abortion access group members, including Hoke, talked to Orloff and demanded that he do his job. Orloff apparently agreed. The next day, the district attorney's office informed D'Alessio that it intended to reinstate both charges against him: disturbing the peace and interfering with a business. Orloff also agreed to assign a lawyer as the district attorney's liaison to the abortion clinic director. That liaison was Creighton.

Kaplan purportedly met with Creighton soon afterward, but nothing came of that. Word around the group was that Creighton was ignoring them. A hearing took place a month later, and the judge refused to reinstate the charges against D'Alessio on the grounds that he hadn't violated the terms of a stay-away order. This incensed Hoke and Barbic, because they felt the stay-away order was nothing more than a slap on the wrist. Once the stay-away order expired, they thought, D'Alessio would be back at 200 Webster Street, and there wouldn't be anything they could do to stop him.

Hoke sent an e-mail blast to the working group, complaining that Orloff had bungled the D'Alessio case. In early 2007, with the approach of both the third Walk for Life West Coast and the first Stand Up 4Life Walk in Oakland, the group put together plans for a meeting. One group member suggested a conference with city officials to denounce Orloff publicly over his handling of abortion cases—a move that would apply significant political pressure on the elected district attorney. The meeting never took place, but discussions about ways to apply political pressure were ongoing in e-mails and at meetings about other matters.

Councilwoman Nadel's working group included lawyers, city staff members, city council members, abortion providers, and members of the public who were either clinic staff members or representatives of sympathetic nonprofits and abortion providers. They met occasionally in 2007 to discuss ways to block D'Alessio. If they could do that, they figured, they could get rid of Walter Hoye, who had become the biggest target of their efforts. Eventually the group decided that a bubble law was the best option.

In August, Hoke sent the group a draft bubble ordinance, which she had prepared with Destiny Lopez, executive director of ACCESS/ Women's Health Rights Coalition, and Helen Hutchinson, president of the Oakland League of Women Voters (LWVC). She also sent a fact sheet that could be used to lobby city council members once the ordinance was introduced. Hoke asked for input and suggestions that Hutchinson could use to make the final edit of the fact sheet in September. Some of the questions it aimed to answer were "Why do we need the ordinance?" and "What would it do?"

Concerns about the bubble law were immediately raised by the American Civil Liberties Union (ACLU). The city attorney's office shared the draft with the ACLU, and the civil rights watchdog saw problems with it right away and rejected it on its face. Nadel hoped to be able to persuade them to be quiet about their objections and not to oppose the law publicly.

Winning over, or at least quieting, the labor unions would be even harder, partly because there were several. Union objections had derailed early talks of an ordinance years before. Councilwoman Nadel would have her hands full trying to square the needs of the abortion lobby and those of her friends in labor. After several months of revising the draft to meet the objections of needed allies, the time had come to introduce the legislation that would create a buffer between workers and clients at abortion clinics and pro-lifers who try to approach them.

Public Safety

On October 23, 2007, the city's Public Safety Committee accepted the bubble law proposal introduced by Councilwoman Nadel. It declared that current law did not adequately protect access to abortion clinics. Specifically, one city policy aide argued, current law didn't prohibit harassment or counseling outside clinics. Federal and state laws also didn't include protective bubbles or zones. The cosponsors of the proposed law were Jane Brunner and future mayor Jean Quan.

Nadel's letter introducing the ordinance laid out the justification for it:

> Currently in Oakland, the intimidation and harassment of women attempting to access reproductive health services is a frequent and recurring problem. The aggressive nature of the harassment and intimidation has noticeably escalated, threatening the public safety of clinic patients, staff, and volunteer escorts by increasing the potential for physical violence.

The letter offered examples of the alleged harassment and intimidation that clients, volunteer escorts, and staff members experienced at the Oakland clinics. The information was said to be taken from clinic escort logs, patient statements, and volunteers.

- A demonstrator regularly pursuing clients down the street and around the corner. When reported to police, officers maintained the street was public property and they couldn't do anything unless the client called the police.
- Clinic escorts and staff frequently being pushed against vehicles, and otherwise being grabbed or physically assaulted.
- Individual demonstrators disobeying stay-away orders, and continuing to harass clinic employees and escorts.
- Demonstrators repeatedly blocking clinic entrances, harassing patients and family members, stopping cars attempting to enter the clinic parking lot, and pushing anti-choice literature (including graphic medical photos and inaccurate medical information) inside cars after people said they did not want them.
- Protestors videotaping or taking photos of patients as they try to enter clinic property.

The letter continued with a description of what the ordinance would do:

The proposed ordinance will address the limitations of federal and state law as follows:

- Prohibiting the use of force, threats, or physical obstruction to intentionally injure, harass, intimidate, or interfere with any person providing or obtaining reproductive health services.
- Within one hundred feet of the entrance, prohibiting approaching within eight feet any person or motor vehicle seeking to enter the facility, without the consent of the person or vehicle occupant, for the purpose of interfering, harassing, injuring, or intimidating the person or vehicle occupant.
- Providing penalties of imprisonment in the county jail for up to one year and/or a fine of $2,000.
- Specifying a safety zone (aka "bubble") of eight feet around an individual to protect against conduct occurring within one hundred feet of the entrance to a reproductive health care facility.
- Broadening the type of harmful conduct prohibited, to include "harassment" or "counseling".

Despite the constant presence of security cameras at all the city's abortion clinics, the letter contains no offer of video evidence that any of the aggressive actions described ever took place. The letter mentions "individual demonstrators disobeying stay-away orders", yet the only known stay-away order was connected with D'Alessio, who, the court ruled, did not violate the terms of the order. The errors and the omissions gave opponents hope that they could persuade the committee to vote the proposal down if for no other reason than its false premises.

Present at the October 23 Public Safety Committee meeting were bubble sponsors Nadel and Quan, Patricia Kernighan, and the committee chairman, Larry Reid. In the room, prepared to handle any questions, were City Attorney Vicki Laden, Police Chief Wayne Tucker, and Deputy Chief David Kozicki, but none of them were consulted. Instead, Reid immediately invited the public comment speakers, after a highly unusual preface: "Certainly, this item will pass by consensus, which means all four of us will be voting in favor, so if you don't want to use your full two minutes ..." Reid's voice trailed off, which elicited laughs from the audience.

Public Testimony

Members of the public who were there to speak against the proposal felt gut-punched. They felt the sting of defeat before they even got started. The audience was diverse, with people from both sides wanting to speak, including Walter and Lori Hoye, Fredi D'Alessio, Mary Arnold, and Ginny Hitchcock.

On the other side were supporters Rachelle Rohrer and Amy Moy of Planned Parenthood, Destiny Lopez of ACCESS/Women's Health Rights Coalition, and clinic escorts such as Terry Sandoval, who was also a member of the National Women's Caucus. All of them were part of the e-mail group established by Nadel and Hoke. There hadn't been any committee debate or discussion, only a presentation of the proposal, which went directly to the public for comment, which at the outset was dismissed as unimportant.

Speakers in favor of the proposal streamed to the microphone and denounced the tactics of anti-abortion protestors, calling to mind violent incidents that had happened in the past or in other states. They described how the people in front of clinics behave to create a dangerous, intimidating environment. Rohrer, an associate director of a Planned Parenthood clinic, told the committee that her clinic on MacArthur Boulevard served twelve thousand clients each year. "We began seeing protestors at our clinic in 2006," she said.

May 2006 was two months after Walter Hoye began outreach at the for-profit clinic on Webster Street and three months after D'Alessio was cited. D'Alessio, who had an active stay-away order from the clinic on Webster Street, took his outreach to Planned Parenthood. Rohrer tried to suggest that a man with a stay-away order from one clinic was doing something illegal and sinister by showing up at another clinic. She did not say what D'Alessio was actually doing at Planned Parenthood.

Clinic escort Sandoval called the sidewalk counselors "anti-choice zealots". She said it was important that a protective zone be established for escorts like her, "to ensure" that they can do their jobs. "I am there on the battleground on a regular basis. I'm there at minimum four times a week, as much as eight times a week. I'm on call 24/7."

Destiny Lopez of ACCESS, based in Oakland, said her organization runs a hotline for reproductive questions. From thousands of calls to the hotline Lopez chose a few examples, including a woman with three children to support who didn't feel she was in a position to have a fourth. "All of these women could have approached a clinic determined to access safe and legal reproductive health care, only to be bombarded with verbal assaults, intimidation, graphic and medically inaccurate images, and the potential for physical harm from people they do not know, have never met, and certainly have no right to infringe on each woman's rights to seek private medical care."

Like Lopez, most of the women who addressed the committee were part of the working group. Their descriptions of what women face going into clinics persuasively presented a need for a bubble law. But according to Walter, the picture they painted did not reflect what was happening in front of abortion clinics in Oakland, specifically, FPS on Webster Street.

If all that harassment and intimidation were happening, Walter asked during his testimony, where were the security camera videos or the police reports to prove it? "They can show you what's actually happening on the sidewalks," he said. "It's not being shown because it's not happening. We are there peacefully. We are within our rights, and we are there to support the rights of all citizens to share their opinions." Walter told the committee that it was the escorts who were aggressive, sometimes bumping into him.

His wife was even more direct. Lori said she was there as a black American woman, "pleading with the city of Oakland to not pass this ordinance." She called it a crime that four of the five abortion clinics in Alameda County were in Oakland:

> The Negro project that Margret Sanger started so many years ago is still alive and well today.... We need to recognize that this buffer zone just gives the advantage to those who want to terminate lives.... You talk about the homicides in Oakland. You need to look at the murders that happen at the abortion clinic. You lose a hundred men to homicide [a year], but you lose fifteen hundred a day to abortion. And we are not even replacing ourselves. We will disappear as a people if we don't start doing something about putting these folks out of business. It's got to stop, and I'm ashamed that you've already agreed to vote for it. It's as if we're standing here expressing our opinion for no reason.... I wish you made eye contact with me, Mr. Reid, like you did with the last lady.

"I can make eye contact with you," interjected Councilman Reid. It was a rare break from decorum for an official to interrupt a speaker making a public comment. He angrily responded directly to Lori as she walked away from the podium. He said the abortion issue is old and ongoing, and people have made up their minds. "So, you've made your decision, and I've made my decision," Reid said. "So, I'm looking at you and making my statement." Then he added that it was the attitude toward the abortion issue in general that educated him on whether the bubble was worth approving.

The bubble law would not stop people from holding graphic signs and making offensive comments from a distance, the kinds of actions that curried sympathy for the clinics, D'Alessio explained. "I spend countless hours on the sidewalk and personally don't know anyone who does that," he said. "What we do out there on the street is provide information that abortion providers may not have provided." By thwarting people like him, he added, the bubble law would simply prevent women from making an informed decision about having an abortion.

Like Walter, D'Alessio asked the committee not to impose a bubble on pro-lifers without looking at videos from the clinics. The videos would prove that his description of their activities was accurate, he said. But at least one person claimed that no such videos were available. Hutchison, from the League of Women Voters, insisted that the clinics don't have the money for video security: "They use all of their money to provide health services.... None of the clinics in Oakland have the money to videotape anybody." Perhaps she was unaware of them, but video cameras can be found at all the abortion clinics in Oakland.

Some opponents of the proposed ordinance presented arguments based on the constitutional right to free speech. One said he was a registered Democrat and a schoolteacher. He extolled the civic virtue of freely expressing one's opinions, using the examples of anti-war protests in San Francisco and anti–death penalty protests at San Quentin. The state prison guards respect his right to free speech, he said and added that it will be "a sad day in Oakland when the city ... stops respecting freedom of speech." His sentiments were echoed by a Berkeley student who said that freedom of speech was important enough to take the time to be there to defend it against the ordinance.

When public comment concluded, Councilman Reid offered a conciliatory remark regarding his earlier comments to Lori Hoye. "If my child, if my oldest daughter was here, she would probably stand up right next to you and choose your side. But in my household, we have a right to agree and disagree.... So I just want you to know I wasn't being disrespectful." Reid was referring to his daughter Treva, who is publicly pro-life and a friend of Walter and Lori Hoye.

Nadel moved the question to a vote, but before the vote was taken, Quan offered a thought: "This image that I'd have to walk so close to you that I'd have to bump you to get into the clinic—that's not trying to talk to me; that's being in my way." Then she added, "To make this an issue of free speech is a bit ridiculous."

The question of free speech turned out to be an important one, however. The financial impact of the law, what it could cost the city to enforce it or to defend it in court, never came up at the hearing. Yet one case alone would end up costing the city $361,269.43. The

Public Safety Committee could not have known at the time that the city would incur such a huge expense as a result of the law, but they surely could have anticipated that there might be legal challenges in the near future.

As Reid predicted, the proposal passed by consensus, and the ordinance was soon sent to the full city council. As council members and the public filed out of the committee room, Police Chief Tucker walked over to Arnold and invited her to talk with him. Arnold was so disgusted by what she had just witnessed in the committee that she declined. She also turned down a newspaper reporter's request for an interview. "I'd given up on them all. I sensed there was no justice to be had and that we as peaceful Christians offering help to troubled women were headed to court or prison or whatever, and that was what happened."

12

Council of Practical Necessity

Walter Hoye was part of the generation of African Americans who grew up during a dramatic political turning point for blacks. While he was coming of age in the 1970s, radical changes were taking place in American society as a result of the efforts of Martin Luther King Jr. and the civil rights movement that began twenty years earlier. The civil rights generation saw many of its cohort work their way into every level of government. In 1971 the freshman members of Congress included a large number of black Americans who took the oath. Having finally reached an influential number in the House of Representatives, they established the Congressional Black Caucus.

The highest-profile black Americans, the best known in their communities, were unsurprisingly the first to gain political influence, and they were most often members of the clergy. Those who made their way onto the national stage included Jessie Jackson, an ordained minister from Chicago who marched with King in Selma and worked for his Southern Christian Leadership Conference (SCLC) until King's assassination. Another was Al Sharpton of Brooklyn, New York, who was ordained at age ten and also worked with the SCLC, in its Operation Breadbasket program. Sharpton was fresh out of high school in the early 1970s when he established his own organization.

Sharpton and Jackson both opposed abortion early in their political careers. In the 1970s, Jackson declared that since God creates life, man doesn't have the right to destroy it. Sharpton made similar statements. But over time they altered their views, or at least they softened their public rhetoric. "Women must have freedom of choice over what to do over their bodies," Jackson said while running for president in 1988. Compare that with some of his statements in 1977. "Those advocates of taking life prior to birth do not call it killing or murder; they call it abortion," Jackson said. "They further never talk about aborting a baby because that would imply something human. Rather, they talk about aborting the fetus. Fetus sounds less than human, and therefore can be justified." This reversal was not a matter of maturity over time but one of practical necessity.

With black political power largely situated in a single political party, black politicians have been pressured to conform to that party's point of view. The Democratic Party has acted as hammer and anvil in shaping the views of Jackson, Sharpton, and other black leaders. Jackson had two moderately successful runs for the Democratic presidential nomination, which would have been impossible if he had not allowed himself to be reinvented. When a black man won the White House in 2008, he was unapologetically pro-choice.

Barack Obama rose to prominence in the model of the post–civil rights era community activist, in the footsteps of Jackson and Sharpton. Obama had been affiliated with a black church in Chicago, and he took the presidential oath of office as a professed Christian. His connection to a church was vital to his rise to power. At the grassroots level, many black Americans are ardent Christians. But as another rule of practical necessity states, the church is a place not only to practice one's faith but also to advance the interests of one's group. In many black churches, there are people willing to support political causes and candidates if they seem as though they will be good for blacks. Whether they are good in themselves can be beside the point.

Black Power in Oakland

Like many major American cities, particularly in California, Oakland is dominated by the Democratic Party. Democrats hold the overwhelming majority of municipal offices, just as they have a supermajority in the state senate and assembly. Because of changes in the state election system, many California general election contests are between two Democrats. Thus, the major contests in the state are decided in the Democratic primary, while the general elections are not much more than a formality. Given the platform of the Democratic Party, only pro-choice candidates need apply.

East Bay officeholders have alliances with unions, community activists, and special interest groups, including the predominantly black churches. They call upon local black ministers to represent their community at political rallies and issues-based public events. The ministers most active in the Democratic Party are the most prominent black leaders. To be a black pastor and at odds with the party platform is to be an outcast.

Reverend Clenard Childress explained that many black religious leaders are privately pro-life but beholden to the abortion money that supports the Democratic Party and its candidates. "Remember, if abortion was not lucrative, it would not be legal. It's not just due to an ideology that these people are such strong advocates of choice. There's money coming into their coffers and the party's coffers. They receive their marching orders from the party.... It's not from their own sentiment. They've been bought."

Enter Walter Hoye

Focused on evangelization and pastoral outreach, Walter had not involved himself in politics. He therefore had not felt compelled to compromise his views on abortion. When those views surfaced more and more, because of concern for the members of his flock being harmed by abortion, his peers in ministry ignored him. As the bubble ordinance moved unimpeded through the city council, they refused to stand by him. Walter's support came primarily from Catholics and a very small but growing national network of black ministers, including Childress.

When journalists asked local black leaders about Walter Hoye and his pro-life activities, Reverend Amos Brown, then president of the San Francisco branch of the National Association for the Advancement of Colored People (NAACP), said that abortion was not a civil rights issue and that he had no plans to take part in pro-life events. "San Francisco's top civil rights issues are education, economic empowerment, and political engagement," Brown said, as quoted by the *San Francisco Chronicle* on January 7, 2008. "African American students are behind every ethnic group in this city academically. People who are learned and informed do the right thing. If not, they engage in destructive behavior."

Reverend Brown could have stopped there, but he moved beyond his point about his priorities and slammed Walter Hoye, although without mentioning him by name. "These pro-life people are demagogues and ideologues and are not receiving overwhelming support from the black community."

Coming from someone as formidable as Brown, these labels could really damage Walter's reputation in the black community. Brown was about sixty-nine years old at the time. Born in Mississippi, he became the leader of the Third Baptist Church in San Francisco in 1976. Among his impressive credentials was having been taught by King at Morehouse College. He had a master of divinity degree from Crozer Theological Seminary and a doctorate in ministry from United Theological Seminary. According to his profile on the NAACP website, "Brown has never seen the issues of society as separate from the mission of the church, especially when the members of the church are directly affected by systems of evil."

Childress had heard that message before and said that the NAACP was silent on abortion for the same reasons politicians were. "The NAACP is well aware that if you ask African Americans if they are pro-life they will take the life position. NAACP has covered up info on abortion at the national convention. They do not reflect the conscience of African Americans. It's sociologically proven they are promoting a position that blacks don't agree with."

Walter Hoye had a choice. He could side with his local brother faith leaders, or he could side with his conscience. The measure of Walter Hoye is the choice he made, which by all accounts was so unpopular that he was ostracized by his peers. In Oakland, of all places, where blacks are the single largest ethnic group, representing 27 percent of the population, he was a man without a country.

When Walter set out to fight the bubble ordinance, he had seen with his own eyes at Family Planning Specialists what reliable statistics demonstrated: black Americans have a disproportionate number of abortions. According to the Guttmacher Institute, in 2008 African American women had about 30 percent of all abortions, but according to the 2010 census blacks make up less than 14 percent of the female population of the United States. The Centers for Disease Control reported that in the United States in 2007, non-Hispanic black women had 36.8 abortions per 1,000 women.

In comparison, non-Hispanic white women had 9.3 abortions per 1,000 women.

City Council

Fresh out of committee, the bubble ordinance was quickly moved to the city council and set for a vote the first week of December 2007, already showing signs of being a juggernaut. One week was hardly enough time for a big campaign against the legislation, but Walter determined to do what he could. Given the prevalence of abortion in the black community, and what it says about the situation many black women are in, Walter thought he would be able to appeal to members of city government who had shown empathy for black Americans in difficult circumstances, those who called themselves champions of the cause. Surely they could be made to understand that black women deserve better than abortion, he thought.

But Walter was no politician. The main lesson he had learned from the experiences of Martin Luther King Jr. was the power of standing up and speaking out. Walter therefore decided to use King's words, and the words of Christ, in an outreach to black members of the council and perhaps the city's mayor.

Those council members were Larry Reid (ten years on the council) and Desley Brooks (five years), two of the most powerful black leaders in Oakland. The longer shot was Mayor Ron Dellums, a San Francisco activist turned politician who was elected to Congress in 1971, when he helped to found the Congressional Black Caucus. Dellums was by far the most powerful and influential person in Oakland, white or black, during the passage of the bubble law. The federal building in downtown Oakland was named after him in 1998. Walter believed that these city leaders understood the struggle and, at the very least, would listen.

Walter called and e-mailed his network in the hope of finding enough volunteers to speak against the proposal. He needed a greater number to oppose it than would speak in favor of it. While he assumed that most of his black peers in the local clergy would decline, he counted on the addition of his new Catholic friends to fill the gaps. The strategy would be simple: defend the right to free speech and raise the point that the clinics were targeting people of color.

There are eight members on the Oakland City Council. Five votes are needed to pass an ordinance, and in the case of a tie, the mayor provides the deciding vote. Walter knew that the law's sponsors—Nancy Nadel, Jane Brunner, and Jean Quan—were sure to vote yes. But he prayed with faith that God would help him to move the hearts of the other five members and Mayor Dellums. As a tiebreaker, Dellums could influence the outcome.

Walter admitted to himself that Dellums, Brooks, and Reid had long ago surrendered their independence to the Democratic Party, which controlled Oakland politics. They did what they considered necessary to hold on to their power and status, and that included positioning themselves as pro-choice, whatever their private views on abortion might be.

But if they would only try to understand the plight of the black women entering Family Planning Specialists, Walter prayed. Those women don't want to kill their unborn children, but without people to offer them alternatives, without anyone to give them encouragement, they think they must have an abortion. Walter was convinced that abortion had become a civil rights issue, particularly for blacks, not only because the black child is deprived of his right to life, but because the black mother is deprived of the support she needs to exercise her freedom to choose life. If only his brothers and sisters in government would be convinced of this too, he prayed.

Up to this point Walter Hoye was not exactly a household name. Media attention was just building, and he could turn back from notoriety if he wanted. The prospect of being launched onto the public stage forced him to take a deep breath. The cost of becoming widely known as a black minster in open rebellion against the status quo could be onerous. He could lose the good opinion of colleagues and friends. He could lose opportunities to exercise his ministry and the little income he made as a pastor.

Yet it frightened him more to be a man so bereft of conscience that he could ignore hundreds of years of black history in America and where that legacy had led many black women—to the doors of the abortion clinic. He recalled the real injustices against his own people, against members of his own family: slavery, lynching, Jim

Crow laws. By every means possible, blacks had been oppressed and diminished. Yes, blacks had achieved equal rights before the law, they had even entered the highest offices in the land, yet the presence of abortion clinics in black neighborhoods appeared to him now as one more tool to keep his people down.

The council of practical necessity would override all these considerations, however, and the bubble ordinance would easily pass. And as he sat in the county jail, Walter Hoye would have plenty of time to think about just how naïve he had been.

13

An Unexpected Brotherly Bond

Walter Hoye was deeply disappointed by the lack of support he received from blacks in both ministry and government. Yet he was undaunted in his opposition to abortion and the bubble law that would restrict his rights to reach out to women at Family Planning Specialists. These words of Martin Luther King Jr. kept running through his mind: "We cannot win the respect of the white people of the South or elsewhere if we are willing to trade the future of our children for our personal safety and comfort. Moreover, we must learn that passively to accept an unjust system is to co-operate with that system, and thereby to become a participant in its evil." Walter believed King's words should have been heard by blacks as a clarion call to extend the cause of civil rights and the black American struggle to the unborn of their community. Ministers in particular, he thought, should stand up for the sanctity of human life.

During Walter's imprisonment, just when he despaired of finding a prominent man of the cloth willing to defend the unborn, and him, he found one: Salvatore J. Cordileone, the Catholic bishop of Oakland.

San Diego

Cordileone was born in San Diego on June 5, 1956, just two months before Walter was born in Detroit. When the two men met decades later and compared notes, they found that they had more in common than their age and pro-life convictions. There was a time when they lived little more than a couple of miles from each other, separated only by a freeway.

Cordileone attended San Diego's Crawford High School when Walter attended rival Patrick Henry. Cordileone played tenor saxophone for the Crawford marching band, and Walter was a running back on the Patrick Henry football team. When the schools faced off for games, both boys were there, but they never met. It was in San Diego that both young men experienced the deep spiritual conversions that would chart their paths in life.

During Cordileone's freshman year at San Diego State University, he attended a vocational retreat and heard the call to the priesthood. He transferred to the University of San Diego, where he graduated with a bachelor's degree in philosophy in 1978. He furthered his studies at the Pontifical Gregorian University in Rome, where he received a baccalaureate in sacred theology in 1981. After Cordileone was ordained in 1982, he took up parish responsibilities at Saint Martin of Tours in La Mesa, California. He returned to the Gregorian in 1985 and completed a doctorate in canon law four years later. Pope John Paul II appointed him auxiliary bishop of San Diego in 2002, and on March 23, 2009, Pope Benedict XVI named him the fourth bishop of Oakland, just two days after a shooting caused a lockdown at Santa Rita Jail.

It was anything but a typical Monday in Oakland when word of Cordileone's appointment reached the people of the city. They were still reeling from the shocking news that on Saturday Lovelle Mixon had gunned down four police officers, killing three and wounding forty-one-year-old John Hege, who was hours away from death in the Highland Hospital intensive care unit.

During and immediately following the shooting, there was a lockdown at Alameda County's Santa Rita Jail. It lasted just a few hours, but the tension in the jail remained high afterward. Brand-new inmate Walter Hoye had hardly gained his bearings when the lockdown began, and when it lifted he was still disoriented from his surreal experiences of entering the prison system. Although news of the new bishop was overshadowed by the endless media coverage of the shootings, it did reach Walter in his cage at Santa Rita.

Walter received word about Cordileone in a letter from Eva Muntean, who expressed her excitement over the appointment and called Cordileone a wonderful and spiritual man. "I don't know if you remember him," she wrote, "but he was the one that Father

Fessio toasted at the Walk for Life dinner, saying something like 'Here's to the new bishop of Oakland.' How prophetic!"

Indeed, Walter first met Cordileone in January 2009, when the bishop traveled from San Diego to attend the Walk for Life in San Francisco. At the time, Walter was on trial for alleged violations of the bubble ordinance in Oakland, and at the Walk for Life dinner, the bishop took an interest in his story.

The following March, when Bishop Cordileone arrived in Oakland to prepare for his May installation, Walter was in Santa Rita Jail. Although the bishop had a lot of work to do, he managed to carve out some time to visit Walter. "I did it more out of a sense of personal support to him. For him to know that we were behind him," Cordileone said. "I didn't do it to try to make any kind of political statement or anything."

The Bishop's Visit

Visiting hours at Santa Rita were limited and complicated, as Walter and Lori Hoye had discovered. So Walter was surprised when on his eighth full day in jail he was told he had a special visitor, someone who needed extra protection and would therefore meet him in the maximum security section of the prison. As a guard escorted Walter to the meeting place on the other side of the jail, he told him that his mysterious visitor was Bishop Cordileone.

Coincidentally, the man Cordileone was replacing, Bishop Allen H. Vigneron, had been appointed archbishop of Walter's hometown, Detroit, and had assumed the post in January 2009. Walter knew and respected Vigneron, who was a speaker at Walter's January 2009 conference. It was one of his last official acts in Oakland. Walter was sad to see him go, but he was happy about his replacement, based on what he had heard from his pro-life Catholic friends. He was even happier that the man came to visit him, just as the Lord asked his disciples to do: "I was in prison and you came to me" (Mt 25:36).

The thick, impact-resistant security glass and the black telephones resembled those in the other visiting area. The two men sat down and picked up their respective phones, smiling through the transparent partition. It didn't take long for the two contemporaries to figure out that they shared some personal history in San Diego.

It also didn't take them long to appreciate the uniqueness of their meeting. While there are many black priests and religious in the Catholic Church, not many are black Americans. Among the black Protestant clergy, not many are publicly pro-life, and none of them had visited Walter. There in the prison the usual alliances and barriers based on black and white, Catholic and Protestant were transcended, for the two men were united in their reverence for God and their respect for his gift of life.

The first thing about Walter that struck Bishop Cordileone was his gentleness, the bishop said. "He's a very courageous man but very gentle." When he asked Walter about his commitment to the unborn, Walter told him that abortion "is annihilating his community and how really it's the African American community who in some ways is being targeted."

Just when the conversation was getting interesting, the phone switched off. A riot had broken out in one of the maximum security cell blocks. Guards locked Walter and Cordileone in the visiting room and vanished. With the phone line dead, the two men shrugged in the silence. The customary thirty-minute time limit for such a visit was suspended, but what could they do without phones? "We started yelling at each other through the glass," Walter said.

"It was kind of frustrating," said Cordileone.

Walter had been explaining where he and his pro-life commitment had come from, and it occurred to him that he had been doing all the talking as if he were in a confessional. But then it was the bishop's turn to tell Walter about himself. "In my mind, it was as if he was in confession with me," Walter said.

The men were surprised by the similarities they shared, he noted. "Some of the issues I was facing with the pastors in my community he was facing with some of the priests in his community. It became evident that we needed one another." As a result, they formed an immediate bond.

"It was a brotherly bond," said Cordileone. "I could tell he was coming out of a place of love. He was doing this out of love for the children, out of love for the women, appreciating that trying to build a culture of life was conducive to a culture of love."

Walter was so impressed by the man of faith on the other side of the glass and felt so close to him that he asked, "Could I be both Baptist and Catholic at the same time?" The bishop said no, Walter recalled with a laugh, "but he said we would talk about it some more."

"I'm sure I said we could talk about it some other time," Cordileone explained, "and I probably said something like, 'You're welcome to come to our services and worship with us, but you can't be both at the same time.'"

It was the beginning of long friendship based on mutual respect and a common purpose, the building of a culture of life.

Eventually Cordileone became the archbishop of San Francisco. He later said that people like Walter Hoye, who are willing to walk the walk, are immensely important. "I mean, anyone who suffered for a cause of justice is immensely important for furthering what is right and good," he explained. "And he continued to be outspoken— but, again, with defensive gentleness. He understands how colossally important this issue is and how [abortion] is tearing our nation apart, and he wants to be an agent of healing."

The jail visit, that long conversation, even with the disconnected phone, and the new bond that it forged with Cordileone buoyed Walter's spirits. He knew that when the bishop promised his prayers he meant it, and Walter counted on those prayers.

Cordileone was one of the few who could visit Walter in jail. Many others who couldn't sent letters. And their letters came in bundles.

Fan Mail

Letters began arriving just a few days after Walter Hoye was incarcerated. They ranged in size—from postcards to large manila envelopes, one of which contained a two-act play. There were short personal messages and long testimonials. Some came from friends and a few from Lori.

The messages came from all over the Bay Area, California, and beyond. There were letters from almost every state in the Union and from foreign countries too. They had two elements in common: an expression of support and "34F" handwritten in red grease pencil next to the address, indicating Walter's pod and cage number. All the mail surprised Walter. He did not realize the extent to which he was making news outside Oakland.

The element of Walter's story that seemed to be attracting the most attention was his race. A woman from Brownstown, Michigan, wrote: "I was an obstetrics nurse in Detroit for 12 years and could not understand why no one cared about the numbers of black babies being aborted each year. Some of my patients would report 5, 10, even 20 abortions. Does no one see?"

Someone from Cape Canaveral, Florida, wrote, "For anything to be accomplished in this country, it is going to take people like yourself (black & pro-life & Christian)." A pro-life black man from Texas wrote, "Walter, you inspire us to stay in the fight."

Some correspondents pointed out the irony of Walter's being in jail: "Is this not a crazy world we live in?" wrote a well-wisher from Sacramento, California. "The day after you are sentenced 4 Policemen are murdered by a man that should not have been let out of jail. Yet Walter Hoye is put in Jail for not killing but saving."

Among the hundreds of letters were a few bright-pink slips. They were return-to-sender notices, showing Walter that the jail received something for him that had to be returned. Sometimes it was a prohibited item, such as rosary beads or food. But mostly it was money. Walter wasn't just receiving letters; he was receiving donations, but they were sent back if the money was not in the correct form. Money orders were preferred.

Most of the donations were permitted, however, and went into Walter Hoye's jail account. They ranged from two dollars to a hundred dollars and were sent for a variety of purposes. One letter said the money was intended to help pay his fine or legal expenses. Another said it was for anything he might need. As it turned out, Walter did not need much, especially since he was fasting, so he gave some of his donations to the men who had nothing in their jail accounts. They usually spent the windfall on snacks. Walter didn't mind that his money was lavished on candy bars and barbecue potato chips so long as he could demonstrate to his cellmates that there were people out in the world who cared about them too.

The letters and the donations were a daily reminder that everything was happening for a reason, Walter said, that his incarceration was not pointless but was serving a greater purpose. He appreciated the words of encouragement and the donations, and he cherished the prayers, especially during a life-threatening illness. But before that part of the story can be told, the passage of the law that put Walter behind bars will be examined.

14

To Fight City Hall

On November 6, 2007, the autumn wind swirled leaves around Frank Ogawa Plaza in front of Oakland City Hall. Also swirling were small pieces of carelessly discarded trash that missed municipal garbage cans conveniently placed along the sidewalks. The sun was setting, but the day seemed to be just getting started as Walter Hoye and people on both sides of the bubble ordinance arrived for the official introduction of the proposal.

Erected in 1914, City Hall is a historic Beaux Arts high-rise topped with a clock tower. Its majestic plaza is a popular staging area for rallies and protests as well as a favorite hangout of homeless men. On any given day they can be seen sharing drugs or napping on the lawn surrounding the city's most famous live oak tree. They regularly use the public restroom in the lobby of City Hall, and as citizens hoping to speak on the bubble law awaited the opening of the city council chamber, they wrinkled their noses at the acrid aroma of urine and marijuana.

Based on some early accounts, members of the public wanting to speak on the proposal were expected to number more than sixty. One newspaper report suggested that those speaking against the ordinance would have a two-to-one advantage over those in favor. The actual ratio might have been more even, but the majority of those who addressed the council that night were against the abortion clinic buffer zone.

Among the pro-life attendees was Terry Thompson of Alamo, California. Thompson made the twenty-five-minute drive to Oakland to speak against the ordinance. He had heard of Walter Hoye but had not met him until that night. Thompson had been an engineer for about thirty-five years, until he went back to school and got a law degree. He then joined the Life Legal Defense Foundation as a board member. Thompson was destined to become an important Hoye ally.

Just after six o'clock, comment cards were distributed. Those wishing to speak on the bubble ordinance first filled out a card to get on the speaker list. They had plenty of time to do so, for the item was at the end of a very long agenda, even though, or perhaps because, it was the most anticipated and controversial matter.

Late-Night Testimony

One hour, two hours, three, four, and five went by. Finally, acting council president and future mayor Jean Quan called agenda item twenty-five. Fifty people had filled out speaker cards entitling them to address the council about the bubble ordinance, Quan noted. "We'll see how many are left."

The small city council chamber had been packed when the meeting began, but the crowd had thinned by the time Marisa Arrona, policy coordinator for Councilwoman Nancy Nadel, introduced the bubble ordinance proposal with a casual good morning, owing to the very late hour, past midnight.

Arrona characterized the proposal as one that would ensure safe and unimpeded access to reproductive health care facilities in Oakland. She claimed that it provided a level of public safety not covered by local state and federal laws. She detailed the key provisions, namely, the buffer zones, which she called "limited medical safety zones". The clinic buffer zone would be one hundred feet, and the personal buffer zone within it would be eight feet for those entering and exiting clinics within the city limits.

Without further discussion, Councilwoman Quan invited members of the public to comment on the proposed ordinance. Unsurprisingly, given the late hour, some of the would-be speakers had already left. Thompson pointed out that many of the people who had wanted to speak on the issue were compelled to leave because the public transportation services were shutting down. "We had thirty-five people here to speak," he said, requesting that the public record show that "we have a de facto abridgment of our rights to public speaking." Quan noted his concern and began a strict enforcement of speaker time limits. Thompson then used his one-minute limit to argue that the ordinance was not needed since there were laws on the books to secure clinics and access to them.

The speakers who followed included both advocates and opponents of the bubble ordinance. Their opinions were varied and often received a smattering of applause from one side or the other. After Thompson came Terry Sandoval, who called herself a pro-choice practicing Catholic and a volunteer clinic escort. She said the ordinance was needed to protect escorts like her and the clients they seek to serve.

Up next were several people from labor groups, who spoke against the ordinance on free-speech grounds. The argument returned to the rights of abortion providers and their clients with comments by Jackie Barbic of Family Planning Specialists. She said the sidewalk counselors were aggressive and confrontational. "For this group to say that they are peaceful and helpful to our patients is an outright lie," she added.

Barbic's description was countered by several women who said they had had abortions. One woman said, "It came to a point I had to go to several priests, because I couldn't forgive myself for what I did." Another said she had an abortion because when she went to a clinic in New York, no one was there to offer an alternative. Another said she wished she had met a sidewalk counselor.

When Walter Hoye came to the podium he was flanked by his curbside companions from Progressive Missionary Baptist Church, Christiana Downer and Sister Elga Kendall. At last he could comment on an ordinance that had everything needed to stop his curbside outreach but his name. Even though he was the real target of the bubble law, he had never been invited to any of the numerous meetings of its drafters, and they had never accepted any of his offers to talk.

"Many of our [church] members are residents of Oakland or are employees of the city of Oakland," he said. "We are not a public safety threat." As he placed a hand on Kendall's shoulder he continued, "This sister is eighty-nine years old. She is not a public safety threat." He explained that they were in front of Family Planning Specialists offering an alternative to abortion one day a week and for just two hours, while the clinic was open nearly every day. "We are not getting the impression the council really fully understands what's happening there," he said. "So, we invite you to come and take a look for yourselves."

The majority of speakers were against the ordinance, but for the city council it was not a night for listening; it was a night for going through the motions. When the time for public testimony was over, the council members made their statements.

Nadel primarily addressed the concerns of labor organizations, as did Councilwoman Jane Brunner. Councilwoman Patricia Kernighan gave the longest statement, which centered on her reasons for thinking that the ordinance was needed. She called the issue a difficult one with strong feelings on each side that would not change. "I'm comfortable with the ordinance," she concluded. "There's no major infringement of free speech here."

Councilwoman Desley Brooks applauded the crafters of the ordinance as she announced that her vote would be in favor. When Quan followed with her support she mentioned Walter's concern that the escorts sometimes bump into him and used those words against him: "In order to get into the clinic, these women had to get close enough to bump into him. I couldn't imagine ... having to bump and fight my way into a clinic." But Walter had referred to the escorts' standing so close that they bumped him, not his bumping into women entering the clinic. It was not clear whether Quan had misunderstood Walter or had deliberately obfuscated the distinction between escorts and clients.

On hand to answer council questions were Police Chief Wayne Tucker and City Attorney Vicki Laden, but the council members asked them no questions and moved to a voice vote. They accepted the proposal, but to become law, the bill required passage by the full council and another long night.

Alveda King

Given the level of interest in the bubble ordinance proposal, many people wrote letters to the city council, asking that they support or oppose the measure. Only a few letters were widely circulated, and only one against the ordinance garnered any attention. It was notable because of the author. The name King, as in a relation of Martin Luther King Jr., commanded such attention.

> To the Honorable Members of the Oakland City Council:
> My name is Dr. Alveda King. I'm a Pastoral Associate of Priests for Life and a lifetime civil rights activist.
> Since my childhood, I have witnessed first hand the long struggle for equal justice in our nation. I lost my father, the Rev. A. D. King, and my uncle, the Rev. Martin Luther King, Jr., in this struggle. These men spoke their consciences and defended those whom society deemed unworthy of inclusion. Because their pleas for justice and compassion were troubling, even threatening to some, they were silenced.
> I urge you, I beg you today not to silence those who seek to speak their consciences and defend those whom our society currently deems unworthy of inclusion, the unborn. Please do not use the power of government, which is supposed to guarantee our freedoms, to gag those whose words may make some uncomfortable.
> I speak to you not only as a defender of civil rights and the First Amendment, but also as a woman who has had two abortions. There may be some who want to live their lives in bubbles where there are no black people or bubbles where there are no pro-lifers. But it isn't government's job to hold down certain people so that we don't come in contact with them. Please, defeat this proposal.

A Last Chance

It was again midnight when on December 18, 2007, agenda item thirty-nine, the proposed bubble ordinance, was called before the full city council for a vote. It was again the final item on the agenda of another very long meeting, and the clock was ticking. There was no updated staff report, no Q and A, and none of the issue updates that were typical in such situations; instead, the council president, Ignacio De La Fuente, pressed on directly to the public comments.

This time around, there were far fewer speakers on the issue. Walter had tried unsuccessfully to recruit more opponents by founding the Issues4Life Foundation. He had hoped it might help him to fight Oakland's bubble ordinance. The organization seemed to have raised awareness of the need for supporters, but the pro-life turnout for the final vote was even lighter than when the bill was introduced.

The supporters also had fewer people. They put forward just one speaker "in the interest of time". Sandoval, the FPS volunteer escort, was back at the microphone. "I'm afraid I'm gonna have to use these words, good morning." She wore an unzipped hoodie, a gray shirt, and reading glasses clasped to her collar. Behind her stood several women, including one holding up an enlarged photograph of escorts and sidewalk counselors interacting.

Before commenting on the photo, she thanked those responsible for the ordinance as if the vote had already been taken and the law had already passed. She thanked sponsors Nancy Nadel, Jean Quan, and Jane Brunner by name and the rest of the city council. Then she mentioned those who helped with the crafting of the language, including Nadel staffer Marisa Arrona, Vicki Laden of the city attorney's office, Lindsey Comey of Feminist Women's Choice Clinic, FPS founder Jackie Barbic, Deputy District Attorney Nancy E. O'Malley, and Police Chief Wayne Tucker.

Pointing to the photograph, Sandoval explained that it represented what happened daily at the FPS clinic at 200 Webster Street. The image appeared to show a gaggle of people standing on a sidewalk. "This is a picture of myself as a clinic escort," she explained, "helping a woman get into the clinic itself. You can see that there is a parking meter there. She had to walk into the street and around a parking meter to get to the clinic. And that's just not acceptable."

By the time the opponents had the chance to speak, it was a formality. The issue had already been decided. Yet at least a few in the room must have been surprised by the tack Lori Hoye took. She said that behind the bill was bitter disappointment that sidewalk counselors had not been present when some of the bill's supporters chose to have an abortion:

> It's about punishing sidewalk counselors for our absence in the past. We were not there when a woman had to make the most difficult decision of her life, to offer her alternatives. We were not there when the woman left the clinic feeling drained and empty, to offer her comfort. So, now the woman is part of the walking wounded, the one out of three women in this country who have had an abortion, and now she's lashing out at

us for not being there. We want her to know that we're sorry and help is still available even now. We love her, we care. Let us continue to be there. Vote no.

Walter followed his wife with some statistics. Abortion is the leading cause of death in the black American community, he said. "Presently, over 1,400 African American babies are aborted every single day. I'd also like to point out that, as of the current U.S. census, black folk are below the replacement level," he said. "There are more deaths than there are live births."

A fifteen-year veteran of sidewalk counseling, Dee Thompson argued that the ordinance would burden an already overworked police force in a crime-ridden city. "With this ordinance, you council members are now asking your police force to take on another peripheral assignment that will divert them from their real jobs. They will be called in to referee whether a leafleter was seven feet or eight from a clinic client, whether the leafleter's arm were extended or not." She called the ordinance un-American.

Terry Thompson of Life Legal Defense Foundation, who had spoken when the bill was introduced, challenged Barbic's use of a photograph in that meeting. It was an image of James Kopp inside her clinic many years earlier. As mentioned in a previous chapter, Kopp was later convicted for the murder of an abortionist in another state. Barbic was waging an old fight and not addressing the realities of the present, Thompson said. "This picture was taken in the late eighties. She acts like any given day she might have to fight her way through a phalanx of militant blockaders," he said. "You're being deceived."

Other speakers were aghast at the chilling effect the ordinance would have on free speech. "Tyranny is a government deciding who may speak and who may not speak," said Cyrus Johnson, a corporate attorney who explained that his interest in this issue was a matter of constitutional rights. "If this law passes I may say, 'Please have an abortion,' and nothing happens to me. If I say, 'Please do not have an abortion,' I may be arrested and thrown in prison. This is the very definition of tyranny."

The last speaker closed with a bit of criticism for the city council. "Regardless of which side of the issue ... you're on," said the man, "twelve thirty in the morning is not a good time to be doing public policy."

Considering the passions stirred up by the issue of abortion, it was a remarkably short comment period, spanning just about thirty minutes. It took many long hours to get to the ordinance, and the discussion was over in an instant. The motion was moved by sponsor Nancy Nadel and, inaudibly to most of those who were there or watching on public access, seconded by the conspicuously silent Desley Brooks, the council's only black woman. The unanimous voice vote came and went, and the meeting was adjourned. A smattering of applause could hardly be heard over the sound of shifting chairs as the council members left the chamber.

It was done. After years in the making, the bubble ordinance was at last law, or so its supporters thought.

Legal Challenge

The legal challenge was nearly instantaneous. On December 19, Hoye, through his attorneys Michael Millen and Catherine Short of the Life Legal Defense Foundation, filed a lawsuit challenging the constitutionality of Oakland Municipal Code §8.52.030(b), otherwise known as the bubble law. They also requested that the ordinance not be enforced as it went through the legal process.

The case was assigned to Judge Charles Breyer, the brother of United States Supreme Court Justice Stephen Breyer. Appointed by President Bill Clinton, Breyer became a federal judge in July 1997. After graduating from Harvard in 1963, he attended Berkeley's School of Law. His legal-work experience included assisting the district attorney in San Francisco. Breyer also had served as a Watergate special prosecutor.

Soon after Judge Breyer was assigned to the case, a teleconference took place between him, Vicki Laden of the Oakland city attorney's office, and Millen. Laden had been instrumental in crafting the bubble ordinance, and during the conversation, Breyer expressed concerns regarding some of the language in the law. Specifically, he questioned the use of the word "persuade" in a subsection of the law.

"It was a whacky line," Millen later explained. "It was one of those things that get into legislation when something's rushed through the process and into law." The law was clearly flawed, and the judge "gently nudged" the city to modify the language, he said. Millen had expected a hearing on the appeal, which was more typical in such cases, but instead the judge took an advisory role and helped the city.

The writers of the bubble ordinance quickly got to work. They decided to tailor the language to mirror the Colorado bubble law more closely. If they could make the changes and pass a revised version of the ordinance soon enough, the judge would deny the motion for the injunction and the temporary restraining order.

Meanwhile, Hoye's Issues4Life organization was closing in on its first annual StandUp4Life Walk in Oakland, which was set for January 18, 2008, just a day ahead of the Walk for Life in San Francisco. One of the chief objectives of StandUp4Life was to voice opposition to the bubble ordinance, which, after rewording, would go back to the city council.

There had to be opposition to the opposition, according to clinic-escort coordinator Barbara Hoke. In a message to the bubble ordinance working group, attributed to Hoke using the generic group e-mail address, she said she had been "angsting" about what to do about the rally. She was certainly not going to let the "extremist invasion" take over the city. Her plan included several key points:

- Protect the clinics: assign ten escorts to each one.
- Engage trusted journalists to cover the story.
- Recruit pro-choice endorsers.
- If there are protesters, create a human tunnel for patients to walk through.
- Lead up to a coordinated rally on March 8, International Woman's Day.

Hoke's draft letter calling on support for the bubble law referred to a fundamentalist "anti", a preacher who wears a cap that says "Got Jesus?" and drives from Union City to prevent women from entering abortion clinics in Oakland. She told the group that the man preaches at a church in Berkeley that abortion is genocide against blacks. She also claimed that Walter Hoye had deep-pocketed

Catholic and right-wing political cronies and that he hoped to bring masses of antis to Oakland City Hall on Friday, January 18, for a huge anti-bubble and anti-abortion rally.

While Hoke rallied the troops to oppose the Oakland pro-life event, Oakland city staff worked on new wording for the ordinance. It took about two weeks to rewrite the bubble law, which was back on the agenda for the next Oakland City Council meeting.

Roll Call

On January 15, 2008, Martin Luther King Jr.'s birthday, the revised version of the ordinance was reintroduced to the city council. There wasn't much for the council to do other than review the wording changes and vote. Of course, it would have to sit through more public comment first.

Supporters of the ordinance rightly assumed that there was no reason to believe it would fail to pass; hence Helen Hutchison of the League of Women Voters, who authored parts of the legislation, was the only pro-ordinance speaker of the sixty-eight people who had filled out speaker cards. The other sixty-seven had turned in requests to speak at the behest of ordinance boosters, even though they had no intention of being present. Hutchison said little more than thank you.

There were only a few speakers against the ordinance, the most committed: Walter and Lori Hoye and a few Catholics who had been there before. Lori wasn't concerned about the vote's being another rubber stamp, or about the time limit, or about the futility of calling yet again for a no vote. She would speak her mind regardless of the expected outcome:

> Sidewalk counselors have been outside abortion clinics in Oakland for over twenty years, but as far as I know, until 2005, few of them, if any, were negro, black, or African American. Personally, I think we need to apologize for being so late to the game. However, now that we African Americans are on the sidewalk it becomes necessary to criminalize sidewalk counseling in the city of Oakland. As we stand here on what would have been the seventy-eighth birthday of Dr. Martin Luther King Jr., you, the Oakland City Council, are again going to vote to criminalize sidewalk counselors, because African Americans are offering the possibility of an alternative choice to the African American women going into

the abortion clinics. I challenge you to vote by roll call vote, not hide behind consensus.

Walter followed his wife to the podium and urged a no vote, reiterating that the sidewalk counselors were peaceful. He was the final public speaker.

Bubble ordinance sponsor Nadel was the only council member to speak when the public comments had ended. She said that her abortion in the past was "the best thing to ever happen" to her and that she did not want anyone praying for her. The job of the government, she continued, is to facilitate free speech and to protect women's access to health services. "This ordinance allows both," she said.

She explained that she had received a call from a clinic regarding aggressive anti-abortion protestors. She didn't say what clinic or where. She projected two photographs that did not look as though they had been taken at Family Planning Specialists. She took the pictures herself on Sunday, she said, two days before that night's meeting. One showed a car with some large poster boards leaning against it. On the posters, she said, were pictures of bloody fetuses. In the other photo were a pair of unrecognizable men who she said used their phones to take pictures of people coming out of the clinic.

"The clients were already inside," she continued. "These folks were staying only to harass the people after they came out of the clinic because there was nobody going in anymore. It's very clear that what is going on is not the peaceful counseling that has been characterized here time after time, after time, after time.

"I'm proud to have a roll call vote," she concluded. "I think everybody here would."

The clerk called the roll, and all the votes were in favor.

Three days later Walter and his supporters held their StandUp4Life event in Oakland.

Final

On February 5, 2008, the bubble ordinance was before the city council for the fourth and final time. It was on the consent calendar, which meant that it would be passed with other items that had previously been agreed to by the majority and not up for debate. There were fifteen consent items grouped together for the single consent vote. The only issue that drew requests for speakers was the revised bubble ordinance.

With both sides exhausted by the process, only a few speakers bothered to address the council. Hoke again thanked the council for their work. She told the council that if it were not so important, it would not be so difficult. The only other voice of support came from Lauren Quan, daughter of Councilwoman Quan. The young woman, possibly in high school, simply asked the council to support the proposal.

There were about eight speakers against the ordinance. Some spoke out on constitutional grounds, calling it a viewpoint crime, a restriction on constitutionally protected speech. Others said it was a matter of life and death. One speaker, Matthew Mason, told the story of a sidewalk counselor who offered to adopt the child of a young woman on her way to an abortion. That woman was being prepped for the procedure when she changed her mind, and that child was himself, Matthew said. His adoptive mother also addressed the council. "Thankfully, I was able to talk to her," said Melinda Mason. "We're asking that we have our freedom of speech, that we are able to talk to these women."

Lori Hoye pointed to the waste of police resources just to prevent people from offering young women an alternative to abortion. "This law is unjust. This law creates a Planned Parenthood–only environment in the city of Oakland. It does not allow alternative views. It does not take into consideration the life of the child, who has a right to live."

Walter followed. Parting from his usual conservative attire, he wore the same blue and gold hoodie, in support of the Golden State Warriors, as the one worn that night by his wife, the team's statistician. But he still wore his iconic "Got Jesus?" hat. On his left and right were the senior companions from his church who accompanied him to the abortion clinic. "We are the ones that this [ordinance] is really all about," he said. "We are not violent." Sadness underscored his soft tone.

The melancholy was also evident on his face and in his posture. He shrugged his shoulders as he spoke with his hands shoved deep into the pockets of his hoodie. "I'm asking you, I'm begging you,

I'm pleading with you to think twice about this," he said. "Please don't restrict our freedom of speech. Please don't restrict the rights we have as U.S. citizens to just state our opinion if nothing else. So, I'm asking you, sir, ladies, and gentlemen, please, please don't do this. God bless you."

When it was Thompson's turn, he said that the new ordinance was still "unconstitutionally viewpoint based" and no better than the previous one. "This revised ordinance simply puts a Band-Aid on the old ordinance," he said. "It's not fixed. It still contains serious constitutional flaws."

Before the vote, Nadel asked to speak. "I have done my homework," she said, referring to her comment in the last meeting, two weeks earlier. She repeated the story of how she had gone out and photographed "protestors" blocking, harassing, intimidating, and photographing clinic clients. "I have seen what is really happening at the clinics, and it is harassment!"

By consensus vote, the city council again passed the following ordinance:

> Within one hundred (100) feet of the entrance of a reproductive health care facility, it shall be unlawful to willfully and knowingly approach within eight feet of any person seeking to enter such a facility, or any occupied motor vehicle seeking entry, without the consent of such person or vehicle occupant, for the purpose of counseling, harassing, or interfering with such person or occupant.

Pro-lifers claimed that the new law was aimed at stopping their speech, and, in particular, Walter Hoye's, outside of abortion clinics. No matter. The following week Walter was back at his curbside post in front of Family Planning Specialists.

15

The Ordinance

One week after Oakland passed its long-awaited bubble ordinance, Walter Hoye stood dutifully near a tree in front of Family Planning Specialists on Webster Street. As he had so many times before, he held his sign saying, "God loves you and your baby. Let us help you." Sister Elga Kendall and Christiana Downer, Walter's steadfast companions, stood across the street. Walter was mindful of the new law. They all were.

Several police cars were parked near the clinic. The escorts in their bright-orange safety vests were gathered near the clinic entrance, talking among themselves. Walter watched the Oakland police officers watching him, and the escorts watched Walter and the police watch each other. All the while everyone had an eye out for arriving patients.

Walter approached the police car parked at the curb across the street from FPS. Seeing the window down, he asked the officer in the driver's seat, "Are you here to arrest me?" They weren't if he didn't break the law, the officer replied. Walter said later that they were polite. "Okay," he responded with a hint of cautious curiosity in his voice. He was fairly certain that he understood the new law, and he was determined to maintain the lawful distance from any person approaching the clinic.

After a while, a buzz began among the escorts. Some young women were headed toward the clinic. Walter remained eight feet away from them and raised his sign saying, "God loves you and your baby. Let us help you." He held out his literature, and some of the women accepted it. The escorts tried to insert themselves between the women and Walter and to block his sign. The police officers watched. It went on like that for two hours.

Inside the clinic, director Jackie Barbic sent an e-mail to Council-woman Nancy Nadel decrying Walter's attempt to test the new ordinance, as she characterized it. Frustrating her even more were the police officers outside, who appeared ignorant of the bubble zones. She told Nadel that she was not able to get anyone on the phone at the city attorney's office.

The police did not arrest Walter or even act as if there had been complaints. When Walter's vigil for the day was over, he walked away, and a few minutes later the black and white patrol car drove off. Apparently the outcome was not what the bubble backers had wanted, for they sent each other a flurry of e-mails.

A Perceived Lack of Enforcement

Escort coordinator Barbara Hoke wrote an e-mail to Vicki Laden in the city attorney's office, copying others in the bubble ordinance working group. She told the recipients that the presence of sidewalk councilors at FPS the previous day was a flagrant and direct violation of the ordinance. The violations were reported to Oakland police, and officers arrived on the scene, she wrote, but they failed to arrest anyone. Hoke claimed the sidewalk counselors were taking advantage of the confused situation to demonstrate how ineffective the law was.

Nadel's aide Marisa Arrona replied to Barbic's complaint that the police failed to enforce the new law. In her message, which she copied to Hoke, Laden, and top police commanders, she explained that a bubble ordinance training bulletin would be prepared and put into the hands of police officers in the Webster Street area. In the meanwhile, she recommended that an emergency contact list be developed for people, including police officers, who might need information about the law. Arrona asked for volunteers to be the first names on the list.

Walter had no idea that these e-mail conversations were taking place, and he was under the impression that his activity on Tuesday morning was in accordance with the spirit of the bubble law, if not the letter. After all, the officers watching him never offered so much as a shake of the head in disapproval of his behavior. As far as Walter was concerned, it was safe to go back to the clinic the next Tuesday.

Throughout the debate on the bubble ordinance, if people in government had wanted to evaluate what Walter was doing for themselves, rather than rely on Barbic's and Hoke's descriptions of his behavior, they could have obtained security-camera recordings of him. At last, after the ordinance became law and was being put to the test, City Attorney Laden asked Barbic for the footage of Walter.

Barbic reminded Laden that FPS was only one tenant in the building on Webster and that the security cameras were not under her direct control, but she offered to check with the landlord. Hoke approved of her getting the videotapes of Walter. From her point of view, he was knowingly and smugly defying the law, and she was confident the tapes would prove it.

A week later, Walter stood off to one side of the clinic, near what some regarded as his tree. He wore his "Got Jesus?" hat and displayed his sign. Kendall and Downer stood across the street. Again the police were called, and again there were no arrests.

Hoke's irritation and frustration boiled over in another e-mail, in which she called the situation a disaster. Hoke directed her complaints to Laden in the city attorney's office and called out the Oakland Police Department for refusing to enforce the ordinance. The failure of the police to arrest Walter empowered the antis, she wrote, by giving them ammunition against the ordinance. The apparent befuddlement on the part of the police could be used as evidence that the ordinance was too confusing to enforce.

Laden responded by instructing Hoke to have her escorts collect the names and the badge numbers of police officers who refused to arrest Walter and claimed to be confused about the law. If Hoke would turn this information over to Laden, she wrote, she would take care of the problem.

Hoke requested a meeting with Nadel, the district attorney, police officers, clinic directors, and escorts to develop a strategy for making the ordinance enforceable. The trouble was, there was confusion on all sides as to whether Walter's actions were, in fact, violating the ordinance.

A week later, on Tuesday, February 26, Walter was back in front of the clinic on Webster Street, sign in hand, with his companions across the street. The escorts walked between Walter and the clinic's clients, blocking his face and his sign with whiteboards. When it was over Hoke sent out another e-mail calling it another frustrating day. She attached a photograph and explained:

> The male escort at the right in this picture arrived before Walter Hoye this morning and stood at the tree. Walter Hoye "approached" him and remained well within 8' of him the entire morning, for 2 hours, even though the escort told him to step back, in compliance with the ordinance. The woman in the vest, in the foreground of the picture is a staff member. Walter was closer than 8' to her, as well as to the escort on the street.

She expressed frustration that clinic director Barbic could not reach the police all morning, despite repeated tries and added, "The antis are making a joke of this ordinance."

That night an e-mail to the bubble ordinance group from a Steve G. described what had happened:

> I took the spot near to Walter's tree, with Suzanne and Phyllis about 10 feet from me on either side. At 8:15 we saw Walter, the Jamaican woman, and the white mean woman approaching. We donned our vests. The white woman and the Jamaican woman crossed the street.... Walter walked right up to me, at his usual tree. I stated "8 feet" to him multiple times.... Then I clarified [to Walter] that he was not allowed within 8 feet of patients, escorts or employees. His only response was "yeah well."

The volunteer escort described it as "a fun little game" as he refused to move and Walter refused to move. Walter stood next to the tree, and the escort admitted he was just a couple of feet away. "My standing next to Walter was extremely effective", he wrote. "He never got more than a 'hi' out. Phyllis and myself did a good job of blocking his sign."

Barbara Hoke praised the work of the escorts. "Great reports and great jobs by you all!" she wrote. "You are our role model for stonewalling Walter, Steve. Very powerful and effective, since Walter's stock and trade is controlling with his phony friendliness and smarmy charm."

A Demand for Action

The meeting with government officials that Hoke had requested convened on Wednesday, March 5, 2008, around noon at the city attorney's office on the sixth floor of Oakland City Hall. Court records show there were various people from the city attorney's office and the district attorney's office. Also present was Oakland Police Captain Anthony Toribio of the Bureau of Field Operations. The Webster Street clinic of Family Planning Specialists was in his area of responsibility. At the meeting Toribio was asked to draft the police training bulletin to govern enforcement of the bubble ordinance.

In a deposition taken on a later date, Toribio said the meeting included five civilians, meaning people who did not work for the city. Apparently, some of these were unhappy with the outcome of the meeting. Hoke criticized the meeting, suggesting that, other than promising to train police officers about the new ordinance, city officials did nothing.

Walter Hoye was the only "demonstrator" named at the meeting. Although pro-life demonstrators in general were discussed, Walter and FPS on Webster Street were the focus of the conversation. "There was a concern that there were incidences going on at this [Webster Street] clinic," Toribio said in his deposition, "and there was a need to make sure that the police department was doing what it was supposed to be doing and that we were all in accord with the policy to ensure that people were not going to get hurt or injured or rights violated in general."

Someone at the meeting suggested that Laden stake out FPS to watch what was going on. Toribio had never heard of a city attorney on a stakeout acting as an agent for law enforcement, but he thought it might be a good idea. That way, if there was a violation of the ordinance, she could offer guidance to the arresting officer. Considering the confusion the ordinance had already caused, Laden liked the unusual idea too. She later explained in an interview that she needed to see what was happening at the clinic before she could articulate it in words. Also discussed was the idea of using undercover officers posing as patients.

Five days after the meeting, a draft bulletin for training police officers about the bubble ordinance was ready for review. Authored chiefly by the city attorney's office, the document had also received input from the police department, Toribio said in a deposition.

In an e-mail to the bubble ordinance working group, he said that the final version would be published in a couple of weeks and distributed to all the police personnel in his area. Their training in how to enforce the ordinance would begin that night. He assured the group that the Oakland Police Department would be prepared to enforce the ordinance should violations of the law occur.

Yet for Captain Toribio it proved to be a complicated and time-consuming task to formalize an understandable, easy-to-follow explanation of what was and was not permitted under the bubble law. In addition to the physical-proximity issue, there was the message issue. According to some interpretations of the law, Walter's "Got Jesus?" cap constituted a sign just like the one he carried. Wearing it in the wrong place, therefore, could be a crime. In explaining how the police in Oakland were trained to evaluate the behavior of people on public sidewalks near abortion clinics, Toribio admitted that he had never before dealt with an ordinance that restricted speech.

Based on the professional opinions offered by the city's attorneys, Toribio concluded that it was a violation for Walter Hoye to come within eight feet of an escort, without consent, when that escort was walking with a patient, when Walter's purpose was to offer a leaflet to the patient. Under the ordinance, according to Toribio's training bulletin, escorts and patients were considered protected within the hundred-foot zone around the abortion clinic, and inside that zone Walter was not permitted to be within eight feet of any workers, escorts, or clients for the purposes of harassing, interfering, intimidating, or counseling. In an interview on the record for this book, Laden explained her logic in making that determination. "I remember thinking of the escorts as auxiliaries. I don't know if that's the right word, but auxiliaries for the clinic, a kind of volunteer clinic personnel," she said.

Thus, as far as the city government was concerned, as long as the escorts wore vests identifying themselves as such, they could walk up to Walter Hoye, and Walter would have to move. The escorts could approach patients on their way to the clinic and ask if they wanted an escort, but Walter Hoye would have to obtain permission from a distance before he could come within eight feet of a patient.

An escort could say to a patient, "Don't listen to the demonstrators" or "It's your right to have an abortion," and such words would not constitute harassing, interfering, intimidating, or counseling. "It is language used to help facilitate their entrance into the facility or maybe their exit," explained Toribio. But Walter Hoye's words, "Can I talk to you about alternatives to abortion?", did constitute harassing, interfering, intimidating, or counseling and therefore violated the ordinance.

Such rules surrounding Walter's mobility and speech, which could be subjectively judged by escorts and police, virtually guaranteed that eventually Walter would be arrested—that is, unless Walter stopped going to the clinic on Tuesday mornings, which was unlikely.

16

Brother Walt and Elder Roe

Walter Hoye had baffled his cellmates and guards. Their disbelief about his crime was the product of misunderstanding and ignorance. Their disbelief about his fast during 40 Days for Life was the product of misunderstanding and denial. The guards thought he was on a hunger strike. His cellmates figured he was gaming the system, faking it somehow. They all thought, *Nobody ever fasts in jail*. But that's exactly what Walter was doing, and the hunger pangs pinched him with every breath.

Besides water, his only source of sustenance was apple juice. It came once a day at breakfast in a four-ounce carton. As the sweet nectar rolled over his parched tongue, the sugar shot through his bloodstream, firing synapses in his brain, which registered the jolt of energy his body needed to survive. But the serving size was so small that the sensation of pleasure was fleeting and the caloric burst minuscule. He really could use another carton.

The first time he was handed a second apple juice, it did wonders, and not just because of the additional calories and vitamins, but because of the source of the gift. His name was Rozier Gibson, an inmate in his mid-forties, easily topping six feet and sturdy. He was a broad-shouldered, muscular black American familiar with jail life. The combination of his physical strength and prison experience made him intimidating when he wanted to be. But he was perceptive and knew when to be gentle, making him even more impressive.

The day of the lockdown, when a cop killer terrified the entire county, Gibson, "Roe" for short, was in the bunk next to Walter's. Lockdown played with the mind in strange ways, even for guys like Roe. "You could have a guy sit on his bunk right next to you and not even notice him as long as the gates were open, but when they were closed, it was the opposite," Roe recalled in an interview with the author at the California State Prison, Solano. Walter, however, didn't put Roe on his guard the way other inmates did. There was something about him that signaled that he was not the type to pull a fast one.

The morning paper was making the rounds in the cell, and as the inmates read it they gave Walter suspicious glances. The paper had an article about Walter's sentencing, and at last one of the cellmates approached Walter, pointed to the story, and asked if it was about him. An anticipatory silence filled the cell as all eyes turned toward Walter. "Yes, I'm the man in the article," he said. The men were surprised that he was in jail for such an odd crime, and even more surprised that he was a minister. Some of the guys shook their heads with audible groans, while others expressed dismay at Walter's plight. Walter could feel their attitude toward him changing. Being featured in the paper gave him a kind of celebrity status; being a black minister imprisoned for trying to help people made him seem trustworthy.

Roe had sensed he could trust Walter before he saw the newspaper. He was a Christian and something of a spiritual leader too, and when the guy with the paper walked away he introduced himself as Brother Roe. Walter said nothing of the coincidence that the name of his first friend in jail called to mind the *Roe v. Wade* decision, but it was a meaningful sign to him.

Due to the proximity of their bunks and the length of the lockdown, Roe and Walter talked together a lot that day. Afterward Brother Roe would regularly turn to Brother Walt for guidance. Others in the cage followed Roe's example. Eventually most of them sought out Brother Walt as if he were holding office hours— morning, noon, and night, and sometimes in the middle of the night. "Some of the guys just didn't sleep at night. They were just up, and we would talk about that," Walter remembered. "They would line up. One would walk over to me, lean against my bunk, and we'd just talk. Then, when he was done and walked away, the next one would come over."

Some of the men gathered regularly to pray and to talk about the Bible. Led by Brother Roe, they met at midnight. As soon as Walter's identity was known, the group expected him to join them. "We thought we knew a lot about the Bible, but Brother Walt's knowledge was way up here," recalled Roe, extending his hand above his head to illustrate his point. At the same time, Walter respected Roe's faith and knowledge and began calling him Elder Roe. The other inmates followed his example, and the honorific stayed with Roe throughout his term at Santa Rita.

Walter knew the Bible better than Roe, but Roe knew the ropes inside the prison. The unwritten rules and the jail's invisible boundaries were tricky to navigate, and, like a guardian angel, Elder Roe guided Walter safely through them. For example, when Walter was about to enter the five-by-five space claimed by the white supremacists in the common area, Roe grabbed his arm and moved him around it. Then Roe explained that crossing the invisible boundaries invited a fight. All the factions have their own spaces, he said, and if Walter wanted to stay out of trouble, he needed to avoid them.

On Walter's first Sunday morning in jail, Elder Roe, knowing that Walter was fasting, gave him his apple juice. Two juices made eight ounces. Another inmate also gave him his juice, so he had three. In the days to follow, other inmates joined in the effort to supply Walter with apple juice, and his daily ration grew to four, five, and six. "After breakfast," Roe said, "they would just walk by and drop them on his bunk, and when he showed up he had 'em all day long."

Collapse

After about fifteen days of his juice fast, Walter felt a little off. He had been growing weaker and thinner, which was expected after not having eaten solid food for weeks, but this feeling signaled that something more was going on. Then, at around 2 A.M., Walter's hunger pangs vanished. Like a man forgetting about the sliver in one toe because a sledgehammer lands on the other, Walter forgot about hunger when a far worse but yet unknown affliction struck him.

He had just finished a counseling session with an inmate, his last of the night, when he decided the new discomfort warranted a trip to the bathroom. He leaned over the sink in the dim light and threw water on his face. "I was trying to wake up," he said. "I thought I was weak from the fasting."

Then he felt an urgent need to lie down. He made his way to the first bunk outside the bathroom and collapsed. "I had just lost all energy," he said. "I was just ... done." Everything was going dark as he was losing consciousness. Then, out of the corner of his eye, Walter saw a person holding his arms out as if to catch his falling body; he recognized the person as Christ. "He [Christ] was laying me down on the floor. That's it. That's all I saw, and I was done. Next thing I knew, I was conscious." Walter was no longer near the bunk by the bathroom, but on the other side of the cage, leaning against a wall, next to his own bunk. "I know I didn't get there [by myself]," he said.

"He just fell," recalled Elder Roe. "Then he was too weak to get back on his bunk."

Near his bunk Walter heard a voice, Elder Roe's possibly, calling out to the guards for help: "We've got a man down!" But the guards were slow to respond. Yelling and game playing happened so often at night that they were suspicious of such outbursts. Somebody yelled into the intercom used to communicate with the guards, and still there was no response. Only after the noise and the panicked calls continued for a while did the guards finally enter the cage and remove Walter. They took him immediately to the infirmary. As Walter's head was spinning he thought of the apple juice and of the time a week or ten days earlier when he had gotten more than he expected from one of the small cartons.

Walter was sitting in the common area, having a talk with cellmates, when he swallowed some apple juice that tasted funny. He could feel the trouble in his throat more than he could taste it. "There's something a little more than just apple juice there," Walter recalled. He knew it had to be mold. The thought turned his stomach, but it was too late to do anything about it. The prudent thing to do was to look closely at the juice before he drank it. From then on, each time he opened a container, he examined it for anything floating in the liquid. Occasionally he found mold, and he tried to avoid it. When he began to feel unwell, he thought that maybe the mold was to blame.

But mold was not the cause of his collapse. Apple juice is very high in sugar, which acts as a diuretic. Without realizing it, Walter was flushing fluids out of his system and dehydrating himself. The high amount of sugar in his bloodstream was also causing a shortage of insulin, which triggered the overproduction of ketones, acids that break down fat for use as energy. Too many ketones can lead to ketoacidosis, a potentially deadly condition familiar to diabetics but not to Walter Hoye.

When the medical staff tested Walter, his ketone levels were dangerously high. The doctor explained the situation and asked some questions. It was a comfort to Walter that the doctor was black, but he was hardly sympathetic. He wanted to know what Walter was "in for", that all too common question asked in all corners of the jail. Walter answered, and the doctor didn't believe him.

A thought jumped into Walter's mind that had nothing to do with ketones. He had made a commitment to some cellmates, a promise to deliver on certain goods, and if he couldn't get back to the cage in time, he would let them down.

The inmates were allowed to buy items such as junk food from the commissary. They could order their chips, candy, and other things and pay for them through their jail accounts, funded by outside family members or other supportive people. Whatever the inmates ordered was delivered to their cage in a small box. It was treated like a special delivery, like a care package of cookies from home.

Some of the inmates had no one funding their accounts, so Walter used the money being donated to him by supporters near and far to brighten the lives of those men. He let them order whatever they wanted, and his right-hand man in collecting orders was Elder Roe. "I remember he asked me to walk around to each bunk in the cage and ask the guys what they wanted," said Roe, with a broad smile. "It didn't matter what it was, as long as it was just one thing. I did that, two or three weeks."

Mostly the men wanted junk food, but Walter didn't mind. Occasionally someone asked for something unusual. "I remember I went back to Brother Walt and said this one guy wants a book of stamps," explained Roe. "It's like more than six dollars."

"I don't care," said Walter.

"But you know he's just going to trade it for something else."

"I don't care. That's between him and Jesus."

There was a catch when it came to the delivery of these items. If, for whatever reason, the inmate wasn't in his cage to receive his package, it was sent back, and he would have to order it all over again and wait until the next week to get it.

While Walter was in the infirmary in the wee hours of the morning, he remembered that a box was to be delivered to him that day. It was a $100 order. Since the doctor didn't believe his story and was going to check on it, Walter tried to bargain with him. "If I'm right, then you let me go back to the general population," he said. "I gotta get back." The doctor said no, and Walter tried again. If the doctor learned that Walter's story was true *and* his ketone levels came down, Walter asked, would he discharge him? The doctor agreed, but his tone indicated that he doubted that Walter's ketone levels would drop rapidly enough for him to do that. "In his mind, I was never going to go back. I was fortunate to be alive."

During what remained of the night, Walter didn't sleep. Somehow, even in his sick and confused state, he had the instinct to bring a book with him. As he lay there in the infirmary bed he read all two hundred pages of *He Leadeth Me* by Father Walter J. Ciszek, S.J.

Ciszek was a Polish-American priest born in Shenandoah, Pennsylvania, in 1904. During his seminary studies, he decided that he wanted to be a missionary in Soviet Russia. But after his ordination, the closest he could get to Russia was Poland, that is, until his Polish village was captured by the Red Army during World War II. After the priest went deeper into Russian territory, he was arrested for spying for the Germans, a charge later changed to spying for the Vatican, and he spent the next twenty-three years in Soviet prisons and labor camps. Despite the hardships and the constant struggle to survive, he continued his ministry by counseling Catholics and offering them the sacraments. To the men without faith, he shared the good news of Jesus Christ.

Walter found a kindred spirit on the pages of that book, even in the description of how Father Ciszek fasted for Lent. He ate only bread and water for forty days. "It was amazing what this priest had endured," Walter said. "I was easily relating to what this guy was going through. I read that book in one night, and then I prayed."

Later that morning tests showed that Walter's ketone levels were in a normal range. "The doctor came back," he said. "He had found out I wasn't lying about why I was in jail. I wasn't in there for selling drugs and all that, and because my levels had come down, he kept his word." Walter was sent back to Unit 34, where he signed for the package. He delivered the items and made some new friends, and that night the prayer group was bigger.

He Leadeth Me

Some social interactions in the cells of Santa Rita Jail were democratic. If an inmate had a problem, he could call a meeting of his cellmates and even ask for a majority-rules vote. Walter Hoye didn't know about the cage meetings at first, so it wasn't on his mind when he brought an issue to Elder Roe. He finally had worked up the courage to address the pornography lining the walls of the shower. "I told him I'm just gonna tear it down," Walter said. Elder Roe warned that tearing down the pictures might be a mistake, might even be dangerous. It could cause a fight, he said. But Walter was insistent. He said the problem was too serious to be ignored. So Roe suggested the meeting. Walter could bring it up and ask for a vote, he said, but the passions of the men would be too volatile to let a simple majority decide the matter. Everyone would have to agree to take the images down, or they would stay. Walter agreed and called the meeting.

A little more than half the cage population was black. There were also some Latinos and a couple of non-Hispanic whites. Walter sat on his bunk, and they all gathered around, as was the quasi-tribal custom. Walter looked priest-like with a gold wrap around his neck. It was there for warmth, but it suggested a minister's collar. By then all the men had become familiar with Walter and knew he was a pastor. Most of the inmates in Walter's cage respected him for that reason.

"I want to take down the pornography," he told them. "That's why I'm calling the meeting. I want to know if we can take this down." There were some angry looks, mumbles of disbelief, and derision from the gathered men. But there was also some silence, some consideration, and it was palpable. The way Walter read the response, most of his cellmates understood that pornography was wrong and should not be plastered all over. "Some were Catholic, some were Protestant, and they knew," he said. He got the impression most of the men were willing to go along with a ban on porn, if for no other reason than out of respect for Walter. But one faction, big tough guys with reputations for violence, jumped up and threatened that respectable idea.

The lines in the young men's arms firmed up, and streaks of white appeared around their knuckles as they made it clear that somebody would get hurt if he tried to take down the pictures. They made their threats with puffed-out chests and darkened eyes. But Walter wasn't ashamed of the request, and he was unwilling to be intimidated. "Don't listen to that," Walter said to the other men. "We can vote. You know what you oughta do. We're going to take this vote."

The pro-porn faction then threatened everyone in the cage. The vote happened anyway, but Walter's side lost. His supporters, with good reason, got scared and voted no, which didn't sit well with Walter. "Well, then, I'm going to take it down," he said defiantly.

The big guys jumped at Walter on the bunk, and Walter jumped down. They were toe to toe with Walter, fists up and ready for a brawl over pornography. Walter may have been strong in spirit, but he was thin and weak from fasting. He recognized that he was frail, but he thought he had to be ready to fight. It was the way of the jail. But there was no need. Elder Roe stepped in and said the path to Walter went through him. Roe was not the guy in the cage anyone wanted to fight even four against one. The tough guys backed down, but they had a grim warning for Walter about the pornography. "If I touched it that night, they were going to kill me," he said. It was unlikely they would kill him, but they certainly could deliver a lot of pain. Consequently, Walter put his plan on hold for the time being. Little did he know that soon he would have another chance to conquer the porn problem once and for all.

At three o'clock the next morning, the names of three of the four porn toughs were called by the guards over the intercom. They were to prepare to ship out. They had been waiting for transit to San Quentin, and the call had finally come. After they left, Walter walked up to the remaining porn tough and explained his plan. "I'm tearing it down, and it's just you and me now," Walter told his cellmate. "Now, you can tear it down with me. We can do this together, but if you don't, I'm taking it down. And it's just you and me now."

The cellmate was hardly about to help, that was for sure, but he also wasn't going to stand in Walter's way all by himself. Walter went to work collecting and trashing every image of porn in sight. He removed the contraband not only from the shower walls but from the undersides of the bunks. After the offensive images were gone, there were no complaints, and, going forward, the cage was a porn-free zone, at least while Walter Hoye was there.

Amazing Grace

While Lori Hoye stood in line to get on the visitor list early one morning, she struck up a conversation with a lady standing next to her. Her son was incarcerated, and she intended to visit him later that evening. The woman told Lori that her son shared a cell with a Christian minster, and Lori found out that it was Unit 34. That chance conversation would help Walter to grow his midnight prayer group by one.

The young man was in prison for annoying a child, a crime different from but related to molesting a minor. The crime did not require that he be segregated from other prisoners, as child molesters usually are, but it was the kind of thing that could make the young man a target of beatings or worse if the other inmates knew.

Lori recalled the conversation. The woman said, "My son is telling me there's this Bible study and just all black guys. He sits there in this corner and he tries to listen, but he's afraid to go over." The young man was one of the few white inmates of Unit 34, the mother explained, and a "baby Christian" who really wanted to join the meeting. Lori said she would tell Walter, and she never saw the woman again.

That night during her visit, Lori told Walter about the woman she met in line and her son in Walter's cell. It was quite a coincidence, although Lori and Walter dismiss the word "coincidence" when it comes to the Lord's interventions in their lives. Walter said that he had noticed the young man sitting on the edge of a bunk when they held their nightly prayer session. He recalled that the young man was always listening. Walter referred to it as "ear hustling".

Later, as the men in Unit 34 assembled for the midnight meeting, Walter was inspired and energized by the victory over pornography that the Lord had won for them. He began the meeting by saying it was wrong that the white inmate didn't feel welcome in their group.

He called the cellmate over next to him. "This is my friend," Walter said. "He's welcome to be in this prayer meeting. I want you to treat him like you'd treat me." And the others accepted the new man.

As Walter launched into his first prayer, he was suddenly interrupted by a rush of water from the shower. It was inexplicable, Walter said, because there was no one in the shower. As the water flowed and soaked the porn-free tiles, the pipes rattled, and the guys in the prayer group looked at each other with frightened expressions. "There's metal banging up against the wall," Walter explained, "and we're shocked." Next they were stunned by an "eerie, demonic hiss". The hiss slowly faded, and as it did, the water gradually shut off.

"We had a prayer service after that, preaching after that, that we had never had before," Walter said. "We had guys get up out of their bunks and come over and start asking about what they need to do to get saved. We had guys who for the first time wanted to come in and be part of the prayer meeting."

One of those young men was known for a great singing voice. When he confessed that he didn't know the words to "Amazing Grace", the other men in the group taught him the hymn written by an eighteenth-century slave trader after his conversion to Christ. The soulful tune was infectious. Men who were still in bed joined in the singing, and they were followed by inmates in the next cage, and so on. Eventually inmates in all four Unit 34 cages were singing "Amazing Grace":

> 'Twas grace that taught my heart to fear,
> And grace my fears relieved;
> How precious did that grace appear
> The hour I first believed.

17

The Hornet's Nest

The week after the bubble ordinance passed, Oakland abortion clinic advocates began plotting the arrest of Walter Hoye, who in their opinion was "blatantly violating" the law every time he showed up on the sidewalk outside Family Planning Specialists with his "God loves you" sign and his "Got Jesus?" cap. It seemed simple enough—catch Walter inside the protected eight-foot bubble of a clinic patient, employee, or escort; then call police officers to arrest him.

A month later, Walter still had not been arrested. No one had been able to convince the police that he was committing a crime. Officers called to the scene would observe him for a while and then leave, and FPS director Jackie Barbic had not been able to obtain security-camera video showing Walter breaking the law. Thus, Tuesdays came and Tuesdays went with Walter Hoye still at large.

By April, clinic escorts, who numbered four or more whenever Walter was at FPS, were snapping photographs and keeping logs of Walter's behavior. On Tuesday, April 15, the escorts filed an account of their experiences. "Pam, Suzanne, Lucy and Georgia had our hands full today", said the report quoted in an e-mail from escort coordinator Barbara Hoke. "Walter, the older African-American woman and the quiet, well-dressed [African]-American woman arrived about 8:30. Their actions were pretty much the ordinary." Hoke included a photo of an unknown person within one hundred feet of the clinic, whom she called "Clone Man". She asked, "Is that a good name for this jerk?"

The Man with the Camera

The issue of someone taking photographs outside the clinic raised a few questions that, like most issues surrounding the bubble ordinance, were not entirely black and white. Someone suggested that the photographer may have been in violation of the California Freedom of Access to Clinic and Church Entrances Act and recommended requesting a temporary restraining order against him. But according to City Attorney Vicki Laden, there was a requirement to show that the man's actions could cause someone irreparable injury if the order was not issued—that is, that his behavior could cause a woman irreparable harm by preventing her from keeping her appointment at the clinic. But the man was on a public sidewalk, where there was no "reasonable expectation of privacy". Any woman in such a place could be photographed by a passerby.

The man with the camera was Terry Thompson, a lawyer and a board member of Life Legal Defense Foundation who spoke out at the city council meetings when the bubble law was debated. The public place he was in was the same one occupied every Tuesday morning by Walter Hoye. Thompson was outside FPS to obtain a photographic record of what Walter was doing and what the clinic escorts were doing to stop him. No evidence was ever offered that he was photographing clinic clients.

On Tuesday, April 22, escorts reported how they had enjoyed dancing around and blocking the "photographer-man" and Walter Hoye's sign. "We found it helpful to use the boards to block the antis," wrote one escort. "The four of us discussed the use of the boards and agree that it would be helpful for each escort to have one to help guide the clients and block their view of the antis. I'll make a couple more."

Barbic came to a different conclusion. She wrote Laden that the time had come for her stakeout on Webster Street, which they had discussed in March. She wrote, "Is it possible for you to come out to 200 Webster on a Tuesday from 8 A.M.–10 A.M. and anonymously observe what is happening?" The message went out to the core group of bubble ordinance backers.

Laden didn't take long to answer. She replied, "Yes, I can do it this coming Tuesday." The timing couldn't have been better. Captain Anthony Toribio informed the bubble group that the much-anticipated training bulletin was due to be published in a matter of days. Thus, on Tuesday, April 29, both Laden and an officer trained to make an arrest would be ready for Walter Hoye at FPS.

On Monday, April 28, Hoke sent a message to Laden, reminding her to show up at FPS the next day and thanking her "for agreeing to witness the behavior of the antis at 200 Webster Street tomorrow. It, once again, shows your commitment to protecting the women of Oakland and the clinics. We are deeply grateful to you and Nancy Nadel."

Hoke suggested that Laden tell the "antis to stay across the street as they do in SF," informing them of restrictions on how close they can stand next to escorts, staff members, and clients while taking pictures. Barbic, however, did not want Laden to blow her cover. Just a few days before, she wrote, she witnessed "antis" walking up to clients and attempting to force literature on them. "If they realize Vicki is there and if there is a police presence," she added, "I am sure they will act differently."

"Thanks for reminding us of how important Vicki's anonymity is," Hoke replied. "Good luck, Vicki." Vicki Laden wrote that she would be there "incognito", perhaps sitting in her car and would be in touch with Barbic by cell phone.

Bubble Geometry

On the morning of Tuesday, April 29, 2008, there was tension in the air on Webster Street. Later some would say the day felt different somehow, even though all the usual players were in their usual places. The building's security officer stood just inside the clinic lobby, where he authorized access to the elevator. Clinic director Barbic was in her office on the first floor, one story up from ground level. Wearing their orange vests, four volunteer escorts were in front of the clinic. One or two of them had blank white poster boards in hand. Walter Hoye was on the sidewalk to the right of the clinic loading zone with his sign "God loves you and your baby. Let us help." His sidewalk-counseling companions from Progressive Missionary Baptist Church, Christiana Downer and Sister Elga Kendall, were across the street. Kendall also had a sign, a small one that said, "Abortion stops a beating heart."

A moderate-sized moving truck was parked in the white zone, and movers were going back and forth unloading it, a minor divergence from the usual setting. There was another difference. If there is truth to the old saying that one can always feel when one is being watched, it would explain why some reported a strange feeling of unease. Walter Hoye and the escorts were indeed being watched, and not just by Barbic, who was minutes away from exiting the building with a tape measure in her hand. City Attorney Laden was across the street, sitting in her car parked at an angle to allow a clear view of Walter Hoye.

Within an hour of the stage being set, several young black women, apparently clients, approached the clinic. "They looked like they were still in high school, mostly," Laden later recalled. One of the escorts lifted a blank whiteboard and blocked Walter Hoye's sign. Just as he had countless times before, Walter took a few steps, so that the clients could see him, and verbally offered his alternative to abortion. He got within two or three feet of the women "for the purposes of displaying his anti-abortion [sign]," wrote Laden in a lengthy e-mail to the bubble working group sent at 10:18 that morning. She also wrote that she didn't see or hear anything that indicated that the clients gave Walter their consent. She watched as the escorts with whiteboards blocked Walter's message and the women entered the clinic.

So far, nothing unusual for a Tuesday morning at FPS had happened. That changed when Barbic exited the building. Based on a variety of sources, including witness testimonies, Barbic exited the clinic and walked up to Walter, offering some sort of comment, question, or statement. Then she walked over to the movers before reentering the building.

A moment later, according to an e-mail to the bubble group from City Attorney Vicki Laden, based on her personal observations during her stakeout, Barbic exited the building with a tape measure in her hand. She extended it to some distance, about eight feet, "to show Walter that he was not complying with the ordinance." Laden did not indicate that she heard what Walter and Barbic said to each other. She was, after all, in her car, which was parked across the street with the windows up. Barbic's initial testimony would suggest that after this encounter with Walter, she went back in the building and asked someone to call the Oakland Police Department.

A couple of hours later police officers arrived at FPS ready to enforce the city's bubble ordinance for the first time, but Walter

Hoye had left at about ten o'clock, his usual departure time. The investigating officer talked to the escorts and perhaps to Barbic and Laden. What followed was veritable silence, save a few e-mails among the bubble group that suggested that an arrest was imminent. In her response to Laden's e-mail, which was shared with the group, City Councilwoman Nancy Nadel thanked Laden for her work and wrote, "I look forward to hearing from the Captain that Walter was cited. Please include me and Vicki in that confirmation." The wheels of justice were grinding a little faster, and Walter was about to get caught in the cogs.

The Citation

It was a chilly spring morning on Tuesday, May 13, 2008, two weeks after the "tape measure incident". There was no moving van this time, and the scene was familiar—Walter stood on the sidewalk near the tree as several volunteer escorts in orange vests hovered around the entrance. The watching eyes were back, surveilling all of them. This time they would witness Walter Hoye's last day in front of the clinic for a long time.

A black and white Oakland police car arrived. According to their report, the two officers saw Walter Hoye standing in front of the clinic when they arrived. They observed him walk past a clinic escort inside of eight feet. From Walter's perspective, they didn't seem at all concerned about him; rather, they were preoccupied with the group of escorts gathered in front of the clinic doorway. The officers approached the escorts, and to Walter it looked as though they were about to arrest one of them for barring or blocking access. Walter admitted later that the scene made him chuckle under his breath. Next, the officers went inside the clinic building. When they came out they walked up to Walter and asked him a few questions. Walter knew the moment had come.

A lieutenant and a sergeant had arrived to help with the arrest, to make sure certain steps were followed so that the violator was cited properly for the never-before-prosecuted bubble ordinance. First, the officers took witness statements from four people: Barbic, a security guard, and two volunteer escorts. A written statement from City Attorney Laden would follow later. Since Barbic was the person who called the police to report that a crime had been committed, the police deemed her request for a citation the equivalent of a citizen's arrest.

After the officers questioned Walter, one of them told him to put his hands behind his back and handcuffed him. Then the two officers walked him to the police car and opened the back door. Walter felt as though he were in a scene from a movie. As one of the officers helped him safely into the car by cradling the back of his head, he noticed Walter's hat with the words "Got Jesus?" and suggested that it was a sign in violation of the law.

Walter sat in handcuffs on the back seat while the officers wrote out an order for him to appear in court. They were going to release him afterward. During the conversation, one of the officers seemed sympathetic and explained how Walter might continue his sidewalk counseling in the future without violating the new ordinance. He even suggested where he might stand. He concluded his bit of advice with this observation: "When you come to the hornet's nest, expect to get stung." Walter cooperated and signed the ticket. The citing officer then confiscated his sign and his pamphlets as evidence.

All of the officers performed their jobs innocuously and professionally without any racial overtones. Despite the accusations of racism made by anti-police activists, the Oakland Police Department was rather diverse. The squad of law enforcers who handled Walter's nonviolent-misdemeanor citation reflected that diversity. The two initial responding officers were white and Asian. The lieutenant was black, as was the supervising sergeant who turned up later.

It is remarkable that it took two beat cops, two sergeants, and a police lieutenant to hash out the details for Walter's citation when the job was presumed to be a logical interpretation and enforcement of the ordinance. Two weeks after Walter was cited, one of the initial responders was tasked with filing a supplemental report and changed the violation date from May 13, 2008, the day the citation was issued, to April 29, 2008, the day Barbic presented her tape measure to Walter in front of the clinic. The result was that neither the Oakland police nor the witnesses made any allegations against Walter related to May 13, the day of his arrest. Yet the police still cited Walter for alleged violations of the law on the thirteenth.

Then there was the matter of identifying the victim. The state of California Department of Justice collects data on criminal allegations linked to abortion clinics: the alleged perpetrator's birth date, sex, and race along with his violation(s) and victim(s). The worksheet filed for Walter's case indicated just one victim, the abortion clinic itself. Two months later the singular "victim" was changed to the plural "victims".

The citation by committee produced plenty of material that would be used later to build a defense of Walter, but when he was released by the police on May 13, he had no idea what lay ahead and how much his commitment to protect the unborn was going to cost him physically, mentally, and financially.

18

The Jagged Edge of Justice

Life Legal Defense Foundation began its public battle against the Oakland bubble ordinance the first time board member Terry Thompson stood before the city council to testify against it. After the bubble ordinance passed, he challenged it in federal court, which prompted the council to pass a revised version of the law that won the approval of the federal judge assigned to the case. On appeal, Thompson challenged the new version of the law, and as that case worked its way through the system, Walter continued his weekly visit to Family Planning Specialists—that is, until his arrest on May 13, 2008. After he was not only cited for violating the bubble ordinance but also issued a temporary restraining order, LLDF's defense of his right to free speech on a public sidewalk took the fight over the bubble ordinance to a new level.

Alameda County Deputy District Attorney Robert Martin Graff earned his law degree at the University of California, Davis, and passed the bar in December 2005. Little more than three years later he was tasked with the prosecution of Walter Hoye. Graff filed four criminal charges: two related to Hoye's actions at FPS on April 29, 2008, and two related to his actions on May 13, 2008, even though the amendment to the original crime report showed no criminal allegations from the thirteenth.

LLDF's Michael Millen and Catherine Short stood in Walter's corner to act as defense counsel. They won the right for a hearing to challenge both the logic of the criminal charges and the legal authority of the court to issue a restraining order under the circumstances. It was a burden that seemed both arbitrary and forced. "The reason for a restraining order is to protect a witness," said Short. "Case law was clear." But the judge had trouble seeing the matter as clearly as Short did.

Alameda County Superior Court Judge Sandra K. Bean was elected to the bench in 2006 after serving as deputy county counsel for six years. She had less time as a judge than Graff had as a prosecutor, and she was to decide the fate of the restraining order against Walter Hoye. She opened the hearing at the courthouse on Washington Street in downtown Oakland with the question: "In a normal situation, we would consider revisiting the order if there's new facts or new evidence; isn't that true?"

"I believe so," answered Graff. "I don't know that any new facts or new evidence have been presented."

"Mr. Millen, are there any new facts or new evidence?" asked the judge.

"Well, since we were not allowed to present any evidence, I'm not sure what to say," replied Millen.

Millen and Short had subpoenaed two witnesses (FPS escorts) and a police officer and were prepared to go through five specific points to demonstrate the lack of justification for the restraining order. Judge Bean asked Graff to find out whether the two witnesses named in the restraining order wanted it to remain in place, given that it was intended to protect them. After a quick break to make that inquiry, Graff returned and said, "Both of them would like the stay-away to remain in effect." He had asked them whether they felt any threats of physical violence from Walter Hoye. "Both of them replied negatively," he said, "that they don't have a specific belief that there will be physical violence towards them." He added that they did feel psychological intimidation from Walter, "based on his position in this issue and their position in this issue and kind of the hot-button nature of it, for lack of a better term."

When the judge learned that in a previous hearing, a deputy district attorney other than Graff had plowed through the proceedings and won the restraining order without having to prove that Hoye was a threat to the witnesses, she let Millen call them, providing he did so in the "most efficient fashion".

Millen asked that a hearing on discriminatory prosecution be done first, to save time. The judge declined. He also asked that Graff do the questioning, since the burden of proof is on the prosecution, but

Judge Bean pointed out that the court had already found good cause to have the restraining order. "So, what you're asking me to do is reconsider it," she told Millen, "and so I think you have the burden."

Graff objected to moving forward, insisting that the judge who issued the order must have had cause to do so. "Well, I'm assuming that the stay-away is appropriate," said Judge Bean. "I'm going to allow Mr. Millen to show me why it isn't." With that, Millen accepted the burden to show that the order was not justified in the first place.

Escort Witnesses

Millen called Lucy Kasdin to the stand. Kasdin was one of two volunteer clinic escorts the police interviewed on May 13, the day Walter was arrested and cited. She was a witness, not a victim, in that the police report hadn't made any allegations that Walter committed acts directed at her personally. She had been a volunteer at the clinic for about a month and worked Tuesday mornings, when Walter was there.

Kasdin told the court that she wanted the order to stay in effect. "Because I feel intimidated by the defendant and I feel like it's important," she said. "I think it's likely that I would feel intimidated and threatened if I saw him, if he approached me at all."

Short took up the questioning from there. She explored the volunteer's activities while acting as an escort and her physical proximity to Walter Hoye: "Isn't it true that ... when you're holding the sign in front of him, you are actually also making it very difficult for Mr. Hoye to move; isn't that correct?"

"No," Kasdin said.

"You're not trying to block his movement at all?" asked Short.

"I mean, in the context—we're on a sidewalk. So, if I'm standing in front of him, he can back away or move to the left or to the right. I mean, we're not physically—he's not constricted in his movement completely. And in the context of blocking him, it's only done when women are walking up. That's when we really block him, so that the women have a safe passage into the clinic."

Short asked about whether Walter had used force against the women in any way or touched someone. Graff immediately objected to the line of questioning as irrelevant. Short fired back that it was, in fact, directly relevant: "If, in fact, Mr. Hoye didn't use force, threat of force, or physical obstruction against Ms. Kasdin, in fact, she was the one who was obstructing him, I think it greatly detracts from the notion that there was good cause for an order keeping Mr. Hoye away from Ms. Kasdin." The judge allowed the questions to continue. "Do you have any reason to believe Mr. Hoye would seek you out and attempt to communicate with you or intimidate you before the trial?" Short asked the witness.

"I have—I mean—other escorts have had experiences where he has approached them."

"Where?"

"And I've only—I'd like to say two things. Number one, I've only been escorting for a brief period of time, so I think that's something. But other escorts have had times when he—for example, there was an escort who was giving a talk and he did approach them afterward and said, 'I see you drove today,' and they found that very intimidating that he knew how they arrived at this talk they were giving. And it's experiences like that as well as the issue itself which makes it very intimidating if I would see him. So, have I ever seen him [approach an escort]? No. But would I be very intimidated if I did see him? Absolutely." She admitted that Walter Hoye had never touched her or used physical force against her.

Short continued with questions about which person, the escort or Walter, was physically obstructing the other's movement. Kasdin answered, "We were both, you know—when a client came, we were both attempting to—you know, I was attempting to block him. He would be attempting to approach them. And so, I don't know what you mean by 'block.' Our movements certainly, you know—I mean, if he was approaching, I would be approaching, but I don't— you know, he didn't prevent me from—physically prevent me from talking to them, no."

Kasdin explained that she first heard Walter was charged with violating the ordinance when one of the other escorts received notification that a restraining order had been issued. Up to that point she hadn't talked to police since the day of the citation and hadn't talked to the district attorney's office about charges or a restraining order. In other words, Kasdin hadn't pursued the restraining order herself.

"So, you did not seek that restraining order?" asked Short.

"Correct," replied Kasdin. She had made no specific allegations against Walter Hoye. She never saw him physically threaten anyone or threaten to do anything violent. It was his very presence, which they found intimidating, that was a problem for all the escorts. More specifically, on April 29, 2008, Kasdin said, Walter was more aggressive that day—he was coming closer and closer, not just to patients, but to her.

Graff followed with some questions of his own, and Kasdin explained that she had uncomfortable feelings about being in the same room with Walter for the court proceedings. The reason wasn't personal, she said, but rather a matter of the vast difference of opinion about the issue of abortion. She underscored how close he would get to her in front of the clinic—within arm's reach.

Then it was Millen's turn. "Ms. Kasdin," he asked, "which is more intimidating, coming to court today with Mr. Hoye present or ... going up to Mr. Hoye and holding a sign in front of his face? Which one is more intimidating for you?"

"Objection. Relevance," interrupted Graff.

"Sustained," ruled the judge.

"Does Mr. Hoye approach you and put a sign in your face?" continued Millen.

"I don't know what you mean by that," Kasdin responded. "I mean, he is there with his sign. And when women come, he's actively trying to put his sign there, as are we."

With bewilderment in his voice, Millen then asked, "Let me understand something here—"

"Mr. Millen," the judge interrupted. "I want you to keep your voice in a more modulated tone. I understand that this is an emotional issue, but I want you to be professional." Millen thanked the judge for her admonishment, lowered his voice, and went on.

After questioning the witness, Millen made his best case for why Kasdin's testimony showed there was no need for a restraining order. He said there had been no allegations or evidence that Walter Hoye made threats or used force to dissuade Kasdin from testifying against him. Furthermore, Kasdin never requested a restraining order, nor was she consulted about one. "And I would suggest to you that there is no evidence that would lead a reasonable person to suspect that Ms. Kasdin has any fear about testifying or assisting the prosecution."

Graff argued in favor of the order: "You've heard the testimony from Ms. Kasdin. She said that she was intimidated. She gave reasons for her intimidation."

Millen suggested "that this is simply a fairly transparent fortuitous attempt by somebody with strong feelings on one side of the issue to knock out a speaker on the other side of the issue when they all converge in the same place to do their speaking."

The judge ruled that, based on Kasdin's testimony, "the restraining order is appropriate. And the restrictions are eight feet, which means that Mr. Hoye can still exercise his free speech. He just simply has to stay eight feet away from Ms. Kasdin."

Millen asked for clarification. "If she approaches him as she does, in other words, if she takes her sign and walks over to him, I guess I'm asking at least the restraining order be modified that that's not a violation. In other words, if he has literature and she walks up to him and puts her sign in his face—"

"He has to back away," said Judge Bean.

"He has to back away," Millen repeated flatly.

"Wow," came a voice from the audience.

"Keep it down, please," ordered the bailiff.

"There was a hubbub in the courtroom," said Short as she looked back on the hearing. "People were in shock that the judge decided the order should stay in place. It was one of the most unjust things I've ever seen happen in court."

So the restraining order would stay. But there was a second part to the hearing to determine whether Walter Hoye was facing discriminatory prosecution. The intent was to call the other clinic escort, Sandra Coleman, to the stand for this matter, but Millen wanted it on the record first, as a basis for appeal, where Coleman stood on the restraining order, as she was the other party it was intended to protect. The judge offered to settle that by asking her a few questions before the court considered the issue of discriminatory prosecution.

"It's this court's understanding that there is a restraining order that keeps Mr. Hoye eight feet away from you that was issued by the court on June the 11th of 2008," she posed. "And do you wish to have that restraining order modified at this time?"

"No," said Coleman, who had been an escort only about a month longer than Kasdin.

"And why is that?"

"Because I find having him near is very intimidating. Just—I mean, by virtue of many of the same things that Ms. Kasdin said." Coleman described Walter standing about eighteen inches behind her on May 13, 2008. She was pretty sure she didn't have a blank sign that day, because of her carpal tunnel syndrome. "So I was standing in front of him just in an effort to keep his sign from being quite so visible to people approaching the clinic," she said. "And it was near the edge of the curb."

Coleman described Walter talking to her in a passive-aggressive manner that she found creepy and intimidating. She blamed the general climate surrounding abortion clinics and the abortion issue in the country for the way she felt. "Big intimidation starts small," she said.

"Does this intimidation ever keep you from doing what you do in front of the clinic?" Millen asked.

"No."

"Would this intimidation ever stop you from coming to trial?"

"No."

Then Graff asked her to explain what she meant by the term "passive-aggressive manner".

"There's a sense of his trying to be so nice and very condescending."

The judge gave Millen another chance to make his argument that the restraining orders should be rescinded. "There's one additional item here, which is these counts against Mr. Hoye of using force, threat of force or physical obstruction. The complaining witness says there's—that didn't happen. So, exactly why she needs protection from anything is not entirely clear." Millen paused to consult with Short, then added, "Oh, yes. [Coleman] would not be intimidated from coming to court, nor would she be intimidated if she saw him there again. So, she simply does not meet any of the standards for a [restraining order], nor is there any probable cause for this particular count."

Judge Bean declined again to modify or to nullify the restraining order.

The discriminatory prosecution hearing was next, and it had two parts: (1) to show there was an incident that was not followed up by police or pursued for prosecution, and (2) to show that the bubble law enforcement policy discriminated against people who shared Walter Hoye's views on abortion.

"The police department's policy is that escorts are not to be prosecuted under this, that when Mr. Hoye approaches he is to be prosecuted under this, and that this is not some random rogue action," Millen said. "This is, in fact, official police and city policy from the highest levels of the city." He then explained that he intended to present evidence that escorts engaged in behavior that violated the bubble ordinance and that the police had been told about the violations. In at least one case there was an actual police report taken but not forwarded for prosecution.

Tables Turned

After Walter Hoye was cited but before the charges and the restraining orders were made, the sidewalk counseling and the volunteer escorting continued at 200 Webster Street. On June 3, 2008, a number of people were in front of the clinic. Walter and his elderly companions were there, and so were at least two other anti-abortion sidewalk counselors, believed to be Mary Arnold and Ginny Hitchcock. The volunteer escorts numbered at least four, and escort coordinator Barbara Hoke was there taking photographs. The debate over what was or wasn't a violation of the bubble ordinance was set for another test—this time with a twist.

A sidewalk counselor, possibly Arnold, phoned the police and reported that the escorts were violating the ordinance. Defense Attorney Millen referenced Arnold as the caller, but years later, when she was asked about it, she didn't have a specific recollection of making the call. One of the responding beat officers called for a supervisor, and Sergeant David Elzey responded, bringing with him the police training bulletin. When the police car rolled up to 200 Webster Street, Walter, Christiana Downer, and Sister Elga Kendall moved as far away as possible. They watched as police talked to the reporting party, again believed to be Arnold, who said that two escorts, a man and a woman, violated the ordinance, and she described the specific allegation she was making against them.

Elzey later testified that the woman who called the police left after talking to the first officer on the scene. "Her complaint was that escorts of the clinic there at 200 Webster were contacting patients when they arrived at the facility and escorting them into the facility." On that basis, the woman wanted to file a complaint. Elzey and the other officers talked to the two escorts and then went into the clinic to talk to Jackie Barbic. "The training bulletin identifies the escort as a protected individual," Elzey testified. "And in my understanding from talking with the director of the facility [Barbic],... these were appointment-based appointments, [and] it was implied that these escorts were contacting these—the clients or patients, what have you, when they were arriving. So, [the escorts'] contacting them to say, you know, 'This is the way to go in' or 'follow me,' directions of that sort, would be okay."

"The director informed me that Vicky Laden wanted me to give her a phone call," Elzey testified. "So, the decision was already made at that point how we were going to respond to this and how we were going to address it, so I contacted Vicky Laden subsequent to the decision already being made. So, I did not call her for advice on how do I handle this, it was after merely—because she was requesting that a phone call be made."

Elzey didn't have the reporting officer fill out a police report; instead the officer filled out a field interview card, which is about two pages long and informational and is used when no crime has been committed. He also made one other notable omission. In such cases involving abortion clinics there is a mandate to report incidents to the Federal Bureau of Investigation's Bay Area Counterterrorism Task Force. The form itself says, "Officers shall complete a crime report to document all complaints, including instances in which insufficient evidence exists to make an arrest."

In presenting the case to the court a month later, Millen was trying to show that the bubble law was not applied equally—that anti-abortion speech was illegal inside the bubble outside abortion clinics but pro-abortion speech was not. The court refused to accept the argument, and as that hearing ended, little was resolved other than the deputy district attorney's clear intent to take the case to trial. A higher court would one day revisit the discrimination question, but the most important basis for appeal had yet to play out, and it would do so in a lengthy trial in Oakland.

Barbara Hoke was offended by the accusation that an escort had violated the ordinance, and she demanded that the police chief make enforcement of the bubble ordinance his top priority. Vicki Laden's response from the city attorney's office was to say that the officers who usually work the area were trained, but that there was no way of knowing who would respond when those officers were on emergency calls.

Even with the training bulletin, police officers remained confused about the ordinance. When Walter's arrest finally caught the eye of local newspaper reporters, even they could not get the story straight.

19

The Trial, Part One

On Monday, January 5, 2009, on the fifth floor of the Wiley W. Manuel Courthouse in Oakland, the first witnesses against Walter Hoye were sitting patiently in the hallway. To make sure that they didn't hear the testimony of the others and tailor their answers accordingly, the witnesses had to wait outside the courtroom for their turn to testify.

The two-week trial began when everyone was more than ready to get back to work after the long holiday season. After four days of choosing twelve jurors from a large pool of prospects, a process that began before Christmas, the trial of Walter Hoye was finally at hand. The attorneys were ready with their arguments, and the court recorder and the clerk were in their seats, as were the members of the audience.

The courtroom was packed. The bailiffs were forced to turn people away at the door because all the seats were taken. Sidewalk counselor Mary Arnold, a Walter Hoye supporter, was at the courthouse frequently during the trial, but she didn't always get inside the courtroom because the seats filled up fast. "The audience was mostly supporters of Walter," she said. "It was only a small group of people there on the side of the prosecution. There were almost as many [Hoye supporters] outside in front of the courthouse. We would pray and talk and be there to show our support."

Walter's supporters were mostly Christians from various denominations, and a large number of them were Catholics, including some employees of Ignatius Press in San Francisco and a Catholic priest, Father John Direen, the pastor of Saint Joseph's in Berkeley.

A Dispute over a Witness

All the players but the jury were in place. A last-minute legal question over a witness was being discussed by the attorneys involved and Alameda County Superior Court Judge Stuart Hing. Barbara Hoke, the clinic volunteer-escort coordinator, was set to testify, but about what exactly? Defense Attorney Michael Millen, from the Life Legal Defense Foundation, explained to Judge Hing that since Hoke was not an actual witness, her testimony would be largely a waste of time. "We're wondering if the DA could make some sort of offer of anything this witness might say that wouldn't be objectionable," offered Millen, "since she wasn't there on the day in question."

"The purpose of Barbara Hoke's testimony," argued Deputy District Attorney Robert Graff, "is that she is an escort coordinator, so she is able to testify that the actions taken by the two escorts that will testify later, Lucy Kasdin and Sandra Coleman, that those actions were taught to them by Barbara Hoke and that there is, in fact, some sort of protocol that these escorts follow."

"It could be confusing to the jury," said Millen, "because the question becomes, is she an expert under the law who sets the standard of what is and is not permissible conduct?"

Graff countered, "She would be testifying that she has been in contact with the executive director of the Family Planning Medical Group and has permission from the executive director for not only herself but for escorts that she organizes to be there."

Defense Attorney Allison Aranda suggested that the district attorney was trying to put into evidence that the people entering the clinic had given the escorts permission to approach them, which would be impossible unless Hoke had spoken with every single person entering the clinic that day.

Judge Hing favored the prosecution's argument and suggested that when Hoke testified, it would be possible to take up the objections one at a time. The jury knew nothing about this discussion, and by the time they entered the room and took their seats, it would be hours before they would hear what Hoke had to say.

Opening Statements

When the judge at last invited Graff to make his opening statement for the prosecution, it was a relief to many, including Walter and his wife, Lori. The onus for proof, beyond a reasonable doubt, was on Graff. He introduced himself to the jury as Rob, saying that it was his obligation to tell the jury what he believed the evidence would show. "This case is about personal choice," he declared.

Graff explained the intentions of the Oakland City Council when it passed the bubble ordinance. Their purpose, he said, was to protect people's access to reproductive health care facilities and to protect both patients and care providers from harassment and counseling as defined in the ordinance. There were two days in question, April 29, 2008, and May 13, 2008, the dates for which Walter Hoye had been charged for violating the ordinance. Graff called Walter's activities on those two days outside Family Planning Specialists "protests".

Graff named two witnesses, Lucy Kasdin and Sandra Coleman, and said they were volunteer clinic escorts. He told the jury that the women assisted people who wanted their help in entering the clinic without fear of protesters. "They identify themselves," he said. "They would wear orange vests, they would say to people who appeared to be people coming into the clinic: 'I'm an escort, would you like my help,' words to that effect."

On the dates in question, according to Graff, Walter Hoye wasn't acting himself. His demeanor was different, aggressive. "They had seen him before. Both of these women had been escorts for some two months and had seen Walter Hoye previously. So, they were familiar with him, who he was. It was not as if they were seeing him for the first time." To his credit, Graff didn't attempt to paint Walter Hoye as some kind of monster. He told the jury that they wouldn't hear anything about Walter Hoye hitting anyone, punching anyone, or using any other form of physical violence. "Yet you're going to hear that these two escorts were intimidated by the conduct of the defendant, Mr. Hoye."

Then Graff told the jury to expect the testimony of Jackie Barbic, who was the executive director of the clinic. On April, 29, 2008, he said, "she confronted the defendant personally because she had heard that his actions on this particular day were a little more egregious than on other days." He said Barbic would also assess the reactions of women Walter approached that day. Other witnesses, he added, would bolster her testimony. The evidence would show, he concluded, that "the defendant willingly and knowingly approached within eight feet of women seeking to enter the facility without their consent for the purpose of harassment and counseling" and that two escorts "were intimidated by the defendant because of their positions as clinic escorts. At the conclusion of the evidence," he said, "we're confident you will find the defendant guilty of all four counts charged against him." Graff finished his short opening statement by reminding the jury that there were two subsections of the ordinance violated on two days, making a total of four counts.

Aranda followed with the opening statement for the defense. Walter was not there to protest against abortion, she said, "not there to take away anybody's rights." In fact, Walter was the one whose rights were being denied, she argued. "You have seen persecution of people based on race, religion, political beliefs," Aranda explained. "We saw this in Germany, with Hitler, Tiananmen Square, in China. And you will hear evidence in this case that this is happening still today, in the United States—in Oakland, just down the street."

Aranda described Walter's sign, which said, "God loves you and your baby. Let us help you." His objective outside the clinic, she said, is to offer help to women who find themselves in a difficult situation, to say "there's an alternative." She explained that by offering women alternatives, Walter was a threat to the clinic's bottom line. "Every time someone takes Mr. Hoye's literature and decides: 'You know what, I will take that help, I will change my mind,' they lose money," she said.

The bubble ordinance was a planned persecution to silence Walter Hoye, Aranda continued. The clinic director and the escort coordinator enlisted the help of the city attorney and the Oakland City Council. Once the ordinance was passed, the police were called to enforce the law, but each time they went out, Aranda said, there was no evidence of any crime.

It was so difficult to get Walter arrested, she continued, that the clinic director once again reached out to the city attorney, who conducted her own investigation, an action that seemed unprecedented. "She went on her own private stakeout to investigate this case. She's not the prosecutor in the case, she's not in charge of enforcing this ordinance, but she felt compelled." She was there at the clinic, watching from her own car during the alleged incident of April 29, 2008.

The prosecution was about to present witness testimony about what happened that day, Aranda told the jury, but "you'll be surprised what the evidence will actually show." She then described what happened on the dates for which Walter was charged:

> Nobody [at the police department] was available to take the call that day [April 29, 2008]. Mr. Hoye wasn't arrested that day. Two weeks later [on May 13, 2008], Mr. Hoye is back at the clinic thinking he's done nothing wrong. He's just quietly standing on the sidewalk complying with the ordinance. And on the 13th when Ms. Laden hears Mr. Hoye is there she calls her friends over at the Oakland Police Department and has a lieutenant, a sergeant, and two officers respond code one, priority, to get down there and arrest Mr. Hoye, like this is some sort of homicide.

Aranda then suggested to the jury that it would eventually be said that Walter Hoye was improperly cited for conduct on the thirteenth. "Nevertheless Mr. Hoye was cited, and we're here today. We're not in Salem; these aren't the witch trials. We're not in the Deep South during the civil rights movement. But persecution still exists in this country. The evidence in this case will show you it exists right here in your own community."

Witness Jacqueline Barbic

Without a break in proceedings the prosecution was allowed to call its first witness. Jacqueline Barbic took the stand and identified herself. She seemed professional and clearheaded. She explained that she had been executive director of Family Planning Specialists for twenty-four years. Her previous experience, which began fresh out of college, was as an abortion clinic counselor, a medical assistant, and then eventually a center manager. She said the Webster Street clinic provided abortions, pregnancy testing, ultrasounds, and counseling. That was the background, but what about Walter Hoye?

As the questions began she was asked to describe the events of April 29, 2008. "I received a phone call," she said, "from one of the escorts [saying] that I needed to come downstairs because things were getting out of hand and that Mr. Hoye was more aggressive—was even more aggressive than usual on that day." She then went downstairs and watched Hoye for about twenty minutes from the lobby of the clinic.

She estimated that there were six to eight interactions between Walter and the patients entering the clinic that morning. "I observed patients driving up in their cars, patients and partners, husbands, boyfriends, parents, driving up, walking up. And they were—I observed Mr. Hoye walking up and approaching them," she said, though her recollections were vague. One of the women Walter interacted with, Barbic claimed, put her hands in front of her face to block Walter's contact with her. "The patient parked across the street with her boyfriend ... and Mr. Hoye walked up to the patient and the boyfriend and appeared to be talking with them."

"About how far away?" asked Graff.

"Two feet. The patient seemed to be distressed by it, along with her partner."

"Objection," Aranda protested, "speculation."

"Overruled," said Judge Hing.

"Why do you say that she seemed to be distressed?" Graff began again.

"Because the patient kind of put her hands up," explained Barbic, "and moved away." Barbic put her hands up in a defensive position after Graff asked her to demonstrate for the jury. She then said that the patient's behavior prompted her to grab a tape measure and go outside to confront Walter. She exited the clinic and went up to Walter, stopping about ten to twelve feet away from him.

She explained that she pulled out the tape measure to eight feet, stood on the sidewalk, and said to Walter, "Maybe you are not so good at math, but this is eight feet, and I need you to stay eight feet away from me, the staff, and the patients." She said she didn't identify herself to him at the time. She claimed it was a matter of being nervous about people knowing who she was and getting her name. When asked what happened next, she said Walter advanced toward her.

"In what manner?" asked Graff.

"I found it a very threatening manner. He looked at me with a smirk."

Graff directed Barbic to step down from the witness stand and to demonstrate what happened.

"He moved towards me and went—," she said, indicating a smile on her face.

"And right now, you're making a face," said Graff. "How would you describe the face?"

"He smirked at me and just kind of kept moving towards me."

"Your Honor," interrupted Aranda. "Can the record reflect that the witness is just simply smiling and that she's casually walking towards Mr. Graff, ten feet away?"

"The witness did indicate that it was a smirk," Graff countered, "not a smile. I think it's a significant difference." The judge allowed the questioning to continue.

"He advanced," said Barbic. "I started to back up a little bit, and he came within two feet of me, he continued to advance on me, and I continued to say: 'Please back up, stay within eight feet of me, back down, stay away from me, you're frightening me, you're scaring me, please move away from me.'" Again, Jackie Barbic demonstrated with her arms and hands to show a shielded posture.

"Did you have your hands up like that?"

"I was shocked that he was continuing to come," Barbic said. Her voice began to crack, and her eyes began to tear. "I mean, I'm getting upset because it was really upsetting to me to have him move in on me."

Again, Aranda objected. "Her state of mind is irrelevant since she's not a victim." But the judge overruled the objection.

Graff invited Barbic to sit, asked if she was all right, if she needed water, and then continued. Barbic testified that she reentered the clinic and asked the security guard to call the police. She then went back to her office to see if she had any inside lines to the police department, she said.

The prosecution's case seemed won. But under cross-examination, a few holes appeared in Barbic's version of the events. Aranda walked Barbic through a minefield of questions about who had reported to her the alleged aggressive conduct by Walter Hoye, when she confronted him, and where she was standing at given times.

Aranda asked who called the police on the morning of April 29, 2008. Barbic said it was possibly Ali, the security officer at the lobby kiosk. Or maybe he called the second time, she added, if there was a second time. She explained that she had other ways of reaching the police. "I have some direct lines to the Oakland police, to the sergeants, their cell phones," she said. But again she mentioned that she wasn't sure if she or Ali called the police. She was also not sure whose phone numbers she had. "I would have to look up which one it was," she said, naming two Oakland police sergeants. "They have since retired." Typically she would call the watch commander, she continued, "and they were able to let me know if somebody could come out. It's a more direct line."

"So, you don't go through the general channels of dispatch like everyone else?" Aranda asked. "You just have the back line; is that right?"

"We call 911," Barbic replied. "The response time is sometimes two hours. So, when that does not seem to be getting the police out, we then will use individual lines to see what we can get, who we can get out."

Aranda also asked Barbic about what she told the investigating police officer. At one point, Aranda asked Barbic to reread her own statement in the police report and asked her, "At no point in your statement to the police did you mention that patients had complained about Mr. Hoye; is that correct?"

"It appears not, from my statement," Barbic responded.

Aranda also asked if Barbic had known about the presence that day of Oakland City Attorney Vicki Laden, who was sitting outside the clinic in her car conducting a surveillance. Barbic said she found out only later in the day that Laden was there. Comfortable with the amount of detail Barbic had provided, Aranda suggested the introduction of a video.

"Your Honor, at this time I'd like to play a video and ask Ms. Barbic if this is a fair and accurate depiction of the tape measure incident, so to speak." She was referring to a video recording of activity outside FPS on the morning of April 29. The prosecutor quickly objected.

"Your Honor," argued Graff, "the people had no idea that this video even existed or was going to be proffered into evidence. We don't think it's appropriate for it to be viewed for the first time for the people in front of the jury without the people getting an opportunity to look at it." Graff's argument was that the video violated the rules of discovery, which govern how evidence intended to be introduced in a trial is made available to both sides beforehand.

"You've never seen it?" asked Hing.

"Didn't even know it existed until right now, Your Honor."

"It's going to be excluded for now," ruled Hing.

Hing's decision was a massive blow to the defense. "Your Honor," countered Aranda, "the great majority of my questioning is going to be related to this video. If we could take—it's not very long, Your Honor."

"No, counsel, just finish what you can right now."

That was the end of the video discussion, for the time being. Aranda continued with her cross-examination, and her questions covered a broad section of facts and observations, possibly laying the groundwork for more questions down the road. Barbic explained that the clinic performed abortions three days per week. The prices ranged from $450 to $1,300, depending on the procedure. But those were the cash visits; most were paid by Medi-Cal. On April 29, 2008, approximately twenty abortions were performed.

As for the other date of alleged bubble ordinance violation, May 13, 2008, Barbic wasn't much help.

"You didn't personally observe any sort of violations on the 13th; is that correct?" asked Aranda.

"I did not personally. I was not downstairs at all," Barbic responded.

"Your Honor, I don't have any further questions of Ms. Barbic at this time other than playing the video to impeach her." But that would have to wait. The judge wanted to keep the trial moving.

Barbara Hoke

The prosecution called to the witness stand clinic escort leader Barbara Hoke. She was introduced to the jury as a recently retired real estate broker who first began as a Webster Street clinic volunteer in the late nineties. This was back when the clinic was at a different location. She had become so active in the process that eventually she was responsible for scheduling the escorts at 200 Webster Street and other Oakland-area abortion clinics. She testified that in more recent years she had helped with maintaining the schedule. Robert Graff asked the typical questions, building from the more foundational to the more detailed, so that the jury could understand her relationship with the clinic, Barbic, and the other people involved. Robert Graff questioned her for a very short time, but her time on the stand wasn't without purpose, at least not for the defense.

Hoke explained that she had known Barbic for many years and communicated with her about where and when the escorts would be available, but it was not a situation where she had to ask permission. Hoke added that she also had the responsibility for training the volunteers. "We train escorts, so that our behavior is exactly the same or that—so that the clinic can trust us to act appropriately with people and that we can—they can expect a consistency of behavior to protect women who are entering clinics in Oakland."

"What do you train them to do?" asked Graff.

Hoke answered:

We train them, first of all, that we never approach anyone unless they're being harassed. If there are no protesters, no demonstrators at a clinic, we're totally invisible. We stay in our cars, we do nothing. That's important because the crucial issue in the need for escorts is the invasion of privacy of women walking into a medical facility, people impinging on their—their—they're just walking in to see their doctor. So, we could commit that same kind of invasion of privacy if we were at the clinics for any reason except to protect them. So, first of all, we train people that we're invisible unless there are demonstrators at the clinic. Also, we never approach anyone without asking permission. And there are several other rules. We try to treat everybody with respect. We wear nothing on our clothes other than the vest so that people—for example, we don't even put statements on our clothes because we want to be inclusive, we don't want to make judgments about why people are there or assumptions. We don't want them to be turned off by us, and we don't want to make assumptions even about why they're coming there, because we don't know why they're coming there.

Hoke identified Walter as the man sitting at the defendant's table and said she was familiar with him because he was a regular demonstrator at 200 Webster Street. Graff asked if Hoke was also familiar with Lucy Kasdin and Sandra Coleman, two clinic escorts. Hoke said she knew them as volunteers who joined the effort beginning in early 2008. Graff was brief with his initial round of questions and turned it over to the defense.

Defense counsel Catherine Short picked up the questions from there. When Short asked about training, specifically connected to holding whiteboards in front of a protestor's sign, Hoke claimed the focus was never on the demonstrators, but on the patients, and there was no specific training about blocking signs. "We do the best that we can," she explained "to get women into the clinic as unmolested as possible. Anything that we do in relation to the demonstrators, in regards to that, is secondary."

Short asked, "Simply the view of a sign, someone holding a sign on the sidewalk, is that considered to be molesting a patient if the person is standing still who is holding the sign, is not approaching the patient?"

"If a sign is intended to harm the person," Hoke replied. "Then certainly part of our function is to obstruct that sign, to cover that sign, to make that woman—to make that woman able to enter a clinic without being emotionally traumatized by those signs."

"Do you consider a sign that says 'God loves you and your baby. Let us help'—do you consider that to be an emotionally traumatizing sign?"

"When it is accompanied by: 'Don't kill your baby,' yes."

"Written on the sign?"

"Written on the sign and said by the—by the people. We certainly have had signs that said that in front of the clinics."

Short asked whether a sign that says 'God loves you and your baby. Let us help' by itself would be emotionally traumatizing.

"I think it's emotionally traumatizing in the context of being in front of an abortion clinic. It is absolutely intimidating and hurtful to women." In that case, Hoke explained, it was appropriate for an escort to block a sign.

"And would the same go for someone speaking to the woman, saying: 'May I talk to you about alternatives?' Is that also a harmful and intimidating message?"

"It is, in the context that they truly do not offer any alternatives."

When asked about the escorts making noise to drown out the messages of the demonstrators, she claimed that it was not something they were trained to do. They were, however, coached on what to tell patients about literature they might have received from a demonstrator: "That the literature is inaccurate," Hoke said. "That the literature is invasive of their privacy, and that it is intended to prevent them from exercising their right to reproductive healthcare services."

Short asked if escorts are trained to prevent pro-life literature from entering the clinic. When Hoke said no, Short presented a list of eleven escort guidelines that Hoke had prepared. Pointing to item nine, she asked whether the list includes a rule that a demonstrator's literature should never be brought into the clinic.

"No," Hoke insisted. "We don't have—we don't have rules. We have guidelines. The guidelines are—the guideline is to give women choice."

Hoke's testimony also included details about her understanding of the bubble ordinance. She explained that inside the hundred-foot zone around the clinic, pro-life demonstrators were not allowed to come within eight feet of patients or escorts. Escorts, however, "as an extension of the clinic staff", are allowed to come within eight feet of patients. Escorts are also allowed to come within eight feet of demonstrators, she said, to protect the patients from them. When an escort moves within eight feet of a demonstrator, it is then the responsibility of the demonstrator to move away from the escort in order to maintain the eight-foot distance between them.

Hoke explained that clinic escorts approached patients only when they were being harassed, when demonstrators "aggressively approached people without permission, pushing literature on them, reaching inside their cars, screaming epitaphs [sic] of various kinds, that's when we would intervene." That level of harassment, Hoke insisted, extended to the act of a pro-life demonstrator simply walking across the street and holding up a sign.

After a brief recess, the jury had a short list of questions for Hoke. They were mostly basic questions, but they proved that the jury wasn't dozing off. The final question was the important one. "What," Hing said, reading the question, "is the description of guideline number nine?" Hing then read the answer: "Do not let demonstrator's literature into the clinic that is intended to induce guilt and provide inaccurate information to unsuspecting clients. Explain that to clients, if necessary."

That concluded Hoke's testimony. She did not testify about what she saw at the clinic, because she was not there on either date established in the charges.

20

The Video

When the bubble ordinance was introduced at a meeting of the Oakland City Council Public Safety Committee, abortion clinic employees, escorts, and others spoke at length about harassment or worse at abortion clinics. As a result of this history, many abortion facilities, including Family Planning Specialists, have some sort of video security system. It therefore made sense for Walter Hoye to ask during the public comments on the ordinance: Where are the videos showing the horrible things that are allegedly occurring at FPS? The same question arose during his trial. Given the continuous security-camera surveillance at FPS, where was the video footage proving the charges against Walter Hoye?

According to the police report of Walter's arrest, clinic director Jackie Barbic told police that she might be able to obtain FPS videotape from the morning of April 29, 2008. But there is no indication that she either asked for or acquired any footage from that day. There is no mention of FPS video in the court records, and the prosecution presented no FPS video as evidence against Walter Hoye.

During Barbic's testimony, as mentioned in the previous chapter, Walter's defense attorneys wanted to present a video taken not by the FPS security camera but by someone outside the facility on April 29, 2008. Defense Attorney Allison Aranda did her best to show the video right then and there in front of the jury. "We didn't anticipate that we would need this," she told Alameda County Superior Court Judge Stuart Hing, "except ... the way that [Barbic has] testified is substantially different than what's on the video. Clearly, we didn't think it would be necessary if she had told the truth."

But Judge Hing shut that request down and excluded the video for the time being. Then he called on the defense to continue their cross-examination of Barbic without the benefit of that evidence, which they did.

At the next break, a recess of about fifteen minutes, Deputy District Attorney Robert Graff reviewed the short relevant parts of the video in question. With the jury still out of the room, and Barbic standing by to continue her testimony, the debate over the video entered its second round.

Graff argued that it should be excluded from the evidence because of its late discovery, because the prosecution had not been given a chance to see it ahead of time. Michael Millen responded that the defense had not intended to show the video until they saw that Barbic's testimony seemed to be at odds with it. "So, we don't understand," he argued, "on what authority the prosecution contends that any impeaching evidence we know of we have to tell him even before his witnesses possibly perjure themselves."

Judge Hing said that the video should have been turned over beforehand. Aranda countered. "We had no basis to introduce this as evidence until Ms. Barbic took the stand and came up with this story that is radically different than what is shown on this videotape," she said. "She never told this information to the police, she never told it to Graff, it's in no written statement whatsoever. We had no idea that she was going to come to court and say the things that she said."

The defense further argued that the video was taken by a California-licensed attorney who was present in the hallway and ready to testify. He was an eyewitness who could explain the video, offer a first-hand account of what happened that day, and be cross-examined by the prosecution.

Graff accused the defense of withholding evidence, which can be a serious matter, a violation of state law. The judge could, on that basis, exclude the video, which would all but kill Walter Hoye's defense. Both sides recognized the critical importance of this moment. It's no wonder Graff was so intent. "I think it's extremely disingenuous to suggest," he argued, "especially noting the line of cross-examination that the defense took, that they had no intention of using this video for impeachment."

"We certainly don't believe we have a duty to give impeachment evidence, so the DA can help the witness get their story straight," Millen insisted.

Hing suggested a continuance of Barbic's testimony on the following day, after the prosecution had a chance to view the video in its
entirety. Millen said that a continuance in and of itself would not be
a problem, but it could disadvantage the defense if the prosecution
lawyers and witnesses watched the video and discussed it in order to
change their story. "That kind of hurts our ability to put on our case
and show this witness is disingenuous," he said.

In a victory for the defense, the judge ruled that the video would
be allowed, but giving the prosecution that much time to view the
video and prepare the witness was destined to complicate matters for
Walter Hoye's defense. Jacqueline Barbic was excused from the witness stand but required to return the next day for further testimony.

The Security Guard

Time was running short on day one of the trial, but there was enough
time to introduce one more witness. The jury returned to the courtroom, and prosecutor Graff called a security guard employed by
the management of the building at 200 Webster Street. Mohammed Ali, commonly known as "Ali", was not an employee of FPS,
but he tracked who was authorized to enter the clinic on certain
days. Before there were volunteer escorts, Ali was known to hustle
women past sidewalk counselors like Mary Arnold. "I had to get
better at my message," said Arnold. "I would greet the women and
get to the spiel quickly, before Ali would come out and usher them
in past me and Ginny."

Much of Ali's initial testimony was intended to establish a context
and to set the scene for the events that unfolded on April 29, 2008.
After he described his general duties and some of the basics about
how clinic access operates, he stated that Walter Hoye arrived
about 8:30 that morning, with two black women, and left about
10:00 A.M.

Ali's testimony paused when the court recessed at the end of day
one. When his testimony resumed on day two, Graff focused his
questions on Ali's recollections of Walter Hoye. When asked about
Walter's demeanor, Ali noted nothing out of the ordinary and said
that Walter didn't seem agitated or angry. Ali did say, however, that
Walter was acting differently toward the patients, but Ali wasn't

specific. More than once Walter greeted someone and walked and talked with her almost to the entrance of the clinic, he said. Upon clarification, he explained that the closest Walter got to the clinic was the curbside where the walkway to the clinic began.

"If you weren't able to hear what the defendant was saying, how do you know he was speaking to these patients?" asked Graff.

"Because almost all the patients would come in and comment on what the behavior of Mr. Walter was and why he was out there and why he was harassing them," Ali replied.

When Ali was interviewed by an Oakland police officer on May 13, 2008, he described Walter as harassing the patients entering the clinic. In court, he clarified what he meant. "I would get patients walking up or being dropped off," Ali explained. "And they would come in and ask me who the person outside was harassing them."

"And that's why you used that term in your statement?" asked Graff.

"Yes. And also, just from visual, what I would see, it's the same thing as other days, is him trying to follow patients and hand out material, whereas they're trying to walk past him and enter the building."

Graff asked questions about Walter's sign—whether it could be seen. He asked about the literature Walter handed out, which sometimes Ali collected from patients when they entered the clinic. But Graff didn't delve into Jackie Barbic and her tape measure or inquire about whether she asked Ali to call the police.

In her cross-examination, Defense Attorney Allison Aranda asked Ali about the surveillance cameras that are part of the building's security system. Ali said that the video coverage is extensive, covering virtually every corner and floor of the building. All the cameras record simultaneously, and the security guards can watch the film in real time. The entire day's events on April 29, 2008, and May 13, 2008, would have been recorded, he said.

On April 29, 2008, about twenty patients entered the clinic between eight and ten o'clock in the morning, he continued. He didn't see Walter interact with all of them, but he did see him interacting with some. The escorts never complained to him about Walter, he said. They never mentioned that they were intimidated by him or afraid of him.

Ali remembered quite clearly when Jackie Barbic walked into the lobby to watch Walter, but his recollection was different from Barbic's.

"Did she stop and have a conversation with you?"

"Not that I remember, no," Ali replied.

"Did she stand in the lobby and watch what was going on for a little while?"

"Just a brief overlook and walked right outside."

"So, would you say she was in the lobby for 30 seconds or less?"

"Yes."

Ali testified that Barbic went outside and returned less than a minute later. That's when she told Ali to call the police, which he did. She went back upstairs, returned with a tape measure, and headed directly outside.

"As soon as she walked out, she ... rolled out eight feet worth of tape," Ali said. Barbic walked toward Walter with the tape, measuring the distance between herself and him. Ali saw them with the tape measure between them. Asked to clarify, Ali said the tape measure was extended eight feet, but the distance between them was about two feet. At some point Barbic walked away.

"During this ten minutes that she's outside, did you ever see Mr. Hoye walk aggressively toward her?"

"I wasn't watching him the whole ten minutes, but every time I did see him I did not see that."

"So, there was nothing sort of unusual that caught your eye to make you think, 'Oh, Ms. Barbic is in danger'?"

"No."

When Barbic returned to the lobby, Ali said, she had a conversation with Tammy, a co-worker who had been taking pictures.

"Do you remember Ms. Barbic saying that she was deathly afraid of Mr. Hoye?"

"I don't remember hearing her say that."

"Do you remember hearing her say: 'I'm scared of Mr. Hoye'?"

"I don't."

"Do you remember her coming up to you saying that she was frightened by Mr. Hoye?"

"She was saying—not that, but generally like that his behavior was strange."

Ali had no recollection of an incident with a woman getting out of a car and having to block Walter Hoye with her arms.

"At any point in time did the escorts put their signs up in front of Mr. Hoye?"

"They did."

"And they were the ones blocking Mr. Hoye's sign?"

"The escorts blocking Mr. Hoye's sign?"

"Yes."

"They were standing in front of him with a sign." The line of questioning focused on the proximity of the escorts to Walter and verified that to hold a white blank board in front of Walter's sign was to be within eight feet of him.

When Aranda was finished, Graff had a chance to ask a question that was also on many people's minds. What happened to the surveillance video captured by the security camera? "It was only stored for fourteen days," Ali explained. "It starts re-recording over the file space after that many days."

Aranda asked if the police requested the videotape for April 29, 2008, and May 13, 2008, when they arrested Walter.

"They didn't," Ali replied.

"They didn't ask you for the security video?"

"No."

"And you discussed the security video [with police]; correct?"

"We did."

"You said that you have a DVR on your premises. So, is there an actual physical recording that stays at your location?"

"Yes, at 200 Webster, yes."

The testimony closed Mohammed Ali's contribution to the case and underscored the argument that the only video evidence that still existed was the one procured by the defense.

The Video, Round Two

Earlier on the second day of the trial, a lengthy debate over the defense's video took place without the jurors in the room. The prosecution, more insistent than ever, wanted the evidence thrown out as a violation of disclosure rules. It wasn't hard to see why. The video showed a version of the incident different from the one detailed in Barbic's testimony and could endanger the prosecution's case.

The defense argued that the video evidence had not been intended as the basis for its case, but after Jacqueline Barbic's testimony it became necessary. Graff questioned this assertion. He claimed that the video equipment in the courtroom on the previous day, along with the availability of the man who recorded the footage, proved that the defense had planned to show the video; therefore, they should have turned it over before the trial began.

"Again, this puts the people in a very difficult position," insisted Graff, "having evidence come in mornings of, evenings of—it just doesn't give the people time to prepare." On that basis he asked again that the video not be allowed as evidence, with the understanding that the court gave the people time to review its origin.

"To be clear, Your Honor," Millen followed, "we assumed that the witnesses would be truthful. But because there's always the theoretical possibility it might not happen we wanted to be prepared."

Judge Hing took both sides into consideration and allowed the video as evidence.

Jackie Barbic and the Video for the Defense

The defense set up a monitor so that their video could be viewed by the court and asked Jackie Barbic, who was still sworn in, to watch it and answer questions. The jury was seated, and the defense showed a portion of the video relevant to Barbic's previous testimony. At a point where a woman was talking to a pair of movers next to a moving truck, Barbic identified that person as herself. It was the beginning of a systematic dismantling of her earlier testimony.

Because the prosecution and its star witness were given an opportunity to review the video, Barbic was prepared. More than once she described the video as "very blurry". In one instance, when her behavior on the tape was compared with her previous testimony, she said, "I would imagine that's me, but one hundred percent—I mean, I think it's probably hard for everyone to see."

The portion of the video showed Barbic exit the clinic building and converse with movers unloading a truck parked outside. It also showed her talking to Walter Hoye. She approached Walter while pointing a tape measure at him, and she appeared animated as she spoke with him. Then she talked to some other people standing around. Barbic returned to Walter, again pointing the tape measure at him. He moved away from her, down the sidewalk.

Defense Attorney Aranda asked why the video did not match Barbic's previous testimony. Barbic explained that the video did not capture the episode she had described before. She had forgotten about the moving van, she said. Seeing the video reminded her that "when I got to work the office said there's a moving van that's parked in front of the clinic and they are moving things in and out. And I went down to talk with them about that.... The incident that I talked about [yesterday] happened later on."

"You came outside," said Aranda, "had a conversation with Mr. Hoye, you were pointing the tape measure at him." She asked whether that was when Barbic made the comment "You must not know math. This is eight feet."

"That is not."

"So, it appeared as if you were having a conversation with him in this video. What were you discussing at this point in time?"

"I believe I was talking to the escorts," Barbic said, reasserting that her purpose in going outside was to address the movers, not Walter.

"You just watched the video. And the video shows that the first thing that you did was come out and immediately measure out the eight feet, point it at Mr. Hoye, and it looks as if you're having a conversation with him?"

Barbic explained that she was probably talking to the escorts about the bubble around the clinic and around the patients. The escorts didn't know, she claimed, where the area of one hundred feet began—at the elevator or at the front of the building. But Aranda pointed out that the difference was less than twenty feet and hardly worth a discussion, for, either way, the eight-foot barrier between the patients and the demonstrators applied to the area where Walter's activities and those of the escorts took place.

"I—you know, what you're—when they asked where 100 feet was and also determining—so, we were speculating on a hundred feet and probably rolling out the—I can't precisely remember what—I wasn't rolling out 100 feet. What we were probably to determine was: Well, here's ten feet, and talking with the escorts getting an idea of what was—within 100 feet what the eight-foot bubble was."

Aranda asked whether, in the video, Walter Hoye approached Barbic in a threatening manner, and the answer was no. Barbic conceded that he wasn't aggressive and didn't make any aggressive moves or gestures toward her, but that doesn't mean she wasn't bothered.

"Mr. Hoye always bothers me," Barbic declared.

"Just his general demeanor and presence there bothers you?"

"The treatment of our patients."

Aranda asked what Barbic saw and heard in the minutes shown on the video. Did Walter Hoye threaten any of the escorts?

Barbic said she didn't know. "Again, I was talking to the men who were handling the moving van."

"Could you hear what was going on five or ten feet away?"

"I would have probably been focusing my conversation on the moving van."

"We're about no more than 20 feet away from each other right now, and you can hear everything that I'm saying; is that right? Okay. I just want to know—you didn't hear any threats being made?"

"Not—"

"During the ten minutes on the video?"

"Again, not that I remember."

"During this ten minutes of video, did you see Mr. Hoye push or shove or act aggressive towards any of the escorts?"

"No, I did not."

"The incident that you described yesterday with the tape measure, did that happen before or after this incident?"

"It happened after this incident."

"About how long after?"

"Somewhere probably within the hour."

"Within an hour?"

"Yes."

Aranda tried to nail down exactly when, but Barbic was cagey. They settled on the most likely time period, between nine and ten o'clock that morning. Barbic wanted to clarify. She surmised that she probably heard there were movers moving things up and down the elevator, so she went down to investigate and may or may not have grabbed the tape measure around that time. But she maintained that the reason she went outside was to talk to the movers.

But Aranda replayed a short portion of video, about fifteen seconds. It showed that Barbic didn't walk over to the movers but, rather, walked right up to Walter Hoye. This hit a nerve.

"When a moving van is in front of the clinic it is a security threat," Barbic protested. "Because moving vans can be used to hold a bomb. And when you have men coming in it is a—to me, it's a high security threat that takes top priority. That's one issue. The second issue is that the elevator is being held and used for moving, and patients cannot use the elevator after anesthesia. That is also a major issue. So, that would have been my number one priority. And it was to talk to who was—who were these people and what were they doing in the building."

If the moving van was the priority, Aranda asked, if Barbic was talking to everyone but Walter, why did she walk toward him, point the tape measure at him, and appear to be having a conversation with him? "Are you telling us that you did not speak with Mr. Hoye?"

"I could have spoke with Mr. Hoye."

"Are you sure that this incident with the tape measure is not the incident—same incident that you described yesterday?"

"One hundred percent positive."

Barbic's previous testimony was equally adamant and very specific. She had watched Walter from the lobby for twenty minutes, she said, went outside and confronted him with a tape measure, and then fled for her safety when he intimidated her.

According to her testimony during cross-examination, however, she watched Walter from the lobby for a couple of minutes, not twenty minutes. She went outside not once but twice—the first time to investigate the movers, although she may have talked to Walter Hoye too; and the second time to confront Walter, who then acted aggressively toward her, which happened later and therefore did not appear on the video.

The defense replayed a forty-five-second clip for Barbic, the portion of the original ten minutes that showed Barbic exit the building with a tape measure and approach Walter. "It looks like you're pointing the tape measure at Mr. Hoye in the same capacity that you described yesterday," Aranda said. "Are you 100 percent certain that it is not the same incident that you described for us?"

"I am," she said.

Prosecutor Graff followed up. He wanted to know why Barbic was so certain that the episode on the video was not the one she had described the day before. Barbic replied that the video did not show Walter walking toward her and did not show her backing away in fear, so it could not have been the incident she was talking about.

"So, what's shown on the video and what you described yesterday are different incidences?"

"They are."

Both the prosecution and Walter Hoye's defense team were finished with Jackie Barbic, but there were a few more questions from the jury. They wanted to know if it were common practice to use the tape measure to demonstrate the eight-foot bubble. No, Barbic replied. Did Barbic know that Vicki Laden, the city attorney, was outside FPS the morning of April 29, 2008? Yes, she answered, but she was not sure when she realized it or found out. When she exited the building the second time, did she see escorts with white signs? No, she was focused on patients.

It was finally over for Barbic, but not for the saga of the videotape. After Barbic stepped down, the prosecution again fought against admitting the video as evidence. The admissibility of the video remained an ongoing question until the end of the trial.

21

The Trial, Part Two

Sandra Colemen was one of two escorts presented as parties injured by Walter's alleged violation of the bubble ordinance, and she testified in the afternoon on Tuesday, January 6, 2009, the second day of the trial.

She told the jury that she volunteered as a clinic escort two or three times a month and began in March or April 2008 with the encouragement of the president of the local League of Women Voters. She was a homemaker who volunteered for different organizations, calling herself a citizen diplomat and an activist. "I am retired. I don't work for money," she said.

Prior to her start as a clinic escort at Family Planning Specialists, she received extensive training from Barbara Hoke, the local clinic escort coordinator. Coleman said she received some thirty minutes of verbal instruction followed by more extensive training on the job.

On April 29, 2008, the escorts arrived not long before the "picketers", she said, referring to Walter Hoye and the women who accompanied him, and the escorts were ready for them. "Since Mr. Hoye and one of the other women often carried big signs, we—somebody came up with the idea that we would have blank signs to hold in front of their signs. And I believe that that did happen that day," she said, adding, "I was not holding a blank—a sign at all that day."

The trial recessed at 4:31 P.M., before Coleman could finish her testimony for the prosecution and be cross-examined by the defense. When the trial resumed on Wednesday, however, the first matter of business was the video again. The defense told the judge it intended to introduce the entire video, a portion of which it had shown the day before. The prosecution resisted, and the judge tabled the matter for the moment, in favor of continuing with the testimony.

Coleman returned to the witness stand and described "Walter's tree", which was near the sidewalk, not far from the clinic's loading zone, and where he usually stood. There was a sense of apprehension outside FPS on April 29, Coleman said, because there was no way of knowing how aggressive Walter was going to be, given that his reason for being there was to harass the women going inside.

At the prompting of Deputy District Attorney Graff, Coleman elaborated on the apprehension she felt. She had heard somewhere, she said, that doctors at abortion clinics wear bulletproof vests. She suggested that abortion providers thought violence against them was a real possibility.

Coleman recalled seeing clinic director Jackie Barbic in front of FPS on the morning of April 29, 2008. She came outside for a reason unknown to Coleman and then went back inside. When Barbic came out again she had a tape measure in her hand, Coleman said.

"What did you see Jackie Barbic do with the tape measure?" asked Graff.

"Measure the distance between—or show Mr. Hoye what eight feet is and then measure the distance between where she was and where he was." She said Barbic was about fifteen feet away at that moment. There was a time when it looked as if Walter was inside eight feet, she added, but it was hard for her to tell who moved closer to whom. It was also hard for her to hear all of what they said to each other, she said, but she claimed to have heard Barbic say, "Back off." She assumed that Walter was closer to her than eight feet, she said. The whole incident in her memory lasted five to fifteen minutes. Coleman testified that she was sad over the situation but never felt that her personal safety was at stake.

When asked about how many women she escorted into the clinic that day, Coleman could recall only one. She described it as a fairly routine day, during which others escorted women to the clinic, but none of the incidents stood out to her. She didn't have any recollection of Walter attempting to block a patient from entering.

About Tuesday, May 13, 2008, the other day in question, Coleman described a moment when Walter said something to her about watching her step. She said he made several such statements under his breath, which she could not hear clearly, but which made her uneasy. She found this behavior intimidating and harassing, she said, especially given how close he was. But she was not afraid and was not worried about her safety.

During a brief break, a juror handed a question to the judge about the charges against Walter and the victims of his alleged crimes. The judge explained that on both April 29, 2008, and May 13, 2008, there were two charges against Walter Hoye, for a total of four charges. The victims were the escorts Kasdin and Coleman. Coleman was on the witness stand at that moment.

Defense Attorney Aranda began her cross-examination with the video of April 29, 2008, ready to be replayed. She questioned Coleman's assertion that she did not carry a sign that day. She said that Coleman did, in fact, have a sign and that while Walter was standing still, Coleman walked over to him and blocked his sign with hers. Aranda followed up by playing a portion of the video that showed the scene she had just described.

"I guess I did have a sign," admitted Coleman.

She also admitted that Walter's warning to watch her step could have been a polite gesture to prevent her from falling off the curb. But it still gave her the creeps, she said, likening it to the feeling of being filmed without her knowledge.

It was a public street, and Coleman was aware of the video cameras recording from the building, Aranda said, and Coleman conceded these facts. She also said that even if she did feel uneasy, she did not report her discomfort to anyone.

"Isn't it true that you kept following him?" Aranda asked.

"No."

"Well, if he moved to a different location, didn't you follow him and continue to stand in front of him at the new location?"

"Some of the time."

"So, these feelings that you were experiencing that day, they didn't stop you from continuing to stand in front of Mr. Hoye?"

"That's right."

Aranda turned the attention back to the tape measure incident on April 29, 2008, and asked Coleman if at any point she heard Jackie Barbic say something like "You're scaring me" and start crying.

"If that happened, I did not see it." Nothing stood out to her during that interaction, she said, and she didn't see Walter walking toward Barbic.

After Aranda's questions, the jury had a few of its own. "Do the escorts approach patients within eight feet to offer help?" the judge asked on behalf of the jury.

"Yes, they do," replied Coleman.

In answer to another question, she said that if Walter Hoye moved, she would follow him so that his sign could not be seen. She would block his sign with her blank one.

Lucy Kasdin

After a lunch recess of about an hour and forty minutes, Lucy Kasdin was sworn in as the next witness for the prosecution and told the jury that she works with mentally ill and homeless seniors at an Oakland nonprofit. She started volunteering at FPS in early 2008, after a family friend, who was also a clinic escort, recommended it and introduced her to Barbara Hoke. Kasdin said she went through the training and became a clinic escort a month later.

Kasdin's testimony mirrored Coleman's regarding how her day as an escort began and what the basic practices of the escorts were, including sitting in a car when no one was outside the clinic, dividing up various tasks among themselves, asking patients if they wanted their assistance, and not engaging Walter Hoye in conversation.

On April 29, 2008, she was at FPS, just as she had been on virtually every other Tuesday since she began volunteering in February. She reported seeing Walter arrive with two women. It was her job that day to hold the sign, the blank piece of poster board, she said. Was she worried about her personal safety that day? Like Coleman and Hoke, Kasdin explained that she had her reservations but said that she did not fear Walter.

The first time she saw Jackie Barbic exit the building that morning was before Walter Hoye had arrived, she said. There was a moving truck outside, and Barbic went over to talk to the movers. Then she went back inside. When she came back out again, she walked right up to Walter, who was standing in his usual spot near the tree, and told him he was violating the ordinance. Kasdin said Barbic went back inside and came out with a tape measure. Kasdin testified that she heard Barbic say, "You are in violation of the ordinance, you're within eight feet of me. I'm asking you to back away." Everybody heard Barbic, she said, but Walter did not respond.

Kasdin called the moment scary and startling, because even though Barbic told Walter that he was in violation of the ordinance, he ignored her. "I think that it really—frankly kind of took me aback because he—just his total disregard for it ... and just he had a kind of—almost a smirk on his face. So, I think just the fact that he clearly disregarded ... her request." To Kasdin, Walter's expression appeared smug and defiant.

When a black couple, a man and a woman, exited a car across the street, Kasdin said her job was to hold her poster board in front of Walter's sign. Hoye had to reach around her to offer his literature to the woman, she said. Kasdin described the couple as fearful or angry. The incident took place on the curb, not in the street or near the car the pair had exited, she said.

Kasdin described another time she walked between a patient and Walter to block his sign. "At the point when she's passing him it's less—less than maybe two or three feet. But as she's approaching, again, she's got an escort and my goal is to be between—was to be between Walter and the patient. So, with all of that I would say roughly five feet [was the distance between the woman and Walter]."

That woman also looked fearful, in Kasdin's opinion. "I don't recall exactly what she said, but she certainly was, you know, was fearful and I mean if you can imagine, you know, this whole group walking up the street, you're just trying to go into a clinic."

She recalled one patient's profanity-laced demand to be left alone.

"Was she speaking to the escorts or was she speaking to the defendant?" asked Graff.

"She was speaking to both. I mean, her—you know, she—she said: 'I don't need any assistance.' So, in those instances we back off."

When it was Aranda's chance to ask the questions, Kasdin revealed that she knew that City Attorney Laden was in the area on April 29, 2008, watching the activity outside FPS. She didn't recall how she found out or who told her. Also present that day were four escorts.

During the first interaction between Hoye and Barbic, when Barbic told him he was violating the ordinance and to back away, Walter didn't walk toward Barbic, Kasdin said. "His response was, he didn't move, he wasn't—I don't remember him saying anything, but he certainly didn't—he certainly didn't move. It was—I mean, he had—he didn't move. He looked defiant, and he certainly didn't back up and respond to her request." She said Barbic then went back inside and five minutes later came out with the tape measure. She then confronted him a second time.

"So, when you turned around and you see the whole scene, she has a tape measure extended towards him telling him, 'you're violating the ordinance'?" Aranda asked.

"Correct," said Kasdin.

"How far apart were they?"

"I would say maybe four feet, max."

Aranda asked her if Walter had threatened Jackie Barbic at any time during the tape measure incident. Kasdin insisted that in her mind he did. "He refused to back away when she showed him he was in violation of the ordinance," said Kasdin. "To me, I would consider that threatening. So, did I hear him verbally threaten her, no. But was his action threatening, I would say absolutely."

"So, Mr. Hoye just standing still on the sidewalk, that was the threat? That's what you were afraid of?"

"Mr. Hoye standing on a sidewalk in violation of an ordinance, holding a sign in the whole context of himself, absolutely. It's definitely very threatening."

It seemed Aranda may have touched upon a very important point. Did Kasdin believe that Walter Hoye was in violation of the ordinance simply by standing on the sidewalk holding a sign? she asked.

Yes, Kasdin said, that was her understanding. She had never seen anyone demonstrate the ordinance with a tape measure before, she explained, and she did not see Barbic repeat the performance later that morning.

Aranda again showed video from the morning of April 29, 2008. Kasdin recognized the moving truck and identified herself in front of the clinic in an orange escort vest. She was shown holding a blank poster board in front of Walter Hoye's sign.

"Ms. Kasdin, is this a pretty accurate description ... of the interaction between you and Mr. Hoye on the 29th?" asked Aranda.

"Yes," she said.

"He would stand there trying to hold the sign, and you would hold the sign in front of him?"

"Right. Well, I mean, depending if there was a patient coming, but yes, that was—that's exactly how it was." She conceded that in the video and to her own recollection, she walked up to Walter Hoye; he didn't walk up to her.

"He wasn't preventing you from walking away, was he?"

"No."

The End Nears

During the first days of the trial, Walter Hoye had doubts about the direction of the prosecution—it all seemed so unreal. In the pit of his stomach it felt as though the acids were devouring the words that entered his ears, blasted through his brain, and spiraled down to his gut. Pressing upon his doubts was a heaviness. He trusted God, but he could not help but wonder how the trial would end, and the possibility of his going to jail scared him. While he sat and listened, his pen worked over a notepad and words flowed in a poetic stream of consciousness.

> As I sit in the defendant's chair, at times I
> feel alone, foolish and betrayed.
> As I sit in the defendant's chair, at times I
> have no idea how God plans to unravel my
> circumstances.
> As I sit in the defendant's chair, at times I
> can feel my freedom slipping away.

It went on.

> As I sit in the defendant's chair, I trust in
> God and thank Him for using me.

Not Familiar

On Thursday, January 8, 2008, the fourth day of the trial, Lucy Kasdin returned to the witness stand under oath. Aranda had more questions about what the clinic escort saw in the few minutes of video the court had reviewed. It was the footage of the tape measure incident with Jackie Barbic and Walter Hoye. It was the same clip reviewed by Barbic in cross-examination, the one she insisted was not the incident with the tape measure she had recalled during her initial testimony. Yet the day before, Kasdin said that there was only one tape measure incident and that during it Hoye and Barbic were within four feet of each other.

Aranda questioned Kasdin on the matter. In the evidentiary hearing in June 2008, she said, Kasdin testified that she was afraid of Walter Hoye, but she never mentioned the tape measure incident. Kasdin explained that the incident never came up then.

"You just forgot to mention it in court?" asked Aranda.

"As I said, it was not—that specific incident was not brought up, and so I didn't mention that incident. I—you know, I'm not familiar with—this is only my second time at one of these hearings. I don't know what I can just say, so I didn't say it."

Aranda asked about Kasdin's interview with Graff back in December. At the time, when Graff mentioned the tape measure incident, Kasdin did not say that it had scared her, Aranda said. When Kasdin challenged Aranda's portrayal of her statements to Graff, Aranda had her review the notes from her meeting with him. After admitting that the notes don't mention her fear, Kasdin insisted that she had mentioned it at some point. It was possible that she mentioned it at another meeting a few days later. Yet when Kasdin met with the police and gave a statement on May 13, 2008, Aranda said, she also failed to mention that the incident made her afraid. Kasdin replied that she was never asked about her feelings.

Motion to Dismiss

Aranda saw an opportunity to get at least two of the four criminal counts against Walter Hoye thrown out due to a lack of evidence. The court agreed to hear her argument out of the presence of the jury. Aranda began by asking the judge to dismiss counts two, three, and four, but specifically the two related to Coleman and Kasdin on May 13, 2008. "The primary element in both of those two counts are that Mr. Hoye used force, some threat of force, or physical obstruction to harass, injure, intimidate or interfere.... We have heard no testimony from anyone that they were physically touched or any force was used against them."

It was a sound argument. Both Coleman and Kasdin testified that they had no recollection of any such touching or intimidation. The prosecution's own witnesses appeared to have exonerated Walter Hoye, at least on those two counts.

Furthermore, there was no testimony that on May 13 Walter approached anyone within eight feet for the purposes of counseling, harassing, or interfering with a patient. In fact, there were no patient-witnesses who claimed anything at all. No such patients were even identified. "We've heard a lot of general testimony about his general behavior," explained Aranda, "but there's no specific evidence that he approached a person [a patient] within eight feet and violated this ordinance."

"Though no patient has testified, hopefully for obvious reasons, circumstantially clearly a lack of consent can be shown. So, that's the argument as to that one," countered Graff.

Then he brought up Judge Hing's instruction to the jury, which would be given to the jury when it was time for them to decide upon a verdict. It stated that, for guilt to be established, force, threat of force, or physical obstruction need not be person-specific. "So, that's to say, if there is a threat of force to one person," Graff went on, "that threat of force to person A can be used to intimidate people B, C, D, F, and G. The case or the instance with the tape measure certainly illustrates that with respect to Ms. Coleman and Ms. Kasdin, their reaction to it and them seeing what Mr. Hoye was doing on that day to the executive director of that clinic—it can be argued to the jury, certainly, that it was clearly meant to intimidate."

Aranda countered that Walter's interaction with Barbic is not a case of transferred intent, where, for example, a person committing a crime shoots at one person but hits another. The criminal never intended to harm that other person, because he wasn't the original target. But in the eyes of the law, the intent to harm the first person transfers to the second person. "Mr. Hoye is engaging in some sort of interaction or conversation with Ms. Barbic," Aranda pointed out. "His intentions towards Ms. Barbic don't get applied to every single person who's out there." She added that even in the tape measure incident "Walter didn't make any threatening gesture, didn't make any threatening movement. He simply stood there."

The bubble ordinance contains no prohibition that prevents Walter Hoye from standing on the sidewalk, Aranda said. If an escort or a clinic staff member approached him and demanded that he back up, he was under no obligation to do so. "He doesn't have to back up. That's not the law," she argued.

Moreover, Aranda said, it could not possibly be within "the scope of reasonableness" for the court to find Walter Hoye guilty of a crime "in perpetuity" by claiming that his actions on April 29, 2008, applied to his actions on May 13, 2008, and on every other day he might stand outside FPS.

Judge Hing then asked Graff whether there was any evidence demonstrating that Walter used or threatened force against Lucy Kasdin or obstructed her.

"The interaction with Jackie Barbic," replied Graff, "and the fact that she witnessed that, yes, Your Honor."

"But is there anything directly toward Lucy Kasdin with regard to force, threat of force, or an obstruction?" Hing asked.

"I don't believe directed at her specifically, no."

"And with regard to count two, how about directed toward Sandra Coleman?"

"The same, Your Honor."

It was a moment in the trial when some observers said the tone of Graff's voice changed and hinted defeat. Nobody thought the case would end right there, but that exchange between the judge and the prosecution was so succinct and to the point that it made sense of at least one big question.

An hour later, Judge Hing took a breath and said, "The court is going to grant the ... motion with regard to count two. And with regard to count four it's going to grant it with regard to Lucy Kasdin. But it's going to remain as to Sandra Coleman."

Formally that meant one criminal charge against Walter Hoye was dismissed. The jury, however, had not heard the arguments or the judge's decision and would not hear them until the outcome of the trial was in its hands, for the prosecution and the defense were admonished to refrain from mentioning the debate over the motion to drop some of the charges.

The prosecution followed by announcing it had rested its case, meaning it was handing the trial over to the defense to make its case in chief. The defense strategy was simple. Call one witness and one witness only, a move that promised to send torrents of doubt through the very foundation of the prosecution's case.

Terry Thompson

Much had been made of the video-recorded evidence. Some witnesses viewed portions of the recording and were asked to comment on what they saw. In most cases they agreed that certain moments fairly represented what had happened.

To clinic director Jackie Barbic, the video recording showed *a* tape measure incident, but not *the* tape measure incident. Barbic was the only witness who said there must have been a second tape measure incident because the one on the video did not match her initial description of the episode. The fact that her testimony was at odds with the video was the reason the defense team decided to enter the recording as evidence. It was also the reason Terry Thompson was the witness the defense called for on the fourth day of the trial.

Thompson, of Alamo, California, had been an engineer for more than three decades before he went back to school and got a law degree. He passed the bar and started doing legal work, some pro bono, as he said in the introduction to the jury. He was on the board of the Life Legal Defense Foundation, which was defending Walter Hoye free of charge.

On April 29, 2008, Thompson went to FPS on Webster Street to film the behavior of the escorts. He said that Walter Hoye had been the target of harassment. Any evidence he could collect, he said, would support a request for a temporary restraining order against the escorts.

Thompson was outside the clinic for about two hours, from 8 A.M. to about 10 A.M. When he arrived, he parked his red Jeep Cherokee across the street, paid the meter, and put a sunshade in the window. He then climbed into the backseat, where he set up his Sony 45 SR camcorder on a tripod. The camcorder's thirty-gigabyte hard drive could record for eleven straight hours. Thompson bought it himself at Best Buy specifically to gather evidence at the clinic.

The Jeep was outfitted with cardboard covering the side windows, and it was parked in such a way that Thompson had a clear view of the front of the clinic through his rear window. That explained the black lines that crossed the picture in the video: they were part of the window defrost system. The distance from the Jeep to the sidewalk in front of the clinic was about sixty feet.

During his nearly two hours of recording, Thompson said, he shut off the camera for less than two minutes on just one occasion, when the view was blocked, but otherwise he recorded straight through without a break. Once he was finished, he took the camcorder home, uploaded the digital content, and sent mini hard drives containing the files to Aranda and Millen.

The jury watched one hour and forty-five minutes of the video from April 29, 2008. It was the first time the jury had seen the uninterrupted recording. Thompson testified that he returned to the clinic two weeks later, on May 13, 2008, for the same purpose, parking his car and setting up his camera the same way as before. Thompson said he stayed a lot longer this time because Walter was arrested.

As the fourth day of the trial came to a close, there was a palpable air of fatigue in the courtroom along with a hint of relief that a much-needed weekend break was at hand. When the trial resumed on Friday, it began with Graff's cross-examination of Thompson.

Graff focused on Thompson's coordination with Hoye, making a plan to be at the clinic for recording purposes. "So, with respect to the 29th," Graff asked, "you called him a couple of days ahead of time and said, 'Walter, I'm going to be there on the 29th because I want to ... record what the escorts are doing, make sure that you're there, so I'm not doing this for naught'?"

"Yes, that's correct. And I did tell him I had a video camera, because I had not had it before that." Thompson confirmed that a similar arrangement was made for May 13. Graff wanted to be sure the jury understood that Walter knew that he and the escorts were under surveillance.

Graff also pursued a line of questions related to Thompson's role as part of the defense team. Thompson explained that he had done the video recording before there were charges against Walter, and therefore there was no defense and no need for a so-called defense team. That answer came up again when Graff wanted to know why Thompson didn't turn the video over to police.

"There wasn't any case when I was doing [the video recording]— my role was to gather evidence. And so, I gathered the evidence. I passed it on to Mr. Millen." Thompson's testimony was primarily to authenticate and to provide a foundation for the video recording, the only viewable evidence in the case. There was other evidence, other video recordings from security cameras, but neither the police nor the clinic staff nor the prosecution obtained them.

Without enough time to give the closing statements and the lengthy jury instructions, the court adjourned. The jury was sent home for the weekend with the assurance that they would be able to deliberate on Monday afternoon.

Closing Arguments

On Monday, January 12, 2009, after a brutally long morning session over jury instructions, the trial's final hours were within reach. After the lunch break, an informal poll taken of those entering the courtroom may very well have revealed maximum stress levels. If not, Walter and Lori Hoye had enough angst for everyone.

What are often called closing arguments are more like statements because they do not include points and counterpoints and often are short on facts. The prosecution presents its closing statement first, followed by the defense.

Prosecutor Robert Graff said in part:

> I'm going to leave you where I started which is to say this issue is heated. Certainly, there are a lot of opinions, a lot of different thoughts, but this job for you as jurors is not deciding what the rights should be or how they should be distributed. It's a First Amendment right versus a right to reproductive health, where it clashes, when it meets, who wins when they do meet. The issue is to decide what happened. Just decide the facts. If you think the facts don't match: not guilty. If you think the facts match: guilty.

It's like any other—any other type of case in that regard. You know, was the person driving, were they under the influence of alcohol, yes or no, done. So, keep that in mind as you deliberate, that you're looking for these facts. Don't get caught up in the debate. You also have become good friends. I'm sure you can have the debate afterwards. Now is not that time.

Thank you very much.

For the defense, Allison Aranda said in part:

Bias, prejudice, personal relationship or interest in the outcome. Does Ms. Barbic have an interest in the outcome? She wants Mr. Hoye removed. She doesn't want him on the street corner with his sign. She loses money, and she can't stand the sight of him. That was abundantly clear. You're to consider that in determining whether or not she was truthful when she testified....

If you have any doubt, watch the video. If you have questions regarding the specific incident, you can ask us to play that specific instance. And I submit to you, if you watch carefully each interaction that Mr. Graff has mentioned to you today you will see not all five elements are present. There are times when he doesn't approach, there are times when he's not within eight feet. You must all agree as to each and every element. And I submit to you the only reasonable conclusion at the end of your deliberations is to find Mr. Hoye not guilty—not guilty of count one, not guilty of count three, and not guilty of count four. That is all that is left before you. There is only one logical conclusion.

Thank you for this opportunity to show the truth.

It was then up to the jury to decide.

22

Judgment Day

On Thursday, January 15, 2009, just shy of two o'clock in the afternoon, Walter Hoye got the call. He was having a late lunch at Ratto's in downtown Oakland. With him was his wife, Lori, and his attorney Allison Aranda. Ratto's was a long-standing family-owned deli on Washington Street. Walter recalled the food and the conversation. They were talking about where they had come from and how they had developed such a deep commitment to Christ and the unborn. The three were having such a good time together that they almost forgot why they were waiting around in downtown Oakland in the first place. The pleasant casual lunch turned serious when the phone rang. The jury, which had been deliberating since Monday, had at last decided on a verdict; it was time to head back to court.

The Verdict

Eerily similar to the first day of the trial, a hush fell on the courtroom as the jury filed into their seats. Walter felt boxed in, as if he were already in custody. "The judge is sitting on the bench," he wrote in a diary. "The prosecutor is on my right, the bailiff is right behind me and my chair feels like it is stuck to the floor, effectively locking me into the table where I am sitting." The murmurs from members of the audience speculating on the verdict sounded as if they were rumbling inside his head. The legal formalities plodded along slowly, as if the system were deliberately rigged to draw out the suspense. Finally, the judge asked the jury foreman for the verdict.

Is my confidence in Christ real enough to pass this test? Walter wondered as the foreman rose from his seat. *Can I really believe that God will take care of me and my family no matter what the outcome?* For a fleeting moment Walter was eleven years old again, in church and poised to give his life to Christ. As he did then, he had a mixture of faith and doubt, and the same question of whether he could trust God was again rising to his lips. This time, Walter managed not to blurt out his question for all to hear, and he was consoled by a line of Scripture that came to mind:

> Slay me though he might, I will wait for him;
> I will defend my conduct before him. (Job 13:15, NAB)

The words washed away Walter's fears and seemed to wash away everything and everyone in the courtroom, leaving him alone with the feeling of Christ next to him. He recalled a sudden sense that he had come to a new level of confidence in God. "I realized I had not hurried out of harm's way or collapsed under pressure," he wrote in the diary. "I realized that I was facing the future with a faith I had not had before."

The foreman gave the bailiff a legal-sized manila envelope, which the bailiff handed to Superior Court Judge Stuart Hing. The judge pulled the verdict from the envelope and read it in silence. Then he passed it to the clerk, who read it aloud, beginning with count one, dated April 29, 2008: "We the jury, in the above entitled cause find the defendant, Walter Brisco Hoye II, guilty of a misdemeanor, to wit harassment of persons seeking healthcare, a violation of Section 8.50.3(b) of the Oakland Municipal Code."

As for the similar count two, dated May 13, 2008: "Guilty," the clerk continued.

Then there was count three, the remaining charge related to the escorts: "We find the defendant not guilty."

After the judge thanked the jury and excused them, he told the attorneys that he was thinking about remanding Walter Hoye to custody right there on the spot, then reconvening the next day for the formal sentencing. The prosecutor raised no objections, but Aranda argued against it. After a moment of consideration, Hing said, "I will move the date of sentencing and Mr. Hoye can remain free if he agrees to the following conditions. He will agree to stay 100 yards away from the abortion clinic on 200 Webster Street in Oakland ...

and stay eight feet away from the persons identified in the case until sentencing. Are you willing to obey this order?" he asked, looking into Walter's eyes.

Walter and Allison discussed the question at hand. The maximum penalty for the two guilty verdicts was two years in jail and a $2,000 fine. Walter thought about his previous commitments for the remaining days of January, and Aranda advised him to take the deal. But Walter hesitated, waiting for some inspiration, some intervention from God that would turn things back in his favor. Nothing. Walter looked at the judge and said, "Yes, Your Honor." And with that the judge set a new date for sentencing, which gave Walter a thirty-day reprieve.

Then Aranda brought up another concern. "Your Honor," she said, "it has just come to my attention [that] some people were out in the hallway listening to the escorts discuss going to Mr. Hoye's church in order to force him to be—to leave because there's now this restraining order in effect, Your Honor." She also pointed out that Walter had a previously scheduled public event coming up, one already permitted by the city. "I would like, actually, the restraining order to specify so that they don't show up in these locations with the order in hand, call the police, and say: 'This man's within 100 yards of me,' have him arrested, which could quite possibly be the case unless there's some sort of written record to the contrary." Her request seemed reasonable to both the judge and the prosecutor, and it was agreed.

Outside the courtroom there were tears for what Walter's supporters saw as a travesty. Under the circumstances, how could the jury find Walter guilty on any count? they asked. As Walter left the building they promised to support him no matter what.

The Sentence

On February 19, 2009, Walter was back at the Alameda County Superior Court. At his side were his attorneys, Michael Millen and Allison Aranda. At the prosecutor's table was Deputy District Attorney Robert Graff, the man who had convinced the jury to convict Walter. As the bailiff's words "All rise" echoed off the old oak-paneled walls, there was a collective whooshing from seat cushions, clothes, and elbows rubbing together as members of the audience stood up in the packed courtroom. A keen ear might also have detected the subtle sound of rosary beads colliding between nervous fingers.

As the Honorable Stuart J. Hing took his place at the bench, he could see there wasn't a single available seat. Bailiffs had needed to turn some people away, as usual. If Walter could have turned around he would have taken comfort in the many familiar and sympathetic faces there. But he also might have been reminded of the peril he was in, for there were other faces he knew, employees and volunteers of Family Planning Specialists and staff members of the city council—the very people who had crafted the bubble law, which seemed tailored to stop him.

Outside there were no big protests over a broken justice system, no calls to free Walter Hoye. Trials by public opinion fueled by radicals of this or that sort are regular occurrences in Oakland, but none were staged on behalf of Walter. His cause wasn't as sexy as fighting for a victim of police brutality and systemic racism.

Still, before the sentencing hearing began, some of Walter's supporters gathered outside the courthouse for a small rally on his behalf. There were no angry shouts of "No justice, no peace" with clenched fists raised in the air, as in the kind of spectacles the local media thrive on. Rather, Walter's supporters expressed their opinions by making speeches and joining in prayer.

Some Hoye supporters who could not be there in person wrote letters to Judge Hing, who began the proceedings with an apology. "I've been meeting in chambers with counsel," he said, "as well as reviewing a large number of letters that I received." Many of those letters were in support of Walter, but some were in support of the bubble law too, and the polarity of views on abortion was not lost on the judge, who told the audience, "I do have to remind you that you won't be allowed to stay if you have any recording devices, or if you start to become disruptive during court."

Hoye attorney Michael Millen then asked the judge to defer sentencing because the bubble law was being appealed in court. He explained that the basis of the appeal was the language of the ordinance itself. "It was, on its face, discriminatory to those of pro-life persuasion," he said later. Judge Hing, however, denied the request to put sentencing on hold until the appeal worked its way through the judicial system.

Before Graff gave the judge his recommendation for a sentence, he noted Walter's lack of a criminal record and the "half-inch stack of letters" that had been written on his behalf. Graff acknowledged there was "little doubt as to the man's character." Thus, he would not ask for time in jail so long as Walter agreed to stay away from Family Planning Specialists. If Hoye would agree to a stay-away order, he continued, he would ask for three years of court probation with credit for any time served ("I believe that's one day in jail") and a restitution fund fine of $130. "If Mr. Hoye is not amenable to a stay-away with credit for time served and probation," he concluded, then he would ask "that he serve two years in county jail."

Usually the victims of a crime, or their family members, have the most to say at a criminal sentencing. But at Walter Hoye's sentencing, as at the trial, no victims came forward to request the price he should pay for harming them. Instead, the court heard only from his supporters. Each speaker spoke directly to the judge, with a bailiff posted to the right and to left of the podium. There were two reasons for the deputies to be on either side of the speakers: (1) to encourage brevity and to keep the line moving and (2) to provide security. There was tension in the courtroom, and anger over what many felt was a failure of the justice system boiled up in the voices of the speakers who pled for leniency toward Walter.

Levon Yuille traveled all the way from Michigan "to say this is a good—a great man," he explained, "a soft-spoken man that is only moved by his convictions and belief in our great constitutional rights of freedom of speech."

Stephen Broden of Dallas, Texas, said he found Walter "to be a conscientious person, a man of peace, who sought to operate within the confines of the constitution." He added, "I just ask the court to consider his work that he has done over the years on behalf of children in this city, and his demonstrative love for his church and his pastor through his participation in their effort to be a light in this community."

Finally, Dion Evans, pastor of Alameda's Chosen Vessels Christian Church, strode up to the podium. Aside from being a minister, he was the host of the KFAX radio show *Issues after Dark* and spoke on topics important to the black community. He was one of the few local pro-life pastors who partnered with Walter Hoye for various events. He later explained that at the time, to his "shame" and "dismay", he was already a little late to help Walter. "I didn't even know what was going on," he said. "Who would put a man in jail for handing out literature to the women? When we got the news, that they had convicted him, he's going to jail, I said, 'What!?'"

At the hearing, Evans alluded to the biblical figure of Daniel and those sitting as judges in his day. A big man, Evans had a strong and authoritative voice, and it rang out with the righteous indignation of a man angered by the countless injustices blacks have suffered. "You are here dealing with a man," he said of Walter. "It's not an issue of pro-life or pro-choice. It's an issue of a man having the ability to stand and proclaim his truth without hurting anybody. A man who speaks barely above a whisper unless a train is riding by. You're dealing with a man who's in his community and has been a beacon in his community. And we pray that—pray that you do not allow this unjust ordinance, or this unjust law to persuade truth."

By the time Evans finished, adrenaline was rushing through his body, and when the bailiff on his left grabbed Dion's elbow, he pulled the bailiff off his feet and sent him across into the other bailiff. "I don't need help sitting down, you don't need to put your hands on me," he told the bailiff. There were gasps in the audience as the bailiffs pushed and manhandled him out of the courtroom. In the hallway he fell in the direction of an elderly woman with a cane or a walker. If he hadn't pushed back on the bailiff behind him, he would have landed on her, he said. "I was shocked that he [the bailiff] could deal with a public citizen that way." A black bailiff showed up and restored order, Evans added. "That's when I went outside."

The court stenographer did not indicate that there was any disturbance or note an admonishment from the judge, which is not unusual in such cases. The incident is not mentioned in the court records, but several interviews of eyewitnesses supported Evans' description of the events

Next Judge Hing asked Walter if he would like to make a statement. He said yes, and the already quiet courtroom sank into a deeper silence as Walter began, "Your Honor,"

I believe an unjust law is no law at all.... It is my intention to continue my efforts to save the life of the unborn child, by reaching out to the men and women going into the abortion clinic with the love of Jesus Christ, my Lord and my Savior. If you are asking me if I'm willing to carry a tape measure with me, Your Honor, I will not. I will, however, do my best to comply with this unjust law until the completion of the ongoing civil case that challenges the constitutionality of this law. Thank you, Your Honor, for allowing me to speak at this time.

"All right," said Judge Hing, "I appreciate your speaking. You didn't have to, and I appreciate that." He then asked the defense attorneys to clarify Walter's words about going back to the clinic.

Aranda answered that question by pointing out that the court was able to watch the video of both days. The court was able to hear the testimony of the witnesses who said Walter was never rude. He spoke in a quiet tone. He was friendly. He never used force against anyone. He never tried to harm anyone. He never made threats against anyone. The most he did was walk about, hold his sign, and offer literature and help.

That was the conduct for which the court was imposing punishment, Aranda said. "To incarcerate him would be depriving the community of a leader. It would be depriving his family of a provider. This would be an extreme hardship on his family to incarcerate him.

"And what Mr. Graff has asked is basically for Mr. Hoye to give up his freedom," she continued. "Mr. Hoye has no problems abiding by the law. That is what he has agreed to do. He will abide by the statute and every other law that is on the books. But to say that he's prohibited from going to this location altogether is asking him give up his right to free speech. A right that all of us enjoy."

"In making your sentence," Graff addressed the judge, "I ask that you consider Mr. Hoye's words, and the fact that he believes that an unjust law is no law at all.... That to me sounds like he's going to engage in the same conduct." Graff said that such conduct was already determined by the court to be in violation of the law. "We have the rights of these other people that need to be considered," he said. "So, in making your determination, Your Honor, I just ask that you take all of that into consideration."

Judge Hing again asked Walter if he were "willing to obey or honor and abide by the stay-away". Walter consulted with his attorneys in a hushed whisper. Then Walter said, "Your Honor, I'm unwilling to agree to stay away from the clinic. I am, however, willing to obey the law. Thank you."

Hing called for a recess. He considered his options and spoke in chambers with both sides. When he returned to the bench, he declared that Walter Hoye

> has been sentenced today to three years' court probation, 30 days in the county jail, which may be satisfied in one of three options. He can serve 30 days in jail. You can do 30 days in the Sheriff Work Alternative Program, or in an approved volunteer program. A program approved by the court. He's also ordered to stay away 100 yards, and have no contact with the clinic in question in this case. Pay a restitution fund fine of a $130, and a general fine of $1,000.

"Just so we're clear," Aranda said, "Mr. Hoye is not simply objecting to that one particular term of the probation [the stay-away order]. He's refusing probation in its entirety; all of the terms and conditions of probation as the court set out."

Judge Hing closed the hearing and ordered everyone back at two o'clock on March 20. "Just so you know the court's thinking," he said. "If Mr. Hoye will agree to the protective order, the court was not going to order the 30 days [in jail], and was not going to order the fine. And if Mr. Hoye's mind changes between now and the next time we meet, the court would be open to modify his sentence."

What were the chances he would change his mind?

Black Lives Matter?

On March 20, 2009, dozens of Walter Hoye supporters gathered near the entrance to the courthouse. They were a diverse crowd of whites, blacks, and others; of Baptists, Catholics, and those of other Christian faiths. Some of them held signs with slogans such as "Shame, City Bans Free Speech", "An Unjust Law Is No Law", and "Stop Judicial Tyranny". It was a send-off for their brother who was likely to go to jail that very day.

Walter was easy to spot in his standard black "Got Jesus?" hat and his trademark sunglasses, which sat neatly just below the bridge of his nose, where reading glasses usually rest. He held his own sign, which read, "Pastor Jailed for Free Speech". Proof that the system could not silence them completely, they prayed together and spoke out against municipal oppression in the city of Oakland.

Pastor Dion Evans led the gathering and invited people to speak. Among them was Reverend Clenard Childress of New Jersey. "We applaud the pastors of Oakland and certainly Pastor Hoye," said Childress, "for being a prototypical example of what's needed to expose the entrenchment of the abortion industry's agenda."

After Childress, Walter spoke. As he stepped forward, his face already showed signs of weight loss, for he was a couple of weeks into his 40 Days for Life fast. In his soft-spoken voice, he explained the importance of the abortion issue. "We can talk about welfare, we can talk about minimum wage, we can talk about health care, we can talk about drugs and crimes in our neighborhoods," he said. "Whatever issue you'd like to talk about we can talk about, but there's no other issue more important than life itself."

Speaking to a video camera, Walter reached out to faith leaders and pastors. He pleaded with them to use their pulpits to talk more about the sanctity of life. "Be bold enough to stand where you are, wherever you are, and talk about how important life is, particularly in the African American community." Then he addressed his circumstances, describing the actions for which he found himself facing jail time. "This is a no-Christ zone. If I had the clinic's permission, I would have been able to retain my First Amendment rights, my free speech rights in order to spread the word, the gospel, to the women entering the clinic."

Lori Hoye also addressed the crowd, linking Walter's conviction and sentence to the injustices of the Jim Crow South. "Oakland has taken a step back to Alabama," she said. "I was just listening to George Wallace telling black folk you can't be on the sidewalk; you can't cross this line. There is a zone that you are prohibited from being at.

"Judge Hing is a complete and total coward," she added. "He had the power to make it all blow away, but he decided to abdicate and blame the city council and blame the twelve jurors.... This is a travesty of justice. This is the most egregious miscarriage of justice that I have seen in my lifetime."

The assembled supporters responded with cheers, and Lori contin-ued. "The fact that the city council voted unanimously, on Martin Luther King's birthday, is another issue that needs to be taken up," she said, asking about the appropriateness of the council members' personal investment in the bubble law. "Nancy Nadel, point one," she said. "What is a city councilwoman doing in a courtroom for two days on a misdemeanor trial? The tax dollars of Oakland are being utilized to railroad one man who had the nerve to stand on the sidewalk and say, 'God loves you and your baby.' Stop killing black people in Oakland!"

The cheers only got louder, but Lori wasn't done. She turned her attention to the many silent black American pastors of Oakland, who she said should be ashamed. "Not one of them has shown their face at a city council meeting. Not one of them has shown their face in this courtroom. Not one of them has opened their mouth and said boo to anybody about what's going on here, and yet they want to sit around and say, 'Black life is important.' How is it important? A hundred lives a week are taken at that clinic!"

On the black members of the city council—Larry Reid and Desley Brooks—and on Mayor Ron Dellums she placed even more blame. "The blood is on their hands," she said. "They are African Americans who are allowing the deaths of African Americans in their city. They cannot claim innocence, they cannot claim they don't know. They are complicit in the deaths of thousands of children in this city."

Attorneys Michael Millen and Allison Aranda of LLDF followed Lori's impassioned remarks. "This is social injustice in your face," declared Millen. "A man gentler than just about any you will see doesn't even get to have his sentence stayed while he appeals an unjust law. It's shocking, and we're just gonna keep fighting."

"There are people convicted of robbery, gang crimes, burglaries and sentenced to a long period in prison," said Aranda, "and those people are granted bail pending their appeal. Walter Hoye is convicted of probably the most innocuous crime that you can be convicted of in the city of Oakland [and yet] is not given the opportunity to have his sentence stayed."

Minutes later Aranda and Millen argued one last time in open court for a stay pending the appeal, but Judge Hing shot down the request without hesitation and imposed the sentence. Walter Hoye was led out of the courtroom between the bailiffs. Next stop: Santa Rita Jail.

"It was unconscionable," Millen said in an interview with the author. Of all that had happened up to that point—the arrest, the endless hearings, the motions and the pleas, and the lengthy trial itself—the most shocking to Millen was when the judge refused to stay the sentence pending appeal. "When he refused to stem the sentence, you kind of felt the way Joseph of Arimathea must've felt in the Jewish legal procedure convicting Jesus," he said. "This is the way the system grinds those it doesn't like: get people in the [police department], the county and city, and a private business working together to get rid of this guy. The murder capital of the world spends money it doesn't have to prosecute a gentle man offering options to help women keep their babies."

"One thing it shows is the power of an evil thing like abortion to corrupt everything around it," said Defense Attorney Catherine Short. "The single-minded focus with which they went after Walter. FPS has this power to get DAs to drop everything, get crowded courtrooms to clear, just to get this guy."

The frustrations boiled over as the observers left the courtroom. Mary Arnold found herself face-to-face with clinic director Jackie Barbic. "Congratulations," she said. "Jackie, not only are you murdering babies, [but] because of your perjury, today you put a really good person in prison. Congratulations."

Walter Hoye's mother, Vida Mae Pickens (left), with her two sisters, Mary (middle) and Bernice (right)

Walter (far right) with his mother (behind him), his sister (in the middle), and his maternal aunts and grandparents, Bessie Kate (Odum) and Eltee Pickens

The wedding photo of Walter's parents, August 28, 1954

Walter (left), his sister, Jo-Ann (right), with a childhood friend

The house on Pasadena Street, Detroit, where Walter grew up

Winterhalter Elementary School,
12121 Broadstreet Avenue, Detroit

Walter and his family in San Diego

High school football: Walter wearing the number of Gale Sayers, one of his heroes on the field

Walter Hoye at Michigan State football practice in 1976

Walter's "Father in the Gospel", Dr. S. M. Lockridge,
Pastor of Cavalry Baptist Church in San Diego, 1953 to 1993

Walter and Lori Hoye
wedding photo,
July 15, 1989

Walter Hoye II,
his son, Walter,
and daughter, Erinn

Pro-life leadership meeting in Washington, D.C., 2016:
Alveda King, Walter, and Star Parker

Lori and Walter Hoye
speaking at
National Organization
for Marriage march,
Washington, D.C., 2017

San Francisco
Archbishop Salvatore
Cordileone and
Walter, 2015

Lori and Walter Hoye celebrating the 2017–2018 NBA World Championship of the Golden State Warriors

Walter Hoye, Golden State Warriors chaplain

23

For Good Behavior

Even though Walter Hoye was often up late at night, praying and giving counsel to those who sought his advice, he could not make up for lost sleep in the morning. The early-morning noises inside the prison were like a continuous snooze alarm. After Walter was awakened by something, the moment deep sleep returned, he was awakened by something else. The noises were not intended as punitive, but like a busy hospital, the prison had lots of administrative activity that required an early start. For this reason breakfast service started early enough to make a Marine recruit cringe—at three o'clock.

Among the many morning sounds were the names of prisoners squawked over the loudspeaker with so much static they were barely intelligible. Among these men would be those being transferred to state prison or taken to court. The lucky ones were those scheduled to be released.

On day nineteen of his sentence, April 8, 2009, Walter heard his name among those to be set free. His ears weren't the only ones that perked up. Elder Roe and the other men in the prayer group also took note. They didn't want Walter to leave, he recalled. Walter was not surprised by the announcement because a guard had told him a few days before that he was about to be released early for good behavior. The guards had recommended the move in acknowledgment of what Walter had done for them.

There had been a new inmate who was crying uncontrollably, Walter explained. The young prisoner was a wreck, so emotional that he had become inconsolable. After the guards had tried everything they could think of to calm him down, they pulled Walter out of his cage and asked him if he would talk with the inmate. If the young man could not pull himself together, they said, he would be brutalized by his cellmates. Of course, Walter agreed to do what he could.

The guards led Walter to a solitary-confinement cell. About the size of a closet, it had a single cement-slab bench protruding from the wall. The inhumanity of it was enough to make Walter angry. Next the guards brought Walter the new inmate. He was black, and he was weeping and sniffling like a child. His eyes were bloodshot from so much crying. The guards left the door open a crack, and one of them remained just outside. The inmate was "scared to death", Walter said, but after talking things over with a sympathetic listener, away from the eyes of the other inmates, he finally regained his composure.

Walter had become the de facto chaplain for Unit 34, Pod F, he realized. He was the go-to guy for inmates and guards alike. As he gathered his few belongings, including the many letters he had received from well-wishers near and far, a notion crept into his mind. "There was a part of me that didn't want to go," he said. "There was so much work left to do there."

Santa Rita had its own official chaplain, but some inmates told Walter that they didn't feel any connection with him. He didn't visit them much, they said, and he seemed distant and unavailable. As a result, the inmates didn't care to go to chapel when he was there. Walter didn't understand the dynamic until the day the chaplain, a Protestant, paid him a visit in the Unit 34 common area, where they could be seen by the other inmates. "The meeting went well enough," Walter said, "but I was not at all comfortable, because it underscored the feelings of the inmates. You see, the chaplain had come out to talk to me, but he wouldn't visit them."

As Walter looked around the cage one last time, he thought, *What now?* The guards moved him and the plastic bag with his few possessions to a holding cell to await out-processing. The room was empty, save for two metal chairs, and he sat down. The metal door bolt clanked into the locked position and he was alone, but not for long. In a few minutes, more inmates began arriving, and soon the room was packed elbow-to-elbow with mounting tension. Luckily for Walter, Elder Roe, who had a court appointment for his upcoming release, also entered the room.

The inmate who sat down in the empty chair beside Walter was a frightening fellow. "He was big, racist tattoos, skulls," Walter said, "and there was something not right about him.... He was not mentally all there." A guard shouted to the man that it was time for his meds, and the big imposing figure got up, put his Twinkies on the seat, and left. All eyes turned nervously toward the empty chair, but no one immediately sat down. When someone finally took the seat, there were audible "oohs", as if he had stepped to the edge of a cliff. A smattering of unsolicited advice was heard from various corners of the room: "Get out of the chair, he's coming back." But the seated man insisted he would get up the moment the big tattooed guy returned. He made good on his promise: as soon as the big man returned, the occupant of the chair hopped up and cleared the way.

Too late—the man with the tattoos, noticing that his Twinkies were missing, proceeded to pummel the interloper who dared to take his chair. Walter stood up, and, as if pulled by centrifugal force, he and the other inmates squeezed against the wall. A small gap opened up around the fight, but Walter was so close to the action, he was in danger of being sucked into the fist-flying vortex. "I knew that if I were pulled into the fight," he said, "I wasn't going to get out [on good behavior]." Just as the melee began to collapse on Walter, Elder Roe, with his massive frame, stepped in to protect him. It was as if God had reached down and put a wall between Walter and the fighting inmates, he said.

The door flung open and guards burst into the room. They did not associate Walter or Elder Roe with the fight. To restore order, they moved some other inmates to other rooms. For the large tattooed man, it was most likely a trip to solitary confinement. Such blow-ups between inmates were so common that, when interviewed later, Elder Roe didn't recall shielding Brother Walt. For Roe, it was just another day.

Lori Hoye was waiting for her husband outside. The time passed more slowly for her than for him, because at least he was making some kind of progress through the red tape while she was staring at a door, the one through which inmates stepped out into the world. If those inmates had family members with resources enough to own a car, they could hope to be picked up or, better yet, to have someone standing there to welcome them with a hug or a handshake. Those who did not have anyone waiting for them had to hope instead that they could pay for the bus that daily stopped at the jail. There was no free ride back to Oakland.

Walter thanked God that he had Lori.

Outside

Walter Hoye was a physical wreck when he left Santa Rita that day in early April. He had lost ten pounds during his incarceration. In a few days his fast ended, but it would take a long while for him to regain his strength.

Although weak, Walter was able to visit the Cathedral of Christ the Light and shake hands with the new bishop of Oakland, Salvatore Cordileone. The visit made the Saturday, April 11, 2009, edition of the *San Joaquin Herald*. The newspaper reported that the city and the police department were not interested in arresting Walter again if he showed up outside Family Planning Specialists. Walter told the paper that it was always his intention to return to the clinic and to resume his sidewalk counseling, but he said that he was in no shape to do so right away.

In hopes of finding shelter from media scrutiny, Lori Hoye booked a hotel room in the San Mateo area. "So we could just decompress," she said.

"There were so many people and so much media," Walter added.

The time away from the limelight was also needed to assess Walter's health. The fast had taken its toll not only on his weight but also on his muscles and major organs. He had lost muscle mass, not just fat, and "he was having issues with swelling in his lower body," said Lori.

After two months Walter was still not back to normal. One of the women who wrote Walter in jail operated a health retreat in San Diego. She called Lori, and they talked about how a visit there might help Walter to recover. Thus, both she and Walter spent a week at the retreat the following June. When they left they had new friends and a renewed outlook, but most importantly, Walter had replenished energy.

"She saved me," said Walter of the owner.

While at the retreat Walter and Lori adopted a vegan diet, which meant no meat or fish or dairy. And they have maintained this diet since. "Hear me," Walter said, "it's our diet, not our religion."

With his strength returned, Walter was eager to return to sidewalk counseling. But there was so much work to be done, and not just in Oakland. Walter's story had gained national attention, and pro-lifers all over the country wanted a piece of him. Meanwhile, outstanding legal questions lingered.

24

Appeals

Three months after Walter Hoye walked out of Santa Rita Jail, he received another blow. On August 4, 2009, he lost his lawsuit challenging the bubble law. Federal District Judge Charles Breyer sided with the City of Oakland and declared the ordinance constitutional. Hoye's attorneys from the Life Legal Defense Foundation promptly appealed the decision.

On Friday, October 2, after Judge Breyer refused a temporary injunction against the enforcement of the law pending appeal, the City of Oakland reveled in its victory. According to a widely released press announcement issued by the office of the city attorney, "Judge Charles Breyer upheld Oakland's 'Bubble Ordinance,' which prevents harassment of women entering health clinics by preventing anyone from approaching closer than eight feet without consent. The ordinance was challenged in court by Walter Hoye, a frequent anti-abortion demonstrator from Union City, who in January was convicted by a jury of two misdemeanor counts for violating Oakland's law." The press release added that "demonstrators in Oakland have a long history of intimidating women and health care providers, blocking patients from getting out of their cars and even chasing women to the door of clinics."

While it was Deputy City Attorney Vicki Laden who was most closely associated with the development, then the enforcement, and finally the defense of the ordinance, it was the city attorney himself who was quoted in the press release. "We are committed to upholding the right to free speech," John Russo said. "We are also committed to protecting the right of women to access health care without running a gauntlet of bullying and harassment."

Laden, who left the city attorney's office in 2014, did not describe the behavior of Walter Hoye and his fellow sidewalk counselors as bullying and harassment, even though she helped to craft the law designed to keep them eight feet away from women entering Oakland abortion clinics. "This isn't the guy who exhibits the characteristics of people who had done highly destructive things," she said of Walter. Her expression "destructive things" referred to the violence and aggression that some abortion providers, including Family Planning Specialists, had experienced in the past.

Laden admitted that the pro-life extremism of more than a decade ago was not occurring at FPS when the bubble ordinance was passed to hinder the activities of Walter Hoye. She explained that she nevertheless was concerned about protecting the privacy of women seeking abortion services. She said she spent many hours in research as she helped to draft Oakland's bubble law, which was modeled on one that had been adopted in Colorado and had survived legal challenges. She thought the law balanced both free speech rights and abortion rights, she added, but a higher court eventually decided otherwise.

Court Brief

In November, lawyers from Life Legal Defense Foundation filed their opening brief with the Ninth Circuit Court of Appeals. Submitted by LLDF attorney Michael Millen, the sixty-five-page brief addressed the constitutionality of Oakland's bubble ordinance and the way it had been applied in the case of Walter Hoye.

The brief claimed that the ordinance differentiated between persons on the basis of their speech:

> A panhandler may aggressively approach a woman entering the clinic and demand money, but a sidewalk counselor may not politely approach her with an offer of assistance. Someone may run up to a car approaching a clinic and start washing the windows and ask for payment, but a sidewalk counselor may not simply approach the car to offer the driver a free pamphlet. A peddler may approach and say, "would you like to buy a flower?" but Plaintiff may not approach and say, "would you like some information?"

To prove that the ordinance applied to only one kind of speech, that of pro-lifers, the brief described the behavior of the escorts at FPS, who were exempt:

> Since the passage of the ordinance, pro-abortion activists have exploited the fact that Hoye is unable to approach patients without consent. Thus, he cannot stand near the path of oncoming patients and offer them literature because the activists stand right in front of him, blocking him. When Hoye tries to speak to the patients, these activists talk loudly or make nonsense noise like "LALALALA" to drown out his voice. Thus, when at the required distance of eight feet, he is completely unable to communicate a request to approach, much less his actual message or his proffer of literature. When Hoye made a sign to convey his offer of assistance "God loves you and your baby. Let us help" the activists responded by holding up blank signs in front of his sign "to prevent [women] from seeing his sign" and to "prevent women from reading the message on his sign."

Then there was enforcement of the ordinance. The city's police department, in interpreting the law for officers in the field, expressly targeted a certain point of view in front of the clinics:

> In most cases, unconstitutionality will have to be proved through showing a pattern of selective enforcement or unlawful favoritism; it is undoubtedly the rare case when a government will admit to unconstitutionally interpreting and enforcing a law. This is one of those rare cases. Where a city has clearly stated that it enforces a criminal statute against some individuals, and not against others, based on the viewpoint of their speech, it must be taken at its word. It is not necessary for Hoye to make a thorough record that the police are actually following the policy promulgated by their superiors and the city itself.

Millen's brief further argued; "A public entity must offer evidence to support its justification for a restriction on speech." Furthermore, the California Constitution guarantees equal protection of the law. "The state bears the burden of establishing not only that it has a compelling interest which justifies the law but that the distinctions drawn by the law are necessary to further its purpose." The brief concluded with a call for the appellate court to direct the lower court to reverse its earlier decision in favor of the city and to grant Walter Hoye summary judgment instead.

The Appeal of the Criminal Case

Walter's lawyers were busy. A month after they filed their opening brief with the Ninth Circuit, in an attempt to overturn the bubble law itself, they filed their opening brief in the Appellate Division of the Superior Court of Alameda County, in order to appeal the outcome of Walter's criminal trial. Nine months later, on August 25, 2010, Superior Court Judge Michael Gaffey certified the court's unanimous decision to overturn Walter's criminal conviction.

The court stopped short of ruling on most of the outstanding questions raised by Walter's legal team. Instead, the decision addressed technicalities the court called "instructional errors", which LLDF described in the following way:

> First, the trial court refused to instruct the jury that it had to unanimously agree on the particular incident for which Hoye was to be found guilty. Because the district attorney's office presented evidence of several separate interactions between Hoye and persons entering the clinic, it was unclear whether the jury had all agreed on a single instance where Hoye allegedly violated the ordinance.
>
> Second, the trial court refused defense requests to provide a definition of "knowingly approach," a critical element of the "crime" for which Pastor Hoye was convicted. By failing to provide a definition, the court stated, the trial court left the jury unaware that the ordinance does not apply to stationary speakers who address and proffer literature to persons passing by.

"By golly, I knew we weren't crazy," said Millen in a later interview. "I knew that if someone who isn't involved in the local political scene [reviewed the case] it would be set straight. This is where God puts his finger on the scale. What God does is say, 'You people worked your tail off. You've done your part. Watch this.'"

But the testing of Walter Hoye was not over yet. Because the court's decision hinged on a technicality and not a flaw in the law, it left open the possibility of a retrial. The new district attorney, Nancy

O'Malley, could refile the charges against Walter—a prospect that left a bittersweet taste in his mouth.

The case was sent back to the trial court on September 24, 2010. For a retrial to take place, the law required that Walter be brought back to court within thirty days of that date. "Somebody in that office put the retrial at the bottom of the stack," said Millen. The county had intended to retry Walter, he explained, but through a presumed administrative error the deadline came and went, and all the criminal charges against Walter were dismissed.

Walter felt immense relief. He was no longer under the threat of further prosecution, and he could at last return to his sidewalk counseling outside FPS without fear of arrest. He also felt that his story might empower other religious leaders. When he first heard the news that the court had overturned his conviction, he told LLDF that he hoped the outcome would "encourage pastors to take a public stand against abortion in the pulpit and to minister the love of Christ to the men, women and children going into an abortion clinic. . . . It is time for men of God to come together and end the incontestable evil of abortion, anywhere and everywhere it exists."

LLDF attorney Catherine Short, however, reminded everyone that the battle was not completely won. The appeal in the Ninth Circuit, she said, which would determine the constitutionality of the bubble law, was still pending.

The Decision of the Ninth Circuit

On July 28, 2011, three years after Walter Hoye was arrested for offering alternatives to abortion on a public sidewalk, the Ninth Circuit Court of Appeals issued its judgment on the bubble ordinance. In its 3–0 opinion, authored by Circuit Judge Marsha S. Berzon, the court stated that there were "grave constitutional problems" with the manner in which the City of Oakland "understood and enforced" its law.

Pursuant to the U.S. Supreme Court decision that upheld Colorado's bubble law, the Ninth Circuit failed to judge the Oakland law as unconstitutional on its face. Nevertheless, it reversed the district court's decision that the ordinance was valid in the way the city applied it. The Ninth Circuit found that the city's enforcement policy represented content-based regulation of speech: "The city's policy of distinguishing between speech that facilitates access to clinics and speech that discourages access is not content-neutral." The Ninth Circuit therefore granted Walter's motion for summary judgment while explaining that its decision was a partial judgment in favor of the plaintiff, because the constitutionality of the ordinance was preserved.

Walter recalled an incident from the proceedings of the Ninth Circuit Court. At one point, one of the three judges asked the Oakland city attorney, "If I were running for governor ... and I had a brochure stating I was pro-life, could I hand out my brochure on the public sidewalk in front of an abortion clinic?" The city attorney said no. The judge continued, "If I were running for governor, and I was pro-abortion, could I hand out my brochure on a public sidewalk in front of an abortion clinic?" The city attorney said yes.

"You could hear an audible gasp in the audience," Walter said. "It was so clear that the enforcement of the bubble law violated the First Amendment of the Constitution." Before that exchange, Walter explained, he and Lori assumed there was little chance the Ninth Circuit judges would change the bubble law, but they prayed and trusted in God for the victory anyway. "At that point, however," he said, "it was obvious the tide was turning in our favor."

As a result of the high court's decision, the City of Oakland agreed to revise its enforcement policies to comply with it. Volunteer escorts would be required to follow the same rules as sidewalk counselors like Walter Hoye. The escorts were not "protected persons" after all, and they were no longer exempt from the bubble law.

25

Reverend Walter B. Hoye II

As Walter Hoye awaited the outcome of his appeals, he was fired by the Elder Board of the Progressive Missionary Baptist Church of Berkeley on October 1, 2009. At the time, Walter was out of town speaking at a 40 Days for Life kick-off event in Amarillo, Texas. There were disagreements on the Elder Board about how to handle Walter's notoriety and his expanded pro-life activism, as well as concerns about how best to address a shrinking budget. In the end the Elders decided to let Walter go.

A week later, after negative reactions had surfaced, the Elder Board rescinded their decision and gave Walter a six-month leave of absence, after which they offered him a new employment contract. "But the conditions were unacceptable to us," Lori said. They would have clipped Walter's wings and pinned him down in the office, she explained, and Walter declined the offer.

"For a black man, when you set out to do this, you lose your family, you lose your community, you lose your church," Walter said later. He did lose his church and many of his brothers in the black American community, but Lori remained steadfast. His marriage and his faith in Christ came through the fire of testing stronger than before, and so did his commitment to defend the most vulnerable human beings on earth, the unborn.

The Mission Continues

Through their nonprofit organization Issues4Life, Walter and Lori Hoye continue their campaign for greater awareness of the impact of abortion, especially on black Americans. Lori has left most of her other pursuits behind in order to share in the mission her husband began. "I work with Walter to keep him organized," she said. She still tracks statistics for sports teams, mostly for Oakland's Golden State Warriors, who won the National Basketball Association championship in 2015, 2017, and 2018. It's a fitting relationship, because several Warriors' stars, such as three-point phenom Stephen Curry, are serious about their Christian faith and Walter is an official team chaplain. It's a blessing that the Hoyes are able to join their love of sports with their love of Christ, Lori said.

Another blessing is the growing involvement of blacks in the pro-life movement, Walter noted. He and Lori have observed more and more blacks participating in events such as the Walk for Life West Coast in San Francisco. And not only blacks: the numbers of Latinos and Asians are also increasing—so much so that one hears from counterdemonstrators such insults as "Go back to Mexico!"

Counterdemonstrators also hurl insults at the StandUp4Life Walk in Oakland, which Walter organizes each year to precede the Walk for Life in San Francisco. Owing to the growing success of the Walk, those in favor of abortion rights turn out to disrupt it. In January 2015, they came en masse after promoting the protest on the Internet. Among the slogans they chanted with bullhorns was "Abortion on demand, women can be free; abortion on demand without apology". The crowd was so large and loud that Walter curtailed the event by canceling the walk portion.

"I couldn't guarantee the safety of the women and children," Walter told police. He requested the meeting with police after the disruption in hopes that they would provide more crowd control, as they do at the Walk for Life in San Francisco. He complained that the counterdemonstrators had no permits for their activities, which are required by law, and yet they were allowed to disrupt his event, for which he had obtained the proper permits. The Oakland police reviewed statements and videos posted by the pro-abortion group on its own web page and promised to examine the situation and to make necessary adjustments. The rally occurred as planned in 2016, but Walter canceled the one in 2017 because the police could not guarantee the safety of participants in the face of illegal and sometimes violent protests against the inauguration of President Donald Trump.

The annual StandUp4Life rally takes place at Oakland's Frank Ogawa Plaza in front of the building where the city council pushed through the bubble ordinance. "We do it on Friday afternoon, because I know the pastors and the senior members of their congregations can be available then to attend," said Walter.

"We walk because abortion in the black community is a form of genocide, it is the Darfur of America," says the Issues4Life website. "We walk because abortion in black America is the civil rights issue of our day. We walk because abortion does violence, both physically and emotionally, to men and women, to their children, and to their families." Yet it is still a challenge to share this message in a convincing way within the black community, Walter explained. Lately he has been finding that the most effective approach is to highlight the fact that abortion denies the personhood of the unborn child. "Black Americans understand what it means not to be a person," he said, referring to the legal justification of slavery in the antebellum South.

To defend the personhood of the unborn child, Walter founded an Internet-based nonprofit called the California Civil Rights Foundation. According to its website, the organization is "committed to protecting both the civil and human rights of the child in the womb by recognizing the inherent dignity and unalienable rights of all members of the human family." An outgrowth of that was the formation of the Frederick Douglass Foundation: "A collection of proactive Americans committed to the development of 21st Century approaches to today's problems with the assistance of elected officials, scholars from universities and community activists." Although it is a young organization, 2016 presidential candidates Carly Fiorina, Ben Carson, and Paul Ryan reached out to the foundation.

Walter has also gotten involved in supporting an organization that directly helps pregnant women. He is on the board of the Morning Center, which was founded in 2011 to provide free full-service prenatal and maternity care to women in urban and underserved areas. A project of Samaritan Ministries International, a nonprofit Christian charity, the Morning Center currently has locations in Memphis and Atlanta.

Brother, We Need to Talk

Walter hopes to begin another mobile service, one inspired by his #BrotherWeNeedToTalk, which accompanies his frequent tweets at @WalterHoye. He and Lori dream of buying a customized van in order to travel around the country to spread the pro-life message to other black communities. "We win when there's a conversation," explained Reverend Clenard Childress. "A guy like Walter has weathered the storm to get to the day when there's an exchange of ideas." Through Walter's story, more and more black Americans could learn the facts about abortion, particularly as it affects their communities. According to Childress, when they hear the truth, they will open their eyes and say, "We were lied to."

The mobile ministry would reach into the heart of the most troubled communities and, when possible, meet with gang members. "We are going to go to the ten worst cities in America, and what am I going to find?" Walter asked. "My people." He would like the van to be equipped so that it can project films on the sides of buildings, creating makeshift drive-ins. With this medium, he would like to counter the dominant destructive messages heard by black Americans. "Our people don't hear the [pro-life] message, and what they do hear comes from the wrong side of the equation," he said.

Opposed but Not Crushed

In all his pro-life endeavors, Walter encounters opposition. After his experiences with the Oakland bubble law, he expects it from the people who profit from the abortion industry, including the black American leaders who benefit from their political alliance with the Democratic Party. But he has run into a deeper source of opposition—the lingering lack of trust between whites and blacks that is the legacy of slavery and the black struggle for equal respect under the law. But Walter believes in a power bigger than the one that runs the world and feeds on the darkness hidden in the human heart. He further believes that God brings good out of the suffering of his servants. He even allows it so that they will be purified. If he had not been arrested and sent to prison, he said, he would not be the Christian man he is today. In fact, he would still be a black preacher on a corner with no opportunities to take the pro-life message to those who need to hear it.

CONCLUSION

Politics, Race, and Faith

A society that professes to be enlightened but can't restrain itself to act in a responsible manner when discussing political questions is not truly enlightened. When it comes to matters of race in the United States of America, our history alone, our "long memories", as Walter Hoye calls them, should remind us to be diligent about fulfilling the promises we make as a society to protect the rights of all. To ignore the mistakes of the past or to brush them off as ancient history is to fail in our duties to each other.

Walter Hoye wasn't universally hated by the creators of the Oakland bubble ordinance, according to former City Attorney Vicki Laden, who helped to craft the law. The ordinance was not meant to target him, she said. Yet target him it did, and he went to jail because of enforcement policies that were eventually declared to be unconstitutional infringements on his right to free speech.

The justice system determined that Walter's arrest, prosecution, and incarceration were directly related to the content of his speech. Was it also related to the color of his skin? Perhaps not, if the question is understood as asking whether Walter himself was a victim of racism in this case. But what if the question is understood as asking whether Walter stationed himself outside Family Planning Specialists once a week because black children were the ones most often aborted there. When the question is considered in this light, the destructive effects of racism in American society come into view.

Walter B. Hoye II is an American son. His slave ancestors cultivated the soil of the South, and his free forebears fled Jim Crow laws by heading for new opportunities in the North. But segregation followed them, and so did the general white attitude toward blacks that had justified their subjugation. The family's Christian faith was not diminished by the indignities they endured, and Walter's parents successfully passed on to him their unshakable confidence in Jesus Christ. Without this firm foundation and their commitment to hard work and education, the violent streets of the city might have swallowed Walter up.

When we hear the slogan "Black Lives Matter" we should hear the ring of gunfire and sirens in our inner cities. But we should also hear the ring of politics, because do black lives really matter when unborn black children aren't allowed to be mentioned in the conversation? Reverend Clenard Childress wants to revise the slogan by inserting the word "all", as in "All Black Lives Matter." If violence against and within the black community is to be seriously addressed, he said, the violence of abortion needs to be confronted too.

"If people really want to see what's happening at the abortion clinic," said Reverend Dion Evans, "just go out there when those big trucks are picking up the baby body parts."

Evans was alluding to a feature of the abortion business that few people knew about until the 2015 release of undercover videos by the Center for Medical Progress. The subject of the recorded conversations was the alleged sale of post-abortion fetal parts and organs, which is a federal crime punishable by up to ten years in prison or a fine of up to $500,000.

One recording, dated June 14, 2013, captures the remarks of Perrin Larton, the procurement manager for Advanced Bioscience Resources (ABR), a nonprofit organization in Alameda, California, a ten-minute drive from FPS in Oakland. At the time, according to corporate filings with the secretary of state's office, ABR had a $1.1 million annual income. Its biggest supplier was Planned Parenthood, yet Larton mentions FPS director Jackie Barbic by name in the video. Larton describes how, during abortion procedures on Saturdays, when FPS did "large cases", she collected and preserved baby parts, which were transferred to the labs that had ordered and paid for them in advance using an online form. In 2013 prices ranged from $60 to $515 per part. If the video is true, FPS was getting paid twice for their midterm abortions—first, by the mother or the California taxpayer via Medi-Cal and, second, by the labs buying the parts.

As this book goes to press, both the Center for Medical Progress and ABR are under legal scrutiny in multiple places and at several levels of government. So far, neither FPS nor ABR has been charged with a crime. Nevertheless, in reference to the FPS-ABR connection alleged by the video, Walter Hoye asked on his Issues4Life website, "How far have we come from slavery if we can still buy and sell black lives?"

Regardless of one's opinion about whether a woman should have a right to abortion, there is no denying that an abortion is a violent act, involving the dismembering of a tiny human being. Yet who was arrested and sent to jail for committing a violent crime? Not the people profiting from the distress of usually poor women, by killing their unborn children, but the peaceable preacher offering them help to keep their babies.

During the debate over the bubble ordinance, there were no public statements from Oakland police about problems outside Oakland abortion clinics. There was a good reason for that strategic oversight. Senior police sources later said that there wouldn't have been much to report—only a laundry list of uneventful police visits and blotter entries about complaints that proved to be little more than people standing around with signs.

A senior law enforcement source said that once the bubble law was passed, the level of police involvement relating to the misdemeanor it proscribed reached unusual proportions. "I had never been part of a process like this, based on the type of behavior that I had encountered, that didn't involve a threat or acts of violence, or things that were frequently going to involve violence. I don't remember another time when we had to develop a detailed process when that didn't appear to be the situation," said the source, who agreed to speak on condition of anonymity.

The police were not the only ones who spent disproportionate resources on Walter Hoye. There is no way of adding up the total public costs of arresting, trying, and incarcerating him, as well as fighting his appeals, but it is known that the City of Oakland paid $361,000 in attorney fees to Walter's lawyers at Life Legal Defense Foundation. And for what? In the end, Walter Hoye was exonerated, and all the while the real but hidden violence of abortion continued—unchecked and unregulated—because it is protected by the law.

EPILOGUE

Elder Roe

Walter's most trusted cellmate and protector, Elder Roe, was released from Santa Rita the day after Walter. He never lost contact with his dear friend Brother Walt, and the two men met on occasion on the outside.

Reintegrating back into society meant mixing with old friends and older habits. He was called Roe on the streets, and his drug of choice—crack—was all too common in Oakland. One day while high on the drug and armed with a pen light and a paper bag, Roe entered an Oakland store. It makes no difference that his weapon wasn't a real gun; his crime was still armed robbery. The sentence was about ten years, and his first stop was the state penitentiary at San Quentin. Fortunately for Roe, the stay there was short.

The prison system identified Roe as a skilled and certified welder, and he was soon transferred to California State Prison Solano for its specialized technical-skills programs. There he found new brothers with whom to gather and pray and was once again Brother Roe. Around his neck and over his blue prison shirt he wears a large silver cross. As of the printing of this book, fifty-seven-year-old Brother Roe was still in custody and eligible for parole in 2019.

Family Planning Specialists

Family Planning Specialists, the abortion clinic at 200 Webster Street, Oakland, which won notoriety through the arrest, trial, incarceration, and exoneration of Reverend Walter B. Hoye II, closed its doors in January 2018. The following announcement was posted on its website: "After 33 years of service, Doctors Paul Wright and Carl Watson are retiring and Family Planning Specialists is closing its doors. We want to thank the community and our patients for the honor of providing their medical care."

ACKNOWLEDGMENTS

I wish to thank the many people and organizations that made this book possible: Ignatius Press—Fr. Joseph Fessio, S.J., Vivian Dudro, and others—for deciding that Walter Hoye's story is worth telling and somehow thinking of me for the task of writing it; Walter and Lori Hoye, for their candor and trust as well as their patience with my endless questions and demands on their time; my wife, Melissa, for sticking with me through endless hours of talking about this project and for countless pages of proofreading; Melissa's mother, Louise, for helping with ancestry research; Solano County Undersheriff Gary Elliott, known in the Army Reserve as Colonel Elliott, for his friendship, leadership, and support through this project and many tough challenges in my life, including my long year in Iraq; and the lawyers at Life Legal Defense Foundation.

I would also like to thank the staff at Alameda County Jail Santa Rita in Dublin, California, for their professionalism and courtesy in meeting my request for a tour of the jail, and the staff at State Prison Solano in Vacaville, California. Many thanks to Elder Roe (Rozier Gibson).

My thanks also extend to Dr. Roberta Reynolds at the College of San Mateo and the writers of Creative Writing 161 at the College of San Mateo for the wealth of experience and knowledge they shared with me, and to Dad, Scott, Marina, Lisa, and Jon.

SOURCE NOTES

This published work of nonfiction is based on documents and extensive interviews with participants, witnesses, and parties knowledgeable about people, places, and industries relevant to the story. Court records, transcripts, and other documents related to the criminal proceedings are a matter of public record. The e-mails that helped to shape significant parts of the behind-the-scenes story of how the City of Oakland does business are also a matter of public record. Anyone can request and obtain these public records without offering a reason, but these e-mails were provided by lawyers with Life Legal Defense Foundation as part of legal cases and trial discovery.

This book contains the authorized biography of Walter B. Hoye II and is based on numerous lengthy interviews with him. For that reason, these source notes do not directly attend to every quote, as it would be too repetitive and onerous for the reader. Interviews with Walter Hoye and others in this book took place between December 2014 and February 2018. The names of most of these interviewees appear in the text, but in some situations, anonymity was requested and honored. For the most part, anonymity was reserved for those who faced potential backlash, professionally or politically, owing to the sensitive nature of the subject matter.

Some material and facts, such as statistics regarding Walter Hoye's football career at Michigan State and many historical references, were gleaned from Internet research. In other cases, the online data changed over time or was deleted from its original source. This is the case with much of the data on Family Planning Specialists obtained from its website. Since the facility closed, information on pricing and other details regarding abortion have since been removed. The information is supported by and consistent with trial testimony. In these cases, the original source is identified. Not all sources for facts of United States history are provided inasmuch as these facts are common knowledge.

In some instances, where details are an amalgamation of multiple sources too fine to delineate, only the major sources are given.

The following abbreviations are used in the notes:

ACSC	Alameda County Superior Court
FPS	Family Planning Specialists
LLDF	Life Legal Defense Foundation
OBG	Oakland bubble group
OCC	Oakland City Council
OCC VA	Oakland City Council video archive
OPD	Oakland Police Department
SRJ	Santa Rita Jail

1. Hunger for Justice

Walter Hoye sentencing: ACSC transcript, Dept. 29, February 19, 2009, and March 20, 2009. **Mood and drama in the courtroom audience:** interviews with various witnesses, including Lori Hoye and Mary Arnold. **Hoye in custody:** Walter Hoye interviews with the author; author's tour of the jail with the Alameda County Sheriff's Office SRJ Training Unit, June 2015. **40 Days for Life:** https://40daysforlife.com. **Pruno and jail contraband:** SRJ Training Unit interview with the author, June 2015.

2. Old Memories

Old Memories: Walter and Lori Hoye interviews with the author, December 2014; Vida Hoye interview with the author, February 2015. **Declaration of Independence compromise regarding slavery:** *The Life and Selected Writings of Thomas Jefferson*, ed. Adrienne Koch and William Peden (New York: Modern Library Classics, 1998), 26. **"Nothing is more certainly written":** ibid., 49. **Jefferson's 130 slaves:** *Jeffersonian Legacies*, ed. Peter S. Onuf (Charlottesville, Va.: University Press of Virginia, 1993), 147. **Hoye, Pickens, Odum ancestry:** public records; U.S. censuses of 1910 and 1920; Georgia birth records; celebration-of-life service program, May 30, 1978; funeral program for Mother Viola McAfee, July 16, 1963. **Georgia slave population by county:** slave map of Georgia, *Harper's Weekly*, December 14, 1861, "This Day in Georgia Civil War

History", Digital Library of Georgia, http://georgiainfo.galileo.usg. edu. **Birth of a Nation and the rise of the Klan:** "100 Years Later, What's the Legacy of 'Birth of a Nation'?", National Public Radio, February 8, 2015, https://www.npr.org. **Odum family lynching:** oral history, Walter Hoye interviews with the author; Vida Hoye interview with the author, February 2015. **The Great Migration:** "The Great Migration, 1910 to 1970", United States Census Bureau Library, September 13, 2012, https://www.census.gov. **Hartford Avenue Baptist Church; Reverend Hill Sr.:** Charles A. Hill family papers: 1917–1981, Bentley Historical Library, University of Michigan, https://quod.lib.umich.edu.

3. Detroit

Hartford Avenue Baptist Church history; Reverend Charles Hill biography: Charles A. Hill family papers: 1917–1981, introduction, Bentley Historical Library, Michigan State University, https://quod .lib.umich.edu/b/bhlead/umich-bhl-9977?rgn=main;view=text; Hartford Memorial Baptist Church, http://hmbcdetroit.org/church -history. **Bessie Kate's role at Hartford Memorial Baptist Church:** celebration-of-life service program, May 30, 1978; Vida Hoye interview with the author, February 2015. **"It wasn't enough":** Vida Hoye interview with the author, February 2015. **Walter B. Hoye Sr. biography:** public records; Vida Hoye interview with the author, February 2015. **"I would break my neck":** Jo-Ann Hoye interview with the author, October 2015. **Motown Records history:** "Motown: The Sound That Changed America", Motown Museum, https://www.motownmuseum.org. **Raisin in the Sun background:** Michael Anderson, "A Landmark Lesson in Being Black", *New York Times*, March 7, 1999, https://www.nytimes.com. **Death of Eltee Pickens:** funeral program, January 13, 1968; public records.

4. Lockdown

BGR852: California Department of Corrections records. **Arriving in 34F:** Walter Hoye interviews with the author; author's tour of SRJ; Alameda County Sheriff's Office SRJ Training Unit interview with the author, June 2015. **Jail contraband:** ibid. **"You had to get out there in the dark":** Lori Hoye interview with the author,

September 2015. **Lovelle Mixon:** Sandra Gonzales, "Cop Killer Was Depressed about Heading Back to Prison, Family Says", *Mercury News*, March 22, 2009, https://www.mercurynews.com; Harry Harris, "DNA Evidence Links Oakland Officers' Killer to Sexual Assaults of Two Women", *East Bay Times*, May 4, 2009, https://www.eastbaytimes.com. **Limited background on SRJ lockdown protocol:** SRJ Training Unit interview with the author, June 2015. **March Madness:** Lori Hoye interview with the author, September 2015; "Gonzaga Sneaks Past Western Kentucky with Last-Second Shot, 83–81", NCAA.com, March 21, 2009. **"You don't know how good" excerpt:** personal letter, Lori Hoye to Walter, March 22, 2009.

5. Made by History

"We are not makers of history": Martin Luther King Jr., "Transformed Nonconformist", in *A Gift of Love: Sermons from Strength to Love and Other Preaching* (Boston: Beacon Press, 2012). **Georgia, Tunis Campbell, Rufus Bullock, the Klan, and the 1872 election:** multiple historical sources, including: Russell Duncan, "Tunis Campbell (1812–1891)", ed. Edward A. Hatfield, *New Georgia Encyclopedia*, http://www.georgiaencyclopedia.org; "1872 Presidential Election", electoral map, 270towin.com, https://www.270towin.com/1872_Election/; Jacqueline Jones, *Saving Savannah: The City and the Civil War*, Vintage Civil War Library (New York: Vintage, 2009), 383–84; Douglas R. Egerton, *The Wars of Reconstruction: The Brief, Violent History of America's Most Progressive Era* (New York: Bloomsbury Press, 2014). **Martin Luther King Jr. biography:** multiple historical resources, including The King Center, thekingcenter.org. **"I am in Birmingham", "Injustice everywhere":** Martin Luther King Jr., "Letter from Birmingham Jail", April 16, 1963, https://kinginstitute.stanford.edu/king-papers/documents/letter-birmingham-jail. **Eight Mile Wall:** Jeff Karoub, "Wall That Once Divided Races in Detroit Remains, Teaches", Associated Press, May 1, 2013. **Twelfth Street riots statistics:** "Uprising of 1967", *Encyclopedia of Detroit*, https://detroithistorical.org/learn/encyclopedia-of-detroit/uprising-1967. **"That's no way to act":** Jo-Ann Hoye interview with the author, October 2015. **"Something else that must be said":** Martin Luther King Jr., Address at the Freedom Rally in Cobo

Hall, June 23, 1963, https://kinginstitute.stanford.edu/king-papers /documents/address-freedom-rally-cobo-hall. **Walter B. Hoye Sr. and the NFL:** "Walter Hoye Passes Away", Los Angeles Chargers, July 13, 2012, http://www.chargers.com/news/2012/07/13/walter -hoye-passes-away. **Murder of Malcom X:** Wayne Drash, "Malcolm X Killer Freed After 44 Years", CNN, April 28, 2010, http:// www.cnn.com/2010/CRIME/04/26/malcolmx.killer/index.html.

6. Life Is Not a Game

Not a game: Walter Hoye interviews with the author. **Calvary Baptist Church history:** JoAnn Fields, "Calvary Baptist Church Celebrates 125th Anniversary", *Voice and Viewpoint*, April 11, 2014, http:// sdvoice.info/calvary-baptist-church-celebrates-125th-anniversary/. **S. M. Lockridge biography:** "The Rev. S. M. Lockridge; Prominent San Diego Pastor", *Los Angeles Times*, April 8, 2000, http:// articles.latimes.com/2000/apr/08/local/me-17324; Hoye interviews with the author. **Michigan State football:** Michigan State, http:// www.msuspartans.com/sports/m-footbl/msu-m-footbl-body.html. **Statistics:** Hoye, Walter, 1 reception, 46 receiving yards, 46.0 average. **The Game:** vs. Northwestern, November 12, 1977; results: win; score: 44–3; attendance: 61,238; location: East Lansing, Michigan. **"We cannot win the respect":** Martin Luther King Jr., *A Gift of Love: Sermons from Strength to Love and Other Preachings* (Boston: Beacon Press, 2012), 7.

7. Self-Will

"What I've dared": Herman Melville, *Moby-Dick; or, The Whale* (New York: Penguin Books, 1992), 183. **Preaching license:** January 12, 1982. **Preterm infant survival rates:** Gene Emery, "Survival Rates for Extremely Preterm Babies Improving in U.S.", Reuters, February 15, 2017, https://www.reuters.com/article/us -health-preemies-survival-impairments/survival-rates-for-extremely -preterm-babies-improving-in-u-s-idUSKBN15U2SA.

8. Lori

Christ-centered and Bible-based: Walter Hoye interview with the author, 2015. **Lori Hoye biography:** Lori Hoye interview with the author, 2015. **Baptism and Marriage:** Lori and Walter Hoye interviews with the author, 2015.

9. Voices in the Wilderness

"The conference changed everything": Lori Hoye interview with the author, September 2015. **"Abortion is heavily politicized":** Clenard Childress Jr. interview with the author, September 2015. **Walk for Life San Francisco:** "History", 2005, Walk for Life West Coast, http://www.walkforlifewc.com/history/2005-history/. **About Christiana Downer:** Lori Hoye interview with the author, September 2015. **Fifteen thousand at second Walk for Life:** "History", 2006, http://www.walkforlifewc.com/history/2006-history/. **"With the banner":** Lori Hoye interview with the author, September 2015. **Fredi D'Alessio biography:** Fredi D'Alessio digital communications, September–October 2015. **"It helps if there's a group of people praying":** D'Alessio interview with the author, October 2015. **D'Alessio FPS timeline and events:** D'Alessio digital communications September–October 2015; OBG e-mails. **"I didn't have a pastor or priest in mind":** Mary Arnold interview with the author, September 2015. **Walter was very young-looking:** ibid.

10. The Church of the Eight Steps

FPS backstory and fees and services: FPS website. **Most FPS abortions paid for by Medi-Cal:** ACSC transcript, Jacqueline Barbic testimony, Dept. 29, January 5, 2009. **Jacqueline Barbic biography:** public-records research by the author; FPS website. **FPS revenue, 2015:** corporate filings, California secretary of state's office; FPS appointments on April 29, 2008. **Pregnancies terminated on April 29, 2008:** ACSC transcript, Barbic testimony, Dept. 29, January 5, 2009. **Forty FPS appointments on April 29, 2009:** ACSC transcript, Mohammed Ali testimony, Dept. 29, January 5, 2009. **Planned Parenthood/abortion clinic operations and outreach:** Abby Johnson interview with the author, August 2015. **Barbara Hoke biography:** public-records research by the author; ACSC transcript, Hoke testimony, Dept. 29, January 5, 2009. **Abortion clinic escorts operations and goals:** ACSC transcript, Hoke testimony, Dept. 29, January 5, 2009; trial video evidence. **Hoke,** **"tenacity of the devil":** Karmah Elmusa, "Oakland Nonprofit Helps California Women Locate Reproductive Health Services", OaklandNorth, March 22, 2011, https://oaklandnorth.net/2011/03/22 /oakland-nonprofit-helps-california-women-locate-reproductive -health-services/. **Inside abortion clinics, real dangers, tactics, and escorts:** Johnson interview with the author, August 2015. **Percent of abortion clinic volunteers who have had abortions:** ibid. **Between 1993 and 2015:** Liam Stack, "A Brief History of Deadly Attacks on Abortion Providers", *New York Times*, November 29, 2015, https://www.nytimes.com. **James Kopp:** David Staba, "Life Term for Killer of Buffalo-Area Abortion Provider", *New York Times*, June 20, 2007. **Abortion provider wears bulletproof vest:** OCC VA, October 23, 2007. **Walter Hoye's first days at FPS:** Walter Hoye interviews; Mary Arnold interview with the author, September 2015. **Hoke recruits:** ACSC transcript, Hoke testimony, Dept. 29, January 5, 2009; OBG e-mails, 2008.

11. Forces Rally against Walter

Nancy Nadel biography: public records, campaign materials, numerous public statements and sources, including Nadel's official LinkedIn profile and Oakland City Council biography. **First job after college:** text of a Nadel speech to a pro-choice group, 2002. **Oakland Feminist Women's Health Center background:** womenshealthspecialists.org. **Barbara Hoke and Jacqueline Barbic contact Nadel:** OBG e-mails, 2007, a continuation of a decades-long dialogue and group discussions over clinic access; text of a Nadel speech to a pro-choice group, 2002. **"She was pleased that laws were in place":** Nadel pro-choice speech, 2002. **Jane Kaplan as volunteer liaison; DA accused of bungling case against Fredi D'Alessio; November 2006 meeting:** Hoke OBG e-mail, January 2007. **Reinstatement of case against D'Alessio:** provided by D'Alessio, September 2015. **Notes on the Hoke draft of the ordinance and contributors:** Hoke OBG e-mail, August 2007. **ACLU concerns about ordinance:** Nadel OBG e-mail, September 2007. **Nadel's letter introducing the ordinance:** OCC Public Safety Committee Documents/Agenda, October 23, 2007. **Non–city**

council officials present at committee hearing: Marisa Arrona, Nadel policy aide, OCC VA, October 23, 2007, https://oakland .legistar.com/calendar.aspx. **"Certainly, this item will pass" and remaining quotes from the Public Safety Committee:** OCC VA, Oakland City Hall, October 23, 2007, https://oakland.legistar .com/calendar.aspx. **"I'd given up on them all":** Mary Arnold interview with the author, September 2015.

12. Council of Practical Necessity

"Women must have freedom of choice," 1988; "Call it abortion", 1977: Colman McCarthy "Jackson's Reversal on Abortion", *Washington Post*, May 21, 1988, https://www.washington post.com/archive/opinions/1988/05/21/jacksons-reversal-on -abortion/dd9e1637-020d-447b-9329-95ec67e41fd5/?utm_term =.1061c2a00aac. **"There's money coming into their coffers and the party's coffers":** Clenard Childress Jr. interview with the author, September 2015. **"These pro-life people are demagogues":** Leslie Fulbright, "Berkeley Preacher Calls for Blacks to Fight Abortion", *San Francisco Chronicle*, January 7, 2008, https:// www.sfgate.com. **Dr. Amos Brown biography; "Members of the church are directly affected by systems of evil":** "Dr. Amos C. Brown", NAACP, http://www.naacp.org/naacp-board -of-directors/dr-amos-c-brown/. **"The NAACP is well aware":** Childress interview with the author, September 2015. **Abortion statistics:** Rachel K. Jones, Lawrence B. Finer, and Susheela Singh, *Characteristics of U.S. Abortion Patients, 2008* (New York: Guttmacher Institute, 2010), 6, https://www.guttmacher.org/report/characteristics -us-abortion-patients-2008; Tara C. Jatlaoui et al., "Abortion Surveillance—United States, 2013", *Morbidity and Mortality Weekly Report* 65, no. 12 (November 25, 2016): 1–44, https://www.cdc.gov /mmwr/volumes/65/ss/ss6512a1.htm.

13. An Unexpected Brotherly Bond

"We cannot win the respect": Martin Luther King Jr., *Gift of Love: Sermons from Strength to Love and Other Preachings* (Boston: Beacon Press, 2012), 7. **Bishop Salvatore Cordileone biography:** Cordileone interview with the author, September 2015; San Francisco Archdiocese, https://sfarchdiocese.org/archbishop-cordileone.

"**A sense of personal support**": Cordileone interview with the author, September 2015. **Cordileone and Walter Hoye:** ibid.; Walter Hoye interviews with the author. **News about archdiocese change in leadership:** personal letter, Eva Muntean to Walter Hoye, March 2009. **Personal letters to Hoye at SRJ**: Letters from Walter's personal collection sent to him in March 2009, reviewed and selected by the author. **Jail rules regarding money in correspondence:** Alameda County Sheriff's Office SRJ Training Unit interview with the author, June 2015.

14. To Fight City Hall

Terry Thompson biography: Thompson interview with the author, September 2015. **"We'll see how many are left" and remaining quotes from the November 6 OCC meeting:** OCC VA, Oakland City Hall, November 6, 2007, https://oakland.legistar.com/calendar.aspx. **Dr. Alveda King's letter to the OCC:** reprinted with Dr. King's approval. **"I'm afraid I'm gonna have to use these words", and remaining quotes from the November 18 OCC meeting:** OCC VA, Oakland City Hall, November 18, 2007, https://oakland.legistar.com/calendar.aspx. **Legal challenge of Oakland Municipal Code §8.52.030(b):** court records; Michael Millen and Catherine Short interviews with the author, September 2015. **Judge Charles Breyer biography:** "Senior District Judge Charles R. Breyer", Northern District of California, https://www.cand.uscourts.gov/crb. **OBG meeting regarding Breyer's suggested changes; in attendance: Vicki Laden, Marisa Arrona, Nancy Nadel, Barbara Hoke, Barbara Ellis, Jacqueline Barbic, Rena Rickles, Destiny Lopez, Helen Hutchinson:** OBG minutes; Lopez OBG e-mail, January 3, 2008, 4:00 P.M. **"It was a whacky line":** Millen interview with the author, September 2015. **OBG "angsting":** e-mail from "ordinance", an unspecified sender to OBG attributed to Hoke, January 3, 2008. **Hoke's draft support letter for supporters:** Hoke OBG e-mail, January 11, 2008. **"Sidewalk counselors have been outside abortion clinics in Oakland for over twenty years" and remaining quotes from the January 15 OCC meeting:** OCC VA, Oakland City Hall, November 15, 2008, https://oakland.legistar.com/calendar.aspx. **"Thankfully, I was able to talk to her" and remaining quotes**

from the February 5 OCC meeting: OCC VA, Oakland City Hall, February 5, 2008, https://oakland.legistar.com/calendar.aspx.

15. The Ordinance

"Are you here to arrest me?": Walter Hoye interview with the author, May 2015. **Jacqueline Barbic's e-mail to Nancy Nadel about the test:** Barbic OBG e-mail, February 12, 2008. **Flagrant and direct violation of the ordinance:** Barbara Hoke OBG e-mail, February 13, 2008. **Marisa Arrona responds to Barbic:** OBG e-mail, February 13, 2008. **Webster Street cameras not under Barbic's control:** Barbic OBG e-mail, February 13, 2008. **Get badge numbers:** Vicki Laden OBG e-mail, February 24, 2008. **Another frustrating day:** Hoke OBG e-mail, February 26, 2008. "I took the spot near to Walter's tree": OBG e-mail from a clinic escort known only as "Steve G", February 26, 2008. **Great reports:** Hoke OBG e-mail, February 26, 2008. **March meeting and quotes regarding the bubble ordinance:** deposition of Captain Anthony Toribio, United States District Court, Northern District of California, January 29, 2009. **Laden likes the idea:** Laden interview with the author, October 2015. "I remember thinking of the escorts as auxiliaries": ibid.

16. Brother Walt and Elder Roe

Lockdown, apple juice, shopping list, porn confrontation: Walter Hoye interviews with the author; Rozier Gibson interview with the author, October 2015; Alameda County Sheriff's Office SRJ Training Unit interview with the author, June 2015. **Jail canteen and payment protocol:** SRJ Training Unit interview with the author, June 2015. **Father Ciszek biography:** The Father Walter Ciszek Prayer League, http://www.ciszek.org. **Jail contraband:** SRJ Training Unit interview with the author, June 2015. "Amazing Grace": written by John Newton in 1779.

17. The Hornet's Nest

Escorts' "had our hands full": Barbara Hoke OBG e-mail, April 17, 2008; escort report, Tuesday, April 15, 2008. "Clone man": Hoke OBG e-mail, April 16, 2008. **FACE Act:** Vicki Laden OBG e-mail, April 17, 2008. **Blocking the antis:** OBG e-mail sender redacted, April 21, 2008; escort report, April 22, 2008. **Hoke, Jacqueline Barbic, and Laden discuss stakeout:** OBG e-mails, April 23 and April 28, 2008. **Clients "looked like they were still in high school":** Laden interview with the author, October 2015. **Laden's stakeout report:** OBG e-mail, April 29, 2008. **The arrest:** OPD crime report, April 13, 2008; Walter Hoye interviews with the author; Terry Thompson interview with the author, September 2015. **"Hornet's nest":** Hoye interviews with the author. **Additional bubble law interpretation:** deposition of OPD Captain Anthony Toribio, United States District Court, Northern District of California, January 29, 2009.

18. The Jagged Edge of Justice

LLDF's interest in the bubble ordinance: Terry Thompson interview with the author, September 2015. **Robert Graff biography:** state bar listing; **Arrest details:** OPD crime report, April 13, 2008; Walter Hoye interviews with the author. **"Case law was clear":** Catherine Short interview with the author, September 2015. **The restraining order:** ACSC transcript, Dept. 115, July 18, 2008. **Lucy Kasdin testimony:** ACSC transcript, Dept. 115, July 18, 2008. **"Hubbub in the courtroom": Catherine** Short interview with the author, September 2015. **The court quizzes Sandra Coleman:** ACSC transcript, Dept. 115, July 18, 2008. **Discriminatory prosecution:** ACSC transcript, Dept. 115, July 18, 2008. **The other bubble ordinance complaint:** ACSC transcript, Dept. 115, July 18, 2008; Mary Arnold interview with the author, September 2015; confidential sources familiar with the case. **FBI Bay Area Counterterrorism Task Force form:** ACSC transcript, David Elzey testimony, Dept. 115, July 18, 2008. **Barbara Hoke and Vicki Laden regarding enforcement:** OBG e-mails, March–April 2008.

19. The Trial, Part One

"Mostly supporters": Mary Arnold interview with the author, September 2015. **Trial begins with a dispute; opening statements; Jacqueline Barbic testimony; video controversy; Barbara Hoke testimony:** ACSC transcript, Dept. 29, January 5, 2009; sources familiar with the proceedings. **Escort guidelines:** court papers.

20. The Video

Statements made to police: OPD crime report, April 13, 2008, including handwritten and signed statements. **Dispute over video evidence:** ACSC transcript, Dept. 29, January 5, 2009. **Mohammed Ali testimony:** ACSC transcripts, Dept. 29, January 5, and January 6, 2009. **"I had to get better at my message":** Mary Arnold interview with the author, September 2015. **Jacqueline Barbic cross-examination and the video:** ACSC transcript, Dept. 29, January 6, 2009.

21. The Trial, Part Two

Sandra Coleman testimony, part 1: ACSC transcript, Dept. 29, January 6, 2009. **Coleman testimony, part 2:** ACSC transcript, Dept. 29, January 7, 2009. **Jury questions regarding victims:** ACSC transcript, Jacqueline Barbic testimony, Dept. 29, January 7, 2009. **Lucy Kasdin testimony, part 1:** ACSC transcript, Dept. 29, January 7, 2009. **"As I sit in the defendant's chair":** Walter Hoye trial diary. **Kasdin testimony, part 2:** ACSC transcript, Dept. 29, January 8, 2009. **Motion to dismiss:** ACSC transcript, Dept. 29, January 8, 2009. **Terry Thompson testimony, part 1:** ACSC transcript, Dept. 29, January 8, 2009. **Thompson testimony, part 2:** ACSC transcript, Dept. 29, January 9, 2009. **Closing statements:** ACSC transcript, Dept. 29, January 12, 2009. **Maximum stress levels:** various interviews with participants and persons familiar with the proceedings.

22. Judgment Day

The verdict: ACSC transcript, Dept. 29, January 15, 2009; Walter Hoye interviews with the author. **Facing the future with faith:** Walter Hoye trial diary. **First sentencing:** ACSC transcript, Dept. 29, February 19, 2009. **Tussle with bailiffs:** Dion Evans interview with the author, October 2015; Eva Muntean interview with the author, October 2015; Walter Hoye interviews with the author, April 2015. **Rally for Walter and quotes from Walter Hoye, Lori Hoye, Evans, Clenard Childress, Michael Millen, and Allison Aranda:** digital video, FamigliaFilms channel, YouTube. **Final sentencing:** ACSC transcript, Dept. 29, March 20, 2009. **"It was unconscionable": Michael Millen interview with the author, September 2015. **"The power of an evil thing like abortion to corrupt"**: Catherine Short interview with the author, September 2015. **"Congratulations"**: Mary Arnold interview with the author, September 2015.

23. For Good Behavior

Freedom for Walter; health crisis: Walter Hoye interviews with the author; Rozier Gibson interview with the author, October 2015; Lori Hoye interview with the author, 2015. **Hoye visits Archbishop Cordileone:** John Simerman, "Pastor Pledges Return to Abortion Clinic", *East Bay Times*, April 10, 2009, https://www.east baytimes.com.

24. Appeals

Charles Breyer sides with Oakland: U.S. Federal District Court document: Hoye v. City of Oakland, 642 F. Supp. 2d 1029 (2009). **"We are also committed to protecting ... access"**: city attorney press release, produced by Alex Kats, October 2, 2009. **"This isn't the guy"**: Vicki Laden interview with the author, October 2015. **Appeal filed in Ninth Circuit Court: Press Release in November:** LLDF posted on November 17, 2009, by staff. **Judge Michael Gaffey certifies decision:** LLDF, "Appellate Court Overturns Walter Hoye's Conviction", LLDF, August 26, 2010, https://lifelegaldefensefoundation.org/2010/08/26/appellate-court -overturns-elder-walter-hoyes-conviction/. **"By golly, I knew we weren't crazy"**: Michael Millen interview with the author, August 2015. "Somebody in that office **put the retrial at the bottom of the stack"**: ibid. **Encourage pastors:** Hoye quoted in LLDF, "Appellate Court Overturns Walter Hoye's Conviction", August 24, 2010, https://lifelegaldefensefoundation.org/2010/08/26/appellate -court-overturns-elder-walter-hoyes-conviction/. **Decision of the Ninth Circuit 3–0 Opinion:** LLDF, "Victory!—Pastor Hoye's Constitutional Rights Vindicated at Ninth Circuit", LLDF, July 29, 2011, https://lifelegaldefensefoundation.org/2011/07/29/victory-pastor -hoyes-constitutional-rights-vindicated-at-the-ninth-circuit/. **"The city's policy ... is not content-neutral"**: U.S. Court of Appeals, Ninth Circuit, filed July 28, 2011.

25. Reverend Walter B. Hoye II

Life after trial; conditions were unacceptable: Lori Hoye interview with Ignatius Press, May 2018. **"When you set out to do this":** Walter Hoye interview with the author, May 2015. **Hoye activities at the time of printing:** Walter and Lori Hoye interviews with Ignatius Press, May 2018. **"We walk":** "The Issues4Life Foundation", Issues4Life, http://www.issues4life.org/. **Personhood:** California Civil Rights Foundation, http://www.civilrights foundation.org/. **Fredrick Douglass Foundation:** http://www .tfdf.org/. **Morning Center:** https://www.morningcenter.org /about/board-directors. **"We win when there's a conversation":** Clenard Childress Jr. interview with the author, September 2015.

Conclusion: Politics, Race, and Faith

"If people really want to see what's happening": Dion Evans interview with the author, October 2015. **"All Black Lives Matter":** Clenard Childress Jr. interview with the author, September 2015. **Perrin Larton, procurement manager:** Center for Medical Progress video dated as indicated; http://www.centerformedical progress.org/. **Advanced Bioscience Resources (ABR):** state corporate records, filings and reports. **"I had never been part of a process like this":** confidential source in an interview with the author, 2015.

INDEX